Rethinking Hegemony

Rethinking World Politics

Series Editor: Professor Michael Cox

In an age of increased academic specialization where more and more books about smaller and smaller topics are becoming the norm, this major new series is designed to provide a forum and stimulus for leading scholars to address big issues in world politics in an accessible but original manner. A key aim is to transcend the intellectual and disciplinary boundaries which have so often served to limit rather than enhance our understanding of the modern world. In the best tradition of engaged scholarship, it aims to provide clear new perspectives to help make sense of a world in flux.

Each book addresses a major issue or event that has had a formative influence on the twentieth-century or the twenty-first-century world which is now emerging. Each makes its own distinctive contribution as well as providing an original but accessible guide to competing lines of interpretation.

Taken as a whole, the series will rethink contemporary international politics in ways that are lively, informed and – above all – provocative.

Rethinking Hegemony

Owen Worth

First published 2015 by
PALGRAVE

Palgrave in the UK is an imprint of Macmillan Publishers Limited,
registered in England, company number 785998, of 4 Crinan Street,
London, N1 9XW.

Palgrave Macmillan in the US is a division of St Martin's Press LLC,
175 Fifth Avenue, New York, NY 10010.

Palgrave is a global imprint of the above companies and is represented
throughout the world.

Palgrave® and Macmillan® are registered trademarks in the United States,
the United Kingdom, Europe and other countries.

ISBN 978–1–137–30046–1   hardback
ISBN 978–1–137–30045–4   paperback

This book is printed on paper suitable for recycling and made from fully
managed and sustained forest sources. Logging, pulping and manufacturing
processes are expected to conform to the environmental regulations of the
country of origin.

A catalogue record for this book is available from the British Library.

A catalog record for this book is available from the Library of Congress.

Typeset by Cambrian Typesetters, Camberley, Surrey, England, UK.

Printed in China

To Sammi and the future x

Contents

List of Abbreviations

ALCA	*see* FTAA
ALBA	Bolivarian Alliance for the Peoples of Our Americas
ANC	African National Congress
APEC	Asia-Pacific Economic Co-operation
ASEAN	Association of Southeast Asian Nations
AU	African Union (formerly OAU)
BRICS	Brazil, Russia, India, China and South Africa
CAN	Andean Community of Nations
CIS	Conference of Independent States
CIVETS	Colombia, Indonesia, Vietnam, Egypt, Turkey and South Africa
Comecon	Council for Mutual Economic Assistance
ECB	European Central Bank
EC	European Community
ECOWAS	Economic Community of West African States
ECSC	European Coal and Steel Community
ERM	Exchange Rate Mechanism
EU	European Union
FDI	foreign direct investment
FTAA	Free Trade Area of the Americas (ALCA in Spansh: Área de Libre Comercio de las Américas)
GATT	General Agreement on Tariffs and Trade
GDP	gross domestic product
GNP	gross national product
HIPC	Heavily Indebted Poor Countries Initiative
HSRC	Human Sciences Research Council (South Africa)
HST	hegemonic stability theory
ILO	International Labour Organization
IMF	International Monetary Fund
IPE	International Political Economy
IR	International Relations
IT	information technology
MDGs	Millennium Development Goals

Mercosur/ Mercosul	Trading bloc in South America: Argentina, Brazil, Paraguay, Uruguay and Venezuela
NAFTA	North American Free Trade Agreement: trade bloc comprising Canada, Mexico and the USA
NASSCOM	National Association of Software and Services Companies (India)
NATO	North Atlantic Treaty Organization
NGO	non-governmental organization
OAS	Organization of American States
OAU	Organization of African Unity (*see* AU above)
OEEC	Organisation for European Economic Co-operation
OPEC	Organization of the Petroleum Exporting Countries
PIIGS	Portugal, Ireland, Italy, Greece and Spain
PPP	purchasing power parity
PT	Partido dos Trabalhadores Workers' Party (Brazil)
SAARC	South Asian Association for Regional Cooperation
SADC	Southern African Development Community
TIMBI	Turkey, India, Mexico, Brazil and Indonesia
UKIP	United Kingdom Independence Party
UN	United Nations
UNASUR	Union of South American Nations
USA	United States of America
USSR	Union of Soviet Socialist Republics (Soviet Union)
VE Day	Victory in Europe Day
WEF	World Economic Forum
WSF	World Social Forum
WTO	World Trade Organization

Foreword

As Owen Worth shows in this wide-ranging study, the idea of hegemony remains an indispensable – albeit contested – concept in the toolkit of International Relations. Indeed, it has often been employed to explain some of the most important phenomena in world history. Thus the rise and fall of hegemons from the Greeks through to the Americans and Russian figure in many accounts of why great power wars begin. Hegemons, however, are also deemed by some writers to be essential for world order. Indeed, the theory of hegemonic stability has in many ways been one of the most influential – if not the most influential – in IR since the end of the Second World War. There also remains the knotty and still unresolved problem of what exactly one should call the United States of America, especially in the years following the collapse of the other superpower? 'Superpower' itself no longer seemed to capture the essence of American power under conditions of unipolarity. The idea of 'empire' appeared to carry far too much political baggage. Hence, almost by a process of elimination, if nothing else, we ended up with the idea of a 'hegemon'. But, as many writers have asked: what precisely did this Greek word refer to? A great deal of power, fairly obviously. But, as Ned Lebow has noted, hegemony implies much more: namely a notion of leadership. However, as others in turn have pointed out, this only begs the important questions. How should the hegemon lead and why should followers follow the hegemon's lead? Indeed, is it even possible for a hegemon to lead in a complex world where no single power – the United States included – has the means, the wherewithal, or even the desire, to lead? Are we in fact, as Barry Buzan has suggested, fast moving into a world where there are no 'superpowers', no leaders, no hegemons? And if we are, then what lies ahead? Thus the debate goes on. Intellectually stimulating to be sure. Politically important too. But so far, unresolved.

It is one of the very great virtues of this volume that the author has been willing to step into a minefield strewn with all sorts of dangers. In part inspired by the work of Gramsci, who has over the years influenced quite a few critical thinkers – Robert Cox most notably – Worth does a terrific job in rethinking the concept of hegemony by examining in detail how the term has evolved and the different ways in which it has been (and can be) deployed to illuminate the world around us. Theoretically open yet empirically rich, this intellectually demanding book is not only a significant addition to an already important series: in its own very special way it makes a most original contribution to the field of International Relations.

MICHAEL COX
Director LSE IDEAS
London School of Economics and Political Science, UK

Acknowledgements

I would like to thank Steven Kennedy and Stephen Wenham at Palgrave for taking an interest in this project, and encouraging its development. I would also like to thank Maddy Hamey-Thomas for taking it through to the production stages. I am also extremely grateful to Mick Cox, the series editor, for his encouragement and suggestions as to the direction of the book.

I would also like to acknowledge funding received from AHSS at the University of Limerick, which gave me the time required to complete the final write-up. Also, I would like to add a thank you to the staff at the *Casa Gramsci* in Sardinia during my visit there in 2012. Many of the themes developed here were discussed at length with colleagues and students at a number of different venues and I would like to thank all those who contributed to the many subsequent discussions. In particular, those who have been subjected to the themes of the book in less coherent forms in late-night bars, and on this note I would like to thank especially Luke Ashworth, David Bailey, Claes Belfrage, Scott Fitzsimmons, Gerry Strange and John Turner, who possibly suffered more than most.

On a personal level, I would like to thank Daisy, Rosa, Perys, Mario and Helen J for their support when writing this book. Finally and most importantly, I would like to thank Sammi for being Sammi. The love, support and advice as well as the many debates we share has provided more inspiration that I could ever have imagined and I dedicate this book to her.

OWEN WORTH

Introduction

When we attempt to understand recent world events, the concept of hegemony never seems to be far away. Events in Syria, Crimea and Eastern Ukraine, Iraq and in North-West Pakistan that have attracted a great deal of interest in recent years because of conflicts can all point to a question or a crisis of hegemony. Similarly, ethnic tensions, the prevalence of religious-orientated terrorism and the global financial crisis have also been attributed to the pursuit of hegemony, or its failures. Whether we are referring to hegemony in terms of international leadership, regional hegemony, ideological hegemony or hegemonic contestation, the concept is used in abundance. For example, in Syria, calls for an American presence have been made because it is regarded as the leading international state and as such can exert its military influence in order to stabilize the wider international system. Hegemony in this case refers to the way a powerful state controls and polices the international arena.

Elsewhere, hegemony can be understood differently. For example, the annexation of Crimea and the unrest in Eastern Ukraine has brought a regional hegemon (Russia) into conflict with what used to be called 'the West'. The post-Soviet space that has emerged since the end of the Cold War, dominated by Russia, clashed with the European Union (EU), which has itself grown into a regional power in world politics. The rise of regional hegemonies was a phenomenon predicted by many in the direct aftermath of the breaching of the Berlin Wall in 1989, when it was thought that the old world of 'bipolarity'; where global power is controlled by two superpowers, would be replaced by a number of regional hegemons (Mearsheimer 1990). However, we also see hegemony used when we look at dominant ideas in society. The financial crisis that began in 2007, and of which we are still feeling the effects, questioned certain hegemonic ideas over the ways we act and order our economic lives. Most notably, it scrutinized the way global economics functioned and was governed. As the banking crash created a snowball effect that saw the crisis globalize, the hegemonic crisis within global capitalism became more apparent. Another example where core hegemonic ideas have been challenged is with the rise of religious militancy since the end of the Cold War. Here we have seen the values of liberal democracy, which are viewed as hegemonic by its opponents, challenged by religious interpretation from those who favour alternative values and ways of ordering society.

In each of these, hegemony can provide a different understanding. They seek to explain either how an actor or a set of ideas has sought to assert its supremacy over another, or show how these have been contested or challenged in some way. As a term, hegemony has been used in different ways to aid the understanding of a whole range of phenomena in politics and, as an extension, in social life. The study of International Politics has considered the notion of hegemony to be a central fact when considering war, peace and international stability. From the wars between city-states in ancient Greece to the formulation of the modern state system in Westphalia, hegemony has featured prominently. Similarly, since the academic study of International Relations (IR) formally emerged in 1919 with the David Davis chair at Aberystwyth, Wales, hegemony has continued to play a prominent role as a key concept within the discipline (Porter 1972). From the 1970s, the concept was to appear prominently in the sub-discipline of International Political Economy (IPE). Here, in the light of the fall of the Bretton Woods system, which had been set up near the end of the Second World War, many looked to see which state might replace the USA as the hegemonic leader in the international economy. Yet, as we fast-forward to the 1990s, we see that the USA emerged from the Cold War as the only surviving superpower and not as a declining economic power, and hegemony returned to the forefront of study within IR.

The significance of US hegemony after the Cold War has divided opinion. Some have argued that as the USA had become effectively the world's policeman in terms of its military and economic capability, Therefore it had a responsibility to stabilize the world to some degree (Krauthammer 2004). Others see the USA as an imperial power, seeking to maintain its superiority through the control and accumulation of resources and commodities (Panitch and Leys 2003). These critics might take up opposite poles in their opinions, but both acknowledge the importance of US hegemony as an explanation of the configuration of power since 1991.

Yet this has been coupled with another understanding of hegemony drawn extensively from the work of the former Italian communist leader, Antonio Gramsci, and has been used to understand how one class in society asserts its authority over another. Hegemony is seen as being the sum of social, cultural and political practices that have been used to consolidate power under a certain ideology. Gramsci was imprisoned by the Italian fascist administration from 1926 until just before his death in 1937, in order to 'prevent his brain from working', but while interned he wrote his *Prison Notebooks*, where he outlined his understanding of how hegemony between social classes is achieved. Despite being smuggled out of prison in the 1930s, the note-books were held over by the Stalinist Italian Communist Party before finally being published in the 1950s. By the time they were translated into a number of different languages in the 1970s, his concept of hege-mony was being used and dissected throughout the social sciences. In IR, Gramscian understandings of hegemony were developed by the Canadian academic Robert Cox. Drawing partly on his early career working at the International Labour Organization (ILO), Cox argued that hegemony at the international level is less to do with state leader-ship and more to do with what he termed 'world order' (Cox 1996). This is when a world is ordered through a set of hegemonic practices influenced by a leading state. The use of Gramsci has inspired a number of critical Marxist studies within IR that have used hegemony and class alongside Cox's understanding of world order (Bieler and Morton 2004).

The interest in hegemony as an explanatory term has been obvious in studies within world politics in recent years, yet there has also been a reluctance at times to explore the concept in depth. In political and social theory, the work of writers such as Ernesto Laclau and Chantel Mouffe took the concept to a level that moved beyond class towards one that took on multiple discourses and identities (Laclau and Mouffe 1985). In post-colonial theory, which has become an increas-ingly popular paradigm within IR, hegemony is seen as a governing discourse which undermines 'primitive' or 'indigenous' discourses that might challenge it (Escobar 1995). Hegemony is understood here as a colonial construction whereby a uniformity that began in Europe replaced pre-existing social orders. These post-colonial and post-structural understandings of hegemony provide an analysis that moves beyond the more common accounts we can find through either state-centric or neo-Gramscian understandings.

One of the departure points for this book is that while we have numerous definitions of hegemony, many lack a clear understanding of the term when engaging with it. Consequently, one is left with the impression that the term is not one that has different ontological starting points and meanings. Therefore, for us to rethink what the concept represents in world politics, we need to look at how the term has evolved in different ways. This book provides a comprehensive overview of the term. In doing so it will introduce and explain the history, development and wider usage of it and then show how a more inclusive conception can be understood. Ultimately, this will draw largely on a Gramscian framework, but will also indicate how the lack of clarity from existing neo-Gramscian accounts about the way that hegemony is used and understood as an international process can provide a framework that borrows from the strengths of existing frameworks but adds to its wider fabric as a concept.

Once we understand in greater depth the ways in which hegemony can be seen at a global level, we can then look at the reality of how it exists in global politics and society itself. The various phenomena such as American leadership, globalization, neoliberalism, regionalism and the emergence of the contender BRIC (Brazil, Russia, India, China) countries can be observed, and their place and role within a hegemonic order considered.

Outline of the Book

To provide a comprehensive study of the term that is accessible to students and scholars alike, this book is organized in a way that seeks to explain the different understandings of hegemony, and then to assess how it can be applied to reflect the current global order. If hegemony is a reality, what form does it take, and how (if at all) is it being challenged? Chapter 1 is geared towards discussing what hegemony is and how it can be understood as a basic concept. It suggests that hegemony used in global politics has been generally applied either as state hegemony or ideological hegemony. In contemporary studies, this is largely limited to 'US' or 'American' hegemony or 'neoliberal' hegemony. However, as the chapter suggests, the two are often used interchangeably and this creates a certain lack of clarity in its meaning. In response, it suggests that hegemony needs to be understood from a historical perspective.

Chapter 2 embarks upon the historical usage of the term in International Politics. It looks at the origins of the term itself and how it was understood at the time of Thucydides and in his accounts of the Peloponnesian Wars. Following this, it explores periods in history that are distinguished from each other through their hegemonic characteristics. It does this, both through understanding them as an order led by a dominant state and alternatively as one led by an overriding ideology. Chapter 3 then looks at the idea of US hegemony as it has been understood within the realms of international politics since the end of the Second World War. It examines the emergence of hegemonic stability theory in the 1970s and the idea of unipolarity after the Cold War as two strands of US hegemony. Chapter 4 investigates how the neo-Gramscian reading emerged as an alternative way of understanding hegemony from the more state-centric forms understood in the previous chapter. It shows how the Marxist development of the term emerged as an ideological way of advancing socialism and was heavily drawn upon by Lenin. It was from this Leninist understanding of hegemony that Gramsci's ideas developed. This was an entirely different embodiment of the term that was drawn from Ancient Greece, though, as the chapter shows, Gramsci's version brings out several similarities. This chapter also outlines some of the well-documented problems accompanying the application of Gramsci's form of hegemony at an international level and shows that, by drawing on the manner in which it has been adapted in other disciplines, these problems can be addressed.

The second half of the book focuses on the nature and fabric of the contemporary post-Cold War neoliberal order. It argues that by providing a mindset forged on market empowerment, a global market drawing on the core neoliberal principles has flourished since the end of the Cold War. It also suggests that emerging states, such as the BRICS (Brazil, Russia, India, China and South Africa) can look to challenge the existing order, but can also adhere to and contribute towards it. Just because a state might appear to be one that might challenge US leadership, it does not follow that the hegemonic character of the global system will change. Chapters 6 and 7 look at the emergence of both regional powers, in terms of the BRICS, and regional bodies, to see what role they play in contributing towards the character of hegemony, and their wider transformatory potential.

Chapter 8 looks more closely at the idea of hegemonic contestation and transformation. It looks at the increasingly popular idea of counter-hegemony in order to understand resistance at different levels of global society. Counter-hegemony is a process that looks to ideologically challenge, de-stabilize and eventually replace an existing hegemonic order. It suggests that, by understanding the potential strength of particular counter-hegemonic movements, we can ascertain where a challenge to the contemporary order might come from and which states might emerge to provide an environment in which they can flourish.

By following this plan, the book looks to open the concept up to scrutiny, before showing new ways in which hegemony can be understood at the global level. In this way, it is hoped to provide some responses to the problems that the term and concept have attracted when being used in the international arena, from all theoretical persuasions. Namely, questions such as whether the international or global arena is hegemonic, whether the said form of hegemony is being threatened, and whether hegemony is able to account for the construction of power adequately within international politics. The essence of these questions is certainly addressed in the following pages. In its mission to 'rethink' the term, the book concludes by inviting students of international politics and society to develop the concept in a manner that will open up new avenues for wider and more inclusive research agendas.

1
Hegemony and Global Politics

The concept of 'hegemony' is used in abundance in the study of global politics. It is an essential term for understanding how international systems function and the practices found within global society. It is a term used across the social sciences and the political spectrum, and by a variety of traditions from within the discipline of International Relations (IR). However, it is often used in IR in a way that overlooks its contested meaning, and as a result tends to be underdeveloped as a precise concept. This chapter provides an overview of the various ways that hegemony has been understood within IR and suggests that while the term has often been employed in a manner that assumes some universal meaning, on closer inspection it is highly contested.

This chapter outlines why hegemony remains a key concept in the study of global politics, and introduces two important ways in which it has been understood: as a leading state and a form of ideology. As a result of these two understandings, hegemony as a term has been used to refer to a dominant state or a dominant culture within international (or global) society. In this sense, contemporary hegemons would be identified as the hegemony of the USA and the hegemony of neo-liberalism. This illustrates the potential ambiguity of the term and the need to unravel it for further analysis. This chapter will thus introduce the concept of hegemony and its use within the study of global politics, and illustrate how and why it is a contested and sometimes ambiguous term.

What Is Hegemony?

The term hegemony is one that has been employed throughout the history of international politics. As Ian Clark's (2011) study of hegemony in international society illustrates, the term has not just been understood within international history as one where a dominant state or region asserts control over a wider area, but as a type of institution. In the same way that war, diplomacy and the balance of power have been features of the historical trajectory of international politics, so too has the process of hegemony (Clark 2011: 34). Yet even as we can suggest that hegemony is a key mechanism within IR, the phrase itself remains one that is open to multiple meanings. Two representative dictionary definitions of hegemony are: 'dominance of one social group or nation over others' (*Collins*) or 'leadership, especially by one state in a confederacy' (*Oxford*). While these might contrast in terms of how hegemony is understood, they nevertheless both focus on practices that are central to international relations.

Linguistically, the term also has its origins in the study of international relations. The genesis of hegemony can be seen with the phase 'hegeomai' that came to prominence in ancient Greece in the fifth century BC. Whether derived from the 'hegemonia' that refers to a leader (Williams 1977) or from another common use, its emergence became synonymous with the early struggles that existed within Greek city-states between the 1400-year dynasties that stretched from the eighth century BC to the sixth century AD. Here, it referred to the manner in which a dominant city-state was able to assert its authority through a variety of means over the wider civilization as a whole (see Chapter 2). For scholars of ancient Greece, the term thus explains one particular form of dominance. This was seen when looking at the historical development of the Greek empire, where Athens was replaced by the Delian League as the principle hegemon, and with Sparta subsequently replacing the Delian League. Such a process was to continue throughout the period of Greek civilization, when one city-state gained control and exerted influence over the system of governance as a whole. Thus hegemony appears both as a tool and as a central feature of the workings of ancient Greece, and becomes a crucial concept for understanding the mechanisms of international politics.

As Chapter 2 will show, it was this mechanism that was to resurface in the era of the nation-state system. Here, in the manner that certain city-states assumed dominance over Greece, powerful states would come to dominate the sovereign international system. Hegemony thus followed the logic set down in ancient Greece, where one specific entity asserts its dominance over others through both passive and coercive means. Certain accounts have borrowed from the most significant theorist and historian at that time – Thucydides – to suggest that hegemony can be seen as a form of leadership rooted in the necessity of justification (Lebow and Kelly 2001: 595). The evolution of the term in these accounts also suggests that by the time the Roman Empire emerged it had taken on a new dimension, as 'hegemonia' began to become understood as 'imperium' (Lebow 2003). Expanding on this, commentators such as Lebow and Kelly, and others such as Meiggs, have suggested that if 'hegemonia' in ancient Greece referred to the process where consent is reached through the leadership of a dominant state, then the word '*arkhé*' referred to domination. By the time the term was being used to indicate a mechanism, it tended to combine both the principles of consent and domination (Meiggs 1972; Lebow and Kelly 2001). The evolution of the term, at least in these accounts, tends to indicate that its popular usage in understanding the international politics of the state system moulded the two trends together. This would suggest that, by the time hegemony was being discussed as a process in contemporary (post-Westphalian) international politics, it was seen very much as a form of dominance (Lebow and Kelly 2001).

Here, then, such accounts like to stress the importance of consent within the term, and to imply that hegemony is not something that relies on force. This is a key to the way in which hegemony is understood. A strong hegemon would be one that could rely on its soft power or influence in order to find stability. It is this combination of consent and the more direct forms of domination that has also been the focal point of discussion in considering the social function of hegemony. When looking at Marxist discussions of hegemony, the question of how much one class asserts its authority over another has generally been the departure point, therefore the primary point of interest is not a dominant state but rather the results of having a dominant class.

There are marked differences, however, between the ways in which states are understood in the mechanism of hegemony. For example, in world systems research, hegemony appears in a relatively similar fashion to those that follow the traditional statist line, remaining central within conventional IR. Here, the general assumption is that a dominant state is required to anchor and embed the capitalist world-system (Robinson 2005). The character of capitalism within the world-system can depend on the nature of the hegemonic state that is leading it, and what it intends to bring as the 'hegemon' (Reifer 2004). The longevity of the hegemon and of its 'change of guard' has generated a number of studies within world-systems research. The overall longue-durée of the contemporary system can then be judged, in terms of its sustainability and in terms of whether one hegemon is in decline and another might succeed it (Wallerstein 2004).

Outside the unique discourse of world-systems research, hegemony has found considerable debate within wider Marxist audiences and subsequently within post-structuralism. Here it is understood primarily in terms of class relations and is often confined to a process that legitimizes a particular mode of production. While the general conundrum here is to understand how capitalism sustains its social relations, the solution is that it provides a vision where a form of ideology can be built to accompany a socialist form of production. V. I. Lenin, for example, understood hegemony as a political process through which the working class could gain supremacy over the bourgeoisie (Lenin 1992). For Lenin, the phase is often associated with the notion of 'dictatorship of the proletariat', a strategy that became synonymous with the early years of the Soviet Union, whereby the state would act in a manner that would provide rule on behalf of the proletariat. To a degree, much of this approach was in contrast to the social democratic strategy favoured by Karl Kautsky. Lenin's notorious attacks on Kautsky accused him of lacking a revolutionary strategy for change and of relying on existing bourgeois institutions to facilitate socialist change. For Lenin, Kautsky did not himself have a socialist hegemonic strategy, but instead he became ingrained within the existing system and as a result neutralized any radical potential for transformation (Lenin 1992; see Chapter 4 for a wider discussion).

Yet within Marxist circles the term has become associated with the work of the former Italian Communist Party leader, Antonio Gramsci. Gramsci developed the term while in a fascist prison, having being sentenced to 20 years for political subversion. During his time he kept notes on the political situation and culture of the era and it was while keeping these – his now legendary 'Prison Notebooks' – he sketched out his theory of hegemony. For Gramsci, hegemony provides the basis for class harmonization. It is the collection of ideas and the mindset that allows for the subordination of one class by another (Gramcsi 1971; 1995). It consists of a set of norms and common assumptions legitimized with the aid of social and cultural agents, and as a result it rests on a set of key principles that go far beyond mere ideology. Included here is the primacy of religion, the cultivation of national myths, and the formation of what Gramsci defines as common sense. That is the set of materially constructed practices considered to be logical in nature (Gramsci 1971; 1995).

. The many recreations of Gramsci's conceptions of hegemony have been applied within the historical era in which the writer finds him/ herself. For example, contemporary accounts often refer to 'neoliberal hegemony' or 'free market hegemony', representing the general productive ideology of the current era (Harvey 2005; Hall 2011). Others have shown how earlier processes of hegemony were developed that reflected the common order at that time (Cox 1987; Rupert 1995). This refers to Gramsci's own understanding of 'historical blocs', where he points to the way that certain historical eras become materially and ideological bonded by particular principles and socially ordered in a specific way (Gramsci 1971). The point here is that unlike those within the dominant strands of IR, Gramscian accounts of hegemony rest on the bond between being forged by social classes within a specific era. Yet, interestingly, this is not often the case with those that borrow from Gramsci within IR, or with those who have generally been associated with the so-called 'neo-Gramscian' school (or schools). For while they are keen to stress the fact that, at the international level, hegemony is formed by more than individually dominant states alone, they still seem to remain quite statist in their analysis (Germain and Kenny 1997; Robinson 2005; Worth 2011). For example, while many show that the international system is shaped by ideas and institutions that lead to a certain type of world order, the original impetus for this development remains from a leading or dominant state (Cox 1987). It is the emergence of this dominant state, therefore, that allows for the opportunity to develop hegemony at the international level. Without a leading state that seeks, through liberal aspirations, to expand its influence outside the confines of the nation-state, a hegemonic world order is not possible. Instead, it is likely to create a hostile international arena where competing hegemonic projects lead to potential conflict. This was seen in the latter part of the nineteenth century and the first half of the twentieth, where the lack of a dominant state in the international system led to fierce competition between respective ideological projects (Cox 1987). Therefore, many of the Gramscian understandings of hegemony insist on including the notions of class, culture and popular common sense, but locate its internationalization though the rise of a dominant state.

As with traditional IR theories, it is the influence of the USA that has fuelled the neo-Gramscian understanding of hegemony, yet its initial departure point was in looking at how class elites within the USA have developed international partnerships, and how the process of hegemonic building within American civil society has expanded towards global significance. This brings us to the first set of questions we need to answer to rethink and unravel the problems with understanding hegemony in contemporary world politics. The first question we should ask is if there is actually much difference between the traditional and the Gramscian or Marxian understandings of hegemony? While it is clear that the two stem from entirely different points of enquiry, how much do they differ in actually understanding the set-up of hegemony at the international or global level? If both suggest that the embodiment of hegemony ultimately requires a leading state for it to sustain its legitimacy at the international level, then we could suggest that the two different readings have more in common than we first thought. This is particularly true when certain traditional understandings of hegemony have themselves acknowledged the importance of ideas in the execution of hegemonic power. At the same time, while neo-Gramscian positions provides a normative framework for understanding hegemony, then a similar claim could be made about certain realist or English School readings within IR (Ikenberry and Kupchan 1990; Clark 2011). While it might be said that the former is generally looking to transform a hegemonic order into one of capitalist exploitation, and the latter seems more geared towards creating a more inclusive form of international society, both nevertheless can comprise normative qualities. This is something I will return to in the conclusion. Therefore, one of the first questions we need to ask is whether the distinction between the 'statist' forms of hegemony and the 'ideational' or 'ideological' form of hegemony is in fact that marked.

One of the more noticeable problems in the application of the term in IR is that it seems to be applied both unevenly and without justification at the same time. For example, textbooks and articles in IR use the term within a multitude of different contexts and sub-sections, but often it is merely preceded by the words 'American', 'Western' or 'neoliberal'. In each of these cases it is the preceding word, rather than the notion of hegemony itself which gives a clue to the reader as to what the writer means by the term. For example 'American' hegemony would suggest that the writer understands the process from a largely statist position. 'Western' hegemony, on the other hand, tends to suggest a historical and cultural form of influence, where the colonialism and imperial expansion of European interests led to European forms of governments and customs becoming embedded throughout the world. As a result, the term 'Western' or 'Eurocentric' hegemony is often used in the post-colonial literature (Said 1978). 'Neoliberal' hegemony, on the other hand, tends to refer far more to the growth and dominance of a specific economic ideology and how this has affected all forms of socio-political life (Plehwe *et al.* 2006).

This leads us to the second question we need to ask. If we acknowledge that there is some difference – however tentatively – in the way hegemony is understood, just how coherent are these various differences? For example, while we might be able to ascertain the difference between American and neoliberal hegemony, do they actually fit into one position or do they display differences? This may appear similar to the first enquiry, but it is asking a slightly different question, namely whether those who use the terms 'American' or 'neoliberal' hegemony actually mean the same thing or whether the respective usages are either inconsistent or imprecise in their meaning. Because hegemony is applied and used in so many different ways it becomes difficult to ascertain whether specific ontological streams actually occur, or whether there actually exist firm, coherent schools of application.

These tentative queries allow us to prompt further questions on the nature of hegemony, and will allow us to go back and look at the historical growth of the concept in international politics itself, and how this has developed through alternative understandings of the term. It will also allow us to unravel the problem, with its meaning in the contemporary world of globalization, and see how the concept can be developed further. To do that we need to go back to tackling our first question about understanding hegemony. As the two ways of understanding hegemony commonly used within IR are through the lens of a 'state' or of an 'ideology', it seems best to look at how these separate meanings came about, and how they have been developed and used over time. While subsequent chapters will look at the historical developments of the different usage of the term, I would like to show briefly how the two different departure points for the term have emerged.

Hegemony through State Leadership

The idea that hegemony arises through the role of a powerful state is one that might date back to Thucydides, but it is used within a number of different traditions and perspectives in IR. The post-Second World War environment saw many analysts within the area of international economics point to the necessity of a strong state in order to stabilize a wider international economic system (Kindleberger 1966). Indeed, it was the collapse of the dollar monetary system, agreed at the Bretton Woods convention in 1944, that prompted the first major interest in studying the political economy of international politics (Cohen 2008).

It was not until after the Cold War, perhaps, and the collapse of the Soviet Union that hegemony began to feature in central debates within international affairs. In light of the reality that the USA emerged as the only remaining superpower in the aftermath of the Soviet collapse, conservative readings within IR began to look at the concept seriously. This was particularly true in response to the crisis in structural realism that stressed the need for a balance of power and was perhaps best demonstrated in Kenneth Waltz's highly influential *Theory of International Politics* (1979). Waltz saw the world of international politics as one where states acted as 'units' within a wider international system, as if in an orbit. This almost Newtonian model of international politics saw influential larger units attracting the smaller entities by their pull of influence. When there are a large number of influential units (as was the case from the late nineteenth century to the end of the Second World War), a multipolar system emerges and instabilities occur. The 'bipolar' situation that existed at the time of the Cold War, where two large units controlled the wider system, is preferable to the multipolar one, where a plethora of large units means that certain alliances have to be forged to avoid potential conflict (Waltz 1979: 104–10). The Waltzian perspective after 1989 was to conclude that powers would emerge to contest and challenge the interim period of US domination, and another multipolar system would emerge (Mearsheimer 1990; Waltz 1993).

Yet another position developed after 1989, which was to accept the general principles behind Waltz's structural theory, but dismissed the idea that a single entity could not stabilize the system on its own without a state, or a coalition of states, acting as a balancer. This is where hegemony has emerged as a central principle within core arguments in IR. Michael Mastanduno (1997) queried whether hegemony, in the form of 'unipolarity', could provide an alternative to conventional understandings of the balance of power. Was the construction of hegemony a more viable mechanism for stability than had hitherto been understood? It has been on the proviso of these questions that hegemony has been of interest in the contemporary era. For those on the right of the political spectrum, the question of US hegemony has been one that has become central to understanding America's role in international security. Plans such as the 'Project for a New American Century' and the neoconservative (neocon) doctrine that was influential in the Bush administration after the terrorist attacks in New York on 11 September 2001 ('9/11'), were based heavily on the belief that hegemony needed to be more prominent at the international level for stability to be maintained. This was to keep up the realist tradition of statism and the limitation of the effectiveness of international organizations by stressing the need for state interaction in international affairs (Krauthammer 2004). Yet it was to reject the assumptions of defensive realism that any form of offensive manoeuvre ultimately results in the weakening in strength of a unit in real terms. It also allows for a normative dimension that is also missing from more traditional forms of realism, by arguing that modernization and democracy provide a universal model for stability (Mazarr 2003).

The aftermath of 9/11 coupled with the US campaigns in Afghanistan and Iraq have seen further developments from the right regarding the form that US hegemony could take in future years. Included here is Niall Ferguson's enthusiastic idea that hegemony could be applied in a more formal arrangement of imperialism. In *Colossus* (2004), Ferguson provided a one-dimensional account of hegemony (answering the question 'What is this thing called hegemony?'), by giving a very limited overview of the term, and presenting it almost entirely as a conservative concept and only briefly mentioning world systems theory as providing a different alternative account. His main aim there, and one that was subsequently debated in conservative journals such as *National Interest* and *Foreign Affairs*, was that hegemony could be used as a tool within a wider US imperialist model. This, for Ferguson, was not something that should be shunned or 'un-American', but rather something that is the most productive model for economic growth. Debates were therefore fashioned around whether a form of formal imperialism or of an American empire necessarily contradicts the historical fabric of the construction of America, or whether the USA needs to be less ideological when approaching world affairs and the unique position in which it has found itself (Odom and Dujarric 2004).

Against neoconservatism, those within the more pluralist or internationalist position believe that as the USA has had a greater form of structural power within international society since the end of the Cold War, it has a commitment to create institutional forms of stability at the global level. In the aftermath of the Cold War, the USA had the opportunity to embed an international system through the use of international organizations and through the pursuit of multilateralism. Here, the hegemon is responsible for guiding and leading the international system towards a stable and prosperous world based around the general principles that the USA traditionally espouses. However, unlike the more state-interventionist approach that these conservatives have taken with the aim of unipolarity, internationalists stress the need for a strong hegemon in order to build a strong system based on international law and sustained by international organizations. For this to be realized, the hegemon would need to stress that its main role is not to pursue power and stability for its own purpose but to push for a more democratic international order that moves beyond the state system that had failed to contain the centuries of wars brought on by great sovereignty powers. This was something that had been considered in discussions at the time of the collapse of the Bretton Woods system (Keohane 1984). The end of the Cold War, and of the bipolarity that marked its era, provided fresh potential for the transformation of the traditional state system (Ikenberry 2008). The events of the 1990s gave the impression that this transformation could occur with the greater use of intervention in certain areas of conflict such as Yugoslavia and Somalia (though, tellingly, not in conflicts such as Rwanda). The enthusiasm with which the Clinton administration took over from the 'new world order' mandate that marked George Bush Sr's tenure in the White House indicated that US hegemony might indeed be used as a way of installing a greater sense of governance to the international order.

The tide of this optimism was to turn by the end of the 1990s, however, with the presidential success of George W. Bush over the liberal internationalism of Al Gore. Yet, while the election in 2000 was fought around the issue of how much the USA sought to engage in areas of global society, the events of 9/11 the following year were to change this. The conservative rethink on intervention, however, was as much a response to the liberal internationalism of the 1990s as it was to the original Bush campaign of international retraction. Indeed, the very fabric of neoconservatism was built on the criticism that the 1990s had provided a platform for insecurity as the USA had relied on weak institutions to seek international answers rather than state power and diplomacy (Krauthammer 2004). In layman's terms, this was very much suggesting that there had been too much of the carrot and not enough of the stick. Or to go slightly further, it suggested that the form of liberal institutionalism favoured after the end of the Cold War aided the growth of potential 'enemy' states or movements that threatened the stability of the USA and the rest of the democratic world (Huntington 1996). By this, however, at least greater clarity was given to what purpose hegemony holds at the international level. One can debate whether a strong state in a position of exceptional power should either seek to assert its moral power in order to embed a system capable of transforming the contemporary world, or should it use its powers as a form of international police force, acting when it feels that the equilibrium of this position is under threat.

Yet hegemony at this level does not have to be seen as something that is carried out extensively by just one dominant power. As many have argued previously, for any form of hegemony to be sustained certain coalitions are required to sustain the state in its position as leader (Haas 1997). Historically, leading states have built alliances in order to preserve certain practices. For example, as Watson and Clark respectively have shown, the period of the Concert of Europe relied on a coalition of powers to forge an agreement from 1815, and the Cold War itself required strong coalitions to allow both competing parties to sustain their respective challenges (Watson 2007; Clark 2011). The importance of collectivism and coalition building in the process of hegemony provides greater legitimacy for the leading state to pursue its own moral leadership. In the contemporary era, for example, the more an influential state supports certain proposals, the more legitimacy they have. Again in the post-Cold War era, this has been seen with the wide coalition during the first Gulf War and with the mobilization of organizations such as the G8. Tensions caused within such organizations can also be seen as a weakness within the international order as a whole.

The positioning of other states in relation to the lead state is also something that preoccupies much of the thinking behind world systems understanding of hegemony. Heavily influenced by Fernand Braudel and Immanuel Wallerstein, world systems theory identifies hegemony as a process where a leading state can alter and shape the structures of international capitalism. While states act as supporters of the leading state, it is ultimately this dominant state that maintains and controls the forces of production and order. Yet, for such theorists, the point where a state can no longer maintain its position as a hegemon is seen when innovative changes in production, coupled with the emergence of new contender states, threaten a breakdown of the system (Rennstich 2004). World systems theorists thus aim to look at the stability of the hegemon and pinpoint any potential resistance and change to the system (anti-systemic movements).

World systems theory might largely be influenced by Marx-inspired understandings of capitalist production, but it relies predominately on statist forms of study when looking at the workings of hegemony and hegemonic orders. In this way they appear to be much closer to the neoconservatives in their structural understandings of hegemony than many of the rich ideational Marxian interpretations, discussed below. For as neoconservatives see the preservation of the power of the American state as imperative for the survival of the contemporary hegemonic order, so world systems see the same for the preservation of contemporary capitalism. Conversely, both see the rise of China as a threat to the contemporary order, and maintain that it is this change of guard which allows the very fabric of an international system to change radically (Reifer 2004; Schweller and Pu 2011). Thus, in both cases, it is the leading state that ultimately determines the character and development of a particular international system.

Hegemony as an Ideology

The other way that hegemony can be understood is as an idea that has materialized over time into a working social order. In this way, hegemony has been put to use and understood both as an ideology and as a wider concept within many of the social sciences that do not look on the order of international politics as their primary concern. Hegemony has been a central concept within Marxist social theory and within the framework of both post-structuralism and post-colonialism. The move to use this within the confines of IR was seen as one that would challenge the predominantly statist view of hegemony and allow for the term to be re-thought within the subject as a whole. Yet, despite this, as I will show, it often retains quite a statist outlook, with the focus on US power still being evident. However, with the growth of neo-Gramscian, post-structural, and post-colonial theory within the subject area of IR amid the so-called 'third debate' on epistemology, hegemony was to take on a different form that was to contest its traditional meaning as a state-led entity.

Within IR, the most notable intervention in establishing a rethink in the manner in which hegemony was understood was with the two seminal pieces by Robert W. Cox published in the journal *Millennium* in 1981 and 1983, respectively. Here Cox introduced the notion of Gramsci's concept of hegemony into the arena of international society. For while a state might have the power to lead and structure an international system, it still needs to build forms of consent and an ideological framework to enable it to succeed (Cox 1981, 1983). Since 1945, the USA has thus aimed to inspire a world order based on the liberal capitalist principles of free trade, individualism, pluralism and democracy. Writing and reflecting on an era that was still entrenched within the ideological divide of the Cold War, Cox looked at how the USA shaped the post-war world order by means of productive capability and the building of institutions. The economic might of the USA enabled war-torn European countries to rebuild their economies through aid and allowed for the construction of the United Nations system, which stressed a commitment to decolonialization and liberal internationalism (Cox 1981). The 'social forces' that were created from these interventions allowed for the harmonization of post-war settlements across civil and political society, and it was this development that allowed for an overriding form of post-war liberal hegemony international society.

However, it was the end of the Cold War and the collapse of the state socialist model of governance that really allowed a form of liberal hegemony to flourish. The end of the Cold War brought with it the globalization of the economy that led to the transformation of production as capital flows and technological innovations moved the world into a new 'global era' (Lechner and Boli 2012). This new era was to be shaped by the rhetoric that had become popular with the Republican Party under Ronald Reagan in the USA, and by Margaret Thatcher and the Conservative Party in the UK. The ideology that was later to become known as 'neo-liberalism' believed in minimizing the size of the state and centralizing the market so that it appears as the main vehicle for the creation of growth and prosperity. The creation and ascension of neoliberal social forces from the beginning of the 1990s onwards has seen an increased focus on the nature of 'neo-liberal hegemony' at the global or international level. Following Cox's understanding of how a world order is maintained (1981; 1983), neoliberal ideas have been employed in key economic international institutions for governmental purposes at the global level. For example, many have cited the policies of the World Bank/International Monetary Fund (IMF) in disciplining fiscally developing states that have fallen into economic difficulty during the debt crisis that followed the end of the Bretton Woods system in the 1970s (Robinson 2005). Institutional policy has sought to 'normalize' neo-liberalism and provide an appearance that (to paraphrase Margaret Thatcher) 'there is no alternative' but to embrace market principles and adapt.

While the use of Gramscian-inspired hegemony favoured by Cox might have provided a different avenue for the concept to be approached in IR, it did not mean that questions have not been raised over the form and clarity of such an application. As I shall discuss at length in Chapter 4, Gramsci's own understanding of hegemony was largely based on looking at class dynamics in society rather than at the wider level of international society (Germain and Kenny 1997). The manner in which Cox understands hegemony still relies predominately on the actions of the US state when looking at how the structural leverage of social forces are initially forged. The use of hegemony in the wider social sciences tends to look at the manner in which forms of contest are reached between those in society that are dominant and those in positions open to be dominated. It is, as Anne Showstack Sassoon comments, the result of the way 'one social group influences other groups, making certain compromises with them in order to gain consent for its leadership in society as a whole' (Sassoon 1982: 13). Studies thus look at the way cultural, political and social relationships are formed to enable this consent to be harmonized. Hegemony has been studied in the fields of literature (Williams

1980), cultural studies (Johnson 1986; Hall 1996), and linguistics (Woollard 1985) as well as in the more conventional areas of political and social theory (Buci-Glucksman 1980; Femia 1981; Salamini 1981). As hegemony encompasses a ruling totality that, to borrow from Raymond Williams, saturates society to such an extent that it even 'constitutes the limits of common sense for most people under its sway' (Williams 1980).

If hegemony is used to look at these social relationships at different levels of academic study, then there is also another issue at stake when studying hegemony in this way. Namely, what was the purpose of the theory in the first place? Those closer and more sympathetic to Gramsci's own political agenda have stressed that hegemony should be seen as a political strategy for building socialism. Looking to build on Lenin's idea of a hegemonic proletarian state, Gramsci's engagement with the term was such that, if a socialist state were to be built it had to be so strong in its ideological fabric that it was able to win the 'hearts and minds' of its citizens. For a hegemonic socialist order to be built, every element of social life had to be transformed. Gramsci looked at hegemony through an understanding of the complex bonds within different capitalist forms of social reproduction. His aim was to show how similar relationships were required in order to preserve socialism.

When Gramsci's most notable set of works, basically the various *Prison Notebooks*, written while he was in prison in the 1920s and 1930s, were translated and became widely accessible (1971; 1992; 1995; 1996; 2007), there were those who wished to stress that Gramsci was merely an orthodox Marxist-Leninist, and others against claims that he was validating a more pluralist liberal socialism of the sort the Eurocommunist movement in the 1970s and 1980s supported (Harman 1977). Yet it was this challenge to the traditional Marxist readings of class that propelled hegemony into new directions of theoretical analysis. The reading of Gramsci by Chantal Mouffe (1979) and later her collaboration with the late Ernesto Laclau in the book *Hegemony and Socialist Strategy* (1985) looked at developing the concept of hegemony to enable it to replace class as the central understanding of social development. Laclau and Mouffe's understanding of hegemony, however, was one that would not be tied to a specific form of ideology but rather it was one that was played out through a multitude of different struggles at contrasting levels of society. It has been from these decentralized, post-structural (and post-Marxist) positions that other understandings of hegemony within global politics have also emerged.

Through an *engagement* with the French philosopher Michel Foucault and anthropologist James Scott, newer studies have focused on non-Western-centric struggles and traditions. In doing so they have looked to develop the theory of the subaltern in understanding hegemonic practices. The subaltern was the phrase used by Gramsci to describe the section of society that needed to submit to contest to enable hegemony to function. Such accounts look at the ways that power is produced and reproduced within global society at different levels (Scott 1990; Walker 1994). Hegemony does not play an all-encompassing role here as it does within neo-Gramscian accounts, but provides a framework where different forms of power relationships can be understood at different levels both above and below the state. In wider IR, these contribute to the larger ideas on the relativity and diffusion of power across borders and boundaries. As such, a particular interpretation of hegemony, initially influenced by the work of Laclau and Mouffe, has been used as an explanatory form of understanding power and consent, amid a wide collection of post-positivist accounts that have emerged within world politics since the end of the Cold War.

Approaching Hegemony

As we can see, then, the concept of hegemony appears not as a singular theory, but as a term used in contrasting ways in world politics. We might be able to distinguish between those who understand it as emerging from the actions of a dominant state, and those who see it as more of a social construct based around some form of ideology. We have also seen, however, that there are stark differences and crossovers between and within these two positions. There are also stark disagreements about whether hegemony is understood as a structural form of expression or whether it is the result of the interaction of agency. For example, to those who follow the structural realism of Kenneth Waltz and the world-system approach of Wallerstein, hegemony appears largely to be a systemic product. In addition, while Cox looked to distance himself from the structural nature of such accounts (Cox 1996), he nevertheless favoured a largely structural approach towards his own model of world order. In contrast, those who stressed a greater role for normative ideas in the leading state in response to more neoconservative readings of hegemony look far more to the transformative potential of agency. More post-Marxist accounts, and those who support the post-structural understandings of power and identity and who might use the notion of hegemony in one form or another, try to distance themselves from any arrangement of structure and universality.

These differences have brought us an array of contrasting approaches to the study of hegemony; too many indeed to use the term merely as an explanatory process within clarification. However, many continue to do precisely that, in the justifiable belief that they are using a phase that appears to be self-explanatory. Yet, as we have seen in this brief introductory chapter, what might appear clear as a term is highly contested as a concept and as an approach to the study of IR. For us to try to unravel the puzzle of hegemony, these distinctions are very important. Even more important, these need to be clarified and discussed in depth by students of IR and world politics.

We have also seen distinct differences between the many different political persuasions understand hegemony. Hegemony is in no way a theory of the right or the left. On the contrary, it is used in different ways by those across the political spectrum. As a result, it remains difficult – or nearly impossible – to try to construct a grand theory of hegemony because of the obvious sheer contrast of political subjectivity. Yet there are some very real connections between the various types of application. All point to the fact that hegemony is comprised of a relationship between the dominant and the dominated at a global level, and all point to the idea that it is this relationship, however universal or fragmented it might be, that is central to the fabric of power within global politics. If a more nuanced but at the same time more compact definition of the concept can be used within IR, it might be best to look at how the modern world developed historically hegemonic ideas, states and orders. From here we can assess the way that the different structures and ideas emerged out of the state system to form the basis of hegemony, and in addition, how this developed over time.

Thus, while I shall look in later chapters at the ways in which hegemony has been understood as a concept and as a reality in international politics, Chapter 2 will look at the roots of hegemony and how it developed in the international system. This will allow us to look more clearly at the way hegemony has been approached within both the post-Second World War environment and within contemporary forms of modern capitalism. It will also be useful to show how each historical era has been seen to be shaped either by a specific leading state or by a specific ideological order. This will be the task for the next chapter.

2

Hegemony and Its Origins in World Politics

One of a number of ways of looking at the nature of hegemony as a mechanism within international politics is to use history as the laboratory. In this way we can look back at previous eras and see how hegemony was employed at the international level during different stages of history. Several writers have used history to show that certain eras have been marked by specific dominant characteristics. Furthermore, as Luke Ashworth's excellent survey of the study of particular eras of dominant thought within international society demonstrates, the discipline of international relations (IR) has often not been particularly vigorous or accurate in its historical analysis (Ashworth 2014). Studies of hegemony have generally been more rigorous in their historical analysis than others, however. Some have argued that this shows how one dominant state can create a system in its own image in order to build a stable world environment (Keohane 1984; Gilpin 1987; Watson 1992). At the same time, historical accounts have also been used that focus more on ideology or class formation when looking at the common characteristics of a specific order (van der Pijl 1984; Cox 1987; Murphy 1994). At all levels, studies have focused on the nature, unity and stability of a certain order. In particular, they have examined whether a strong state or ideology existed to make it stable or coherent enough for sustainability within that period of time.

As a result, we can tentatively map out the historical trajectory of hegemony within world politics by looking at the different forms that have emerged over time at the international level. This became particularly prevalent with the beginnings of capitalism, when the nation state emerged and when, as a result of the mercantilist era of the sixteenth and seventeenth centuries, colonial expansion provided the first significant form of Europeanization of the world. From here, we can see how different types of capitalism have emerged alongside different forms of statehood, and how they have transformed over time to reflect the changes to state and material power in the international system.

In looking at the different historical characters of hegemony we can also distinguish the trends that might determine the decline of one particular order and the rise of another. Indeed, both structural realism and world systems theory spend a great deal of time examining previous hegemonic orders in an attempt to determine the health of the present order (Wallerstein 1979, 2004; Waltz 1993; Mastanduno 2002; Layne 2006). As mentioned in Chapter 1, in distinguishing one specific order from another, Gramsci employed the term *blocco storico* (historical bloc). This refers to the solid structure that is created when a hegemonic order is in place. The formation and character of a historical bloc is dependent on the type of hegemony it is based upon, but it can be distinguished by the fact that it has a set of material circumstances, which include the positioning of social relations and the economic means of production (Worth 2005). Each historical bloc differs in the manner in which it is organized and understood, both socially and economically, or, to borrow from Gramsci, material forces are the content and ideology of the form of each historical bloc (Gramsci 1971: 377).

Even when looking at historical transformation through a highly state-centric lens, Gramsci's concept of *blocco storico* becomes useful, because within each bloc or era there exists a unique set of popular beliefs and assumptions. The withering away of one bloc and the formation of another happens over time as ideas, material circumstances and overriding hegemonic forces challenge the prevailing order and replace it with another. This transformation might occur through conflict and war, or through confrontation, but the resulting material conditions brought about by that conflict remain central to such a change. For example, even if we were to understand contemporary hegemony from the standpoint of US state power, the structural reasons why US power was allowed to flourish – the economic destruction of the Second World War – has to be acknowledged (Gilpin 1987). Similarly, the economic, political and cultural ideas that emerged following the end of the Second World War characterized the very fabric of that particular historical era.

In looking at the various historical orders to try to ascertain the roots of the actual workings of the concept, one needs to look at the birth and first use of the term, before moving on to the capitalist era.

Hegemony in Greece and Rome

As we have seen from Chapter 1, the first accounts of hegemony appeared in ancient Greece and became a feature of the Greek system of city-states. A number of prominent writers who look at the history of IR theory have written on the evolution of the term. For example, Richard Ned Lebow mentions that we can see the initial development of the concept in Thucydides' classic work *History of the Peloponnesian War*. Here, Thucydides outlines how Athens moved from being what he terms a successful *hegemonia* towards a failed *arkhé* (Lebow and Kelly 2001; Lebow 2003). The period of Athens' descent into war and ultimate failure to find consent among the other major city-states of the Greek system brought to an end its period of supremacy. In resorting to violence, Athens had broken the trust that had been built up during the successful period of the Athenian empire and the whole idea that bound the Greek system together – that of leadership and the construction of harmony among the different parts – was to come crumbling down.

Thucydides, as understood by Lebow and Kelly, saw hegemony not in the form of military might, but as a form of moral leadership that ultimately rested on consent and on building trust, hierarchy and popularity across the system of *Hellas* as a whole (Lebow and Kelly 2001: 598). The strategy of *arkhé*, on the other hand, was geared towards force and militarism and relied on fear and repression. For Thucydides, it was the end of the leadership of Pericles that proved to be the watershed for Athenian hegemony. Despite coming under attack from the Peloponnesians, Pericles at least remained true to the commitment of building support among his citizens (Thucydides 1972: 156–65). This legitimacy was not sought by his successors, who looked instead for expansion and relied on coercion to succeed. To a degree, we see a further similarity with Gramsci here, with his understanding of the balance between coercion and consent with hegemony. For Gramsci, unless these were formulated in the right way, a policy he described as Caesarism might emerge (Gramsci 1971: 272–83). This would be a situation where a leader relies on his state's military might and his own personality to maintain legitimacy. The moral here is that one can only rely on such a strategy for so long until it is necessary to build on a hegemonic project. For Thucydides, contest and coercion, or *hegemonia* and *arkhé* could exist together but *arkhé* alone would only lead to instability (Lebow and Kelly 2001: 601).

The Greek hegemonic system based around the principles of *Hellas* does provide us with our first insight into the workings of an inter-state organization. Yet the Greek system did not produce any pretence of internationalism. Indeed, its expansion was limited very firmly within its territorial sphere. Rome, however, did expand its authority, using the first significant invading land army and spread its might as far north and west as England, and east and south as Mesopotamia. Its senatorial provinces could be understood as being similar in some way to the Greek city-states in that, while Rome was the dominant partner, the other provinces were seen as vital cogs within its administration. The imperial provinces, however, were expansive outposts of a regime where citizens were controlled and subjected to Roman law and were inferior to the ethnic inhabitants of greater Rome. This led to the birth of the term 'imperialism', which denoted the territorial expansion of an empire and its continued maintenance (Kiely 2010: 2). It is the word *imperium* rather than the terms *hegemonia* or *arkhé* that are associated with Rome.

Yet the Roman empire is still used as a form of successful hegemony in some accounts of world politics. Indeed, both Robert Gilpin and Robert Keohane, pioneers behind the theory of hegemonic stability (see Chapter 3) suggest that the *Pax Romana* established a successful form of hegemony, which ensured stability from conflict and sustained economic prosperity (Gilpin 1981: 151–3; Keohane 1984: 31). Here hegemony does seem to take on a more coercive form, though as classical historical accounts have argued, one of the more salient features of the Roman empire was that elites were formulated and maintained in the aftermath of conquest and those elites were rewarded with Roman citizenship (Syme 1939). The same form of rule could be seen in other ancient civilizations such as the rival Parthian empire in Persia, or with the expansion of Chinese civilization in the Far East. Yet the *Pax Romana* is seen as the first systematic *international* form of governance.

While it might have provided a useful understanding regarding the roots of power in international politics, the Roman empire does not necessarily provide the best example of hegemony. The leadership of

Rome over Italy and its nearby upgraded regions shared similarities with Greece; its expansion provides us with the first example of imperialism and empire. This is not to say that hegemony cannot be a factor within the wider process of empire building, but that a hegemonic relationship is one that is formed through an informal hierarchy of power, whereas an empire requires a formal process of governance. While there are many new accounts of imperialism and empire that rely on informal sources of control as opposed to formal imperial governance (Hardt and Negri 2000; Harvey 2003; Panitch and Gindin 2003; Kiely 2010), the point here is that imperial systems do not rely on the forms of consent that are required for hegemony to be maintained. We also cannot use the system of the Roman empire to understand the wider international forms of hegemony, as while it did provide the first system of governance over a wider territorial area, there has never been a situation of a formal 'global empire' within world politics. The Roman empire existed in a part of the world in the same historical time-frame as other civilizations were operating separate systems in other parts of the world. It therefore lacked universality. It was not to be empire, or *imperium*, that would provide a truly international form of cohesion, but religion, which neither the Greeks nor the Romans could provide.

The Holy Roman Empire

If the first Roman empire was built on imperialism and expansion, the second one provided a moral leadership that influenced and maintained control over the leading medieval European countries and beyond. It was also based on a feudal system that was by no means global or expansive in its productivity. In his classical historical study on the development of world order, Robert Cox identifies two forms of productive relations that are apparent within the timescale of medievalism: that of the peasant–lord relationship and the primitive labour market (Cox 1987: 35–50). The former was based on the concept that a 'lord' owned the land on which a feudal settlement was situated, and as a result ordered the position and social status of the villagers. For this to be realized, a bond was required between the two groups and a legitimacy was forged from the emergence of the ethnic nation that had arisen through centuries of tribal struggle. Here, social hierarchies had been formed by tribal leaders adopting a monarchic title and appointing hereditary lordships, which allowed for the social settlement of the order. Christianity provided an additional form of social and cultural morality that bonded the social hierarchies together.

The primitive labour market can be seen to some extent as being the precursor of modern capitalism. At one level, the European model of feudalism developed alongside trade fairs until the territory of the feudal village expanded in tandem with commerce, industry and urbanization (Braudel 1983). However, European feudalism was by no means the only significant form of production during this period of history. Nor was the Holy Roman Empire the only sphere of modern influence. The equally significant rise in Islam provided not just a different form of moral leadership but also a threat to Christendom, as was demonstrated by the many crusades. The work of Janet Abu-Lughod has shown that, in addition to the different forms of religious faith that developed in other parts of the world outside Europe, there also existed a thriving merchant and trading system in parts of the Far East and Middle East. Therefore, if we are to understand the state system and capitalism emerging from a specific form of production, innovations such as the circulation of paper money, banking and merchant communication can be traced back to the Middle East and the Orient (Abu-Lughod 1989).

The medieval/feudalist era did not have a universal hegemonic project as such and was certainly not centred on Europe, or indeed Christendom. In some way, it could be seen as an era where contrasting civilizations existed. However, this would not necessarily be seen as a clash of civilizations of the sort associated with Huntington, despite attempts to link up the contemporary era with the medieval world (Ruggie 1993; Huntington 1996). Instead, such civilizations were not really prone to clash except on questions of religion and on the spheres of influence such religions would have in certain parts of the world. The world was thus more defined by regional civilizations, which were in no way interconnected or necessarily threatening. The one factor that was evident, however, was the rise of religion as a ruling form of ideological control. The authority driven by elders of Islam through devolved forms of acceptance, and more structurally from the Holy Roman Empire, provided the basis of hegemony for this specific period in history.

Religion was also a central determinate within Gramsci's own understanding of hegemony. Much of this was geared towards understanding the role of the Catholic Church in Italy during its unification and in the development of fascism (see Chapter 4). Yet Gramsci also spent a large proportion of his writing in the 'Prison Notebooks' commenting on its key social significance (Gramsci 1995). Here, religion played a significant role in the construction and governance of a specific hegemonic and is particularly noticeable in the channelling of faith and belief at a bottom-up level. The fact that religion is constructed in a manner that devolves its leadership throughout levels of society provide it with a unique position in terms of moral leadership (Fulton 1987). It was also a form of agency that could be employed effectively by leaders once the state system began to emerge and take over legitimacy from the church.

Mercantilism or Spanish Hegemony?

The emergence of Spain and Portugal as the first expansionist European powers began to transform the feudal system into one that placed commerce and the attainment of goods and produce at the centre. While one specific date cannot be given for the exact start of this transformation, the event that is often used as the symbolic moment of change is 1492 with the discovery of the Americas. The discovery and conquest of new lands and the first process of colonialism not only brought in a form of intercontinental production and an international economy but it also introduced the first form of capitalism, which was to formalize the nation state through the economic arrangement of mercantilism.

Mercantilism was more of a practice than an economic theory in reality. The basic premise behind it was that a country would control its own trading system and look for material to make it as wealthy and as powerful as possible. In doing so it would also gain a significant foothold in world affairs. The territorial expansion of Spain allowed for the extraction of precious metals, which, until the circulation of money became common, was seen as the first measurement of national wealth in comparative terms. Along with the establishment of the slave trade (instigated by the Portuguese), the extraction of metals allowed the Spanish empire to gain considerable leverage in the international system, especially when such metal was to stimulate monetary supply and a comprehensive trading system.

Yet the Spanish Empire did not fare well either in sustaining a hegemonic order as a state, or providing conformity to the mercantilist system, the flamboyant extravagance of Seville making way for the corrupt paranoia of Cadiz, when the empire changed its centre in the eighteenth century. Mercantilism as a theory was to benefit far more as a concept in France, from the much-lived realities of Jean-Baptiste Colbert, the Minister of Finance under Louis XIV, and the theories of Jean Bodin. It also thrived in Austria, where Philipp Wilhelm von Hornick (Baumol and Strom 2010) set out a national protectionist strategy in order to stave off the potential threat from Turkey. No one, however, exemplified the spirit of mercantilism better than Thomas Mun. Writing in England from a position that sought to challenge any supremacy from Spanish expansion, Mun outlined the steps needed to maximize a national economy. Central to this was the principle of a positive balance of trade; for a state to prosper it must do everything in its power to increase what it exports and reduce what it imports. While oversees conquests play a large part in realizing this end, such territorial expansion should be geared specifically towards providing resources that will bring down imports and provide a surplus of materials that are already in good supply for export purposes (Mun [1519]/2000). In addition, Mun suggested that states should seek to increase consumption and productivity, which would further increase its competitive advantage against other countries (Mun [1519]/2000).

Mercantilism became the first school of capitalist expansion and, despite it being the Spanish who brought it into existence as a result of the nature of their overseas discoveries, it was others that codified and theorized the economic practice to greater effect. Indeed, as Friedrich List later remarked, it was precisely the success of mercantilism in Britain that allowed the country to argue for free trade once it had gained significant economic advantage (List 2005b). However, the more significant long-term effect of sixteenth- and seventeenth-century mercantilism was that it led to the move towards statehood. By the time Machiavelli's *The Prince* ([1532]/1984) was published (and roundly condemned), the nation state was already on its way towards autonomy. The period when Spain gained ascendency was certainly one where the practices of diplomacy and statehood gained momentum. The era of formal national bargaining around the Spanish court was one that was to represent what was regarded as 'pure' diplomacy in its mythological sense, as the power of the national ambassador gained considerable stature (Der Derian 1987).

What did this all mean in terms of hegemony, though? The period of Spanish dominance is certainly omitted from many historical accounts looking at periods of hegemony. However, the Spanish and the Portuguese explorations led to a mindset that placed expansion and strategic state aims to the fore. It also prompted the beginnings of the culture of sovereignty and oversaw the first transformation from feudalist production to mercantilist capitalism. Moreover, it provided the first example of internationalism or globalization, and certainly marked the beginnings of the process of Europeanizing the world. The moves by Spain prompted the first era of state-building in Europe as countries departed from their medieval political and social systems and embarked on statehood and capitalist expansion. But by doing so it brought an era of distrust and competitiveness that was to spark centuries of conflict between the emerging powers. At a more mundane level, the transformation of everyday life during the sixteenth and seventeenth centuries was substantial as new forms of productivity emerged. This is perhaps best illustrated by Fernand Braudel's epic account of societal transformation during the period. Here, the radical changes to consumerism, employment and the family are discussed in depth, and the relationship at each level of society explored reveals just how transformative the period was in terms of the change in values and assumptions (Braudel 1979).

Westphalia or Dutch Hegemony?

If the sixteenth century and the early part of the seventeenth trans-formed the very nature of production and set Europe on the road towards global supremacy, then the period that followed institution-alized these moves. The 1648 Treaties of Westphalia provided legiti-macy for the European states legitimacy, while the Dutch East India Company developed and embedded the processes of capitalist expansion.

The Treaties of Westphalia were set up to end the 30 Years' War that had divided the Catholic and Protestant fraternities, and perhaps more substantially ended the longer 80-year dispute between the Spanish empire and the Dutch. In terms of the latter, it could be said that the banner of hegemony passed from the Spanish and was taken up by the Dutch. Westphalia gave the state institutional legitimacy over the use of violence and allowed it to 'legitimise the system of domestic and external – national and international – relations based on private property and territorial expansion' (Wallerstein 1979). As each party present accepted the exclusive sovereignty of themselves and others over their own lands and their governance, then legitimation within European affairs formally passed to the nation state. While these were not conceived originally at Westphalia and had in fact been agreed as early as the Peace of Augsberg in 1555, it was here that states finally compiled.

In strategic terms, the treaty also allowed the Dutch to break the link with Spain and ensure that sovereign legitimacy lay with the Dutch state. Any account that has stressed the importance of the Dutch in the establishment of capitalism points to the significance of Westphalia in providing a platform for hegemony (Arrighi 1993). It was here that the Dutch set the precedent for further hegemonic orders by laying the foundations for the future state system after realizing that the Thirty Years' War revealed a deeply chaotic atmosphere and a set of rules were required to enable some sort of international system to be implemented. By taking the lead, the Dutch reaffirmed their status as a strong state and, in the aftermath of Westphalia, providing a strong intellectual and moral leadership, and the potential to dictate a system that would finally remove the remains of the medieval system of rule (Arrighi 1993: 161).

The Dutch Republic's freedom from Spain allowed them to develop their colonies in South East Asia and to develop the Dutch East India Company, which had been established in 1602. The company held a monopoly over trading in the Netherlands and was organized into a body that orchestrated Dutch productivity in a manner that far outstripped its opponents (the British and later the French). In these terms it was a perfect example of mercantilism in action, as the Dutch East India Company was charged with organizing, transporting and trading goods on behalf of the Dutch state (Boxer 1965; Ames 2008). As a result, the Dutch Republic succeeded in increasing its own economic position and subsequently added to the establishment of international capitalism. As the trading routes increased and new parts of the world were being colonized by emerging European powers, capitalism, at least in its mercantilist form, was developing into a sophisticated institutional system that served to consolidate Europe's position as the master of international production.

However, despite the significant role of the Dutch East India Company in the mercantilist era, it remains questionable to suggest that the Dutch had great hegemonic influence over the system as a whole. It remains even more questionable when we look at the types of hegemony understood by contemporary hegemonic stability theorists, who stress the need to lead, dominate and police a system where necessary (O'Brien and Cleese 2002; Ikenberry 2006). The Dutch emerged as the front-runners in institutionalizing trade links in the way that both the Spanish and the Portuguese failed to do, and did emerge initially as the main benefactor of Westphalia. However, Westphalia itself did not lead to institutions that would strengthen the role of the state in Europe but instead nurtured a system of international law and diplomacy that reinforced and legitimized the anarchic state system. In stabilizing diplomatic institutions it stabilized a climate for both the growth of trade relations and the management of colonial expansion. As such, it allowed states to develop their own forms of national political economies within their own boundaries, while applying to them a universal set of principles. Unlike free trade, mercantilism ensured that national states would compete aggressively against each other for economic supremacy rather than look to mutually advance national economies.

The key hegemonic characteristics from this period were that, first, capitalism was developed into an institutionalized international system and as such became increasingly normalized as a social system. Second, the acceptance within Europe of sovereignty legitimized the state system as a territorially bounded entity which in the following centuries would lead to the establishment of European power as states became greater entities on the world stage. It also, through its structure, allowed for the formal development of alliances and coalitions that would provide the basis for the balance of power in the years to come (Bull 1977).

Liberalism or British Hegemony?

The emergence of the British state and its seaborne supremacy saw the first significant dominance of the world by one state arguably since the Roman Empire. British supremacy was based largely on economic might, on the ability to forge an economic ideological mandate to its advantage, and on the expansion and development of its overseas colonies. Central to the premise of British hegemony was the birth and the development of liberal economics, and of the doctrine of free trade through notions such as Ricardo's 'comparative advantage' theory, which showed how free trade might be beneficial to all. The enactment of British hegemony is also used categorically by hegemonic stability theorists (Krasner 1976; Gilpin 1981; Keohane 1984; O'Brien and Cleese 2002) as the first example of a hegemonic state. While this period has been understood as a distinct hegemonic era, there remains much discussion over when it actually began and ended. For some, the period extends from the Napoleonic Wars up to the beginning of the First World War. This spans the period of the so-called Hundred Years' Peace and explains how, in the broader context of international stability, one state has the capacity to bring stability to a wider state system (Friedberg 1988).

The period between 1830 to around the end of the 1880s is generally seen by most to be the time when British supremacy was at its strongest. It was then that the gold standard was enshrined into the international economic system, and when a free trade system was encouraged (Gilpin 1981; Darwin 2009). However, the British share of world trade peaked later and the zenith of Britain's empire in terms of overseas possessions did not occur until the start of the twentieth century (Hobsbawm 1975). In historical terms its pre-eminence came from two distinct parts. First, from the transformation of production as a result of the Industrial Revolution, and second, from the transformation of the British economy and society through the liberalization of its economy from government control.

Industrialization and the Napoleonic Wars

In the same way that exploration and conquest provided the main thrust for change during the fifteenth and sixteenth centuries, so the Industrial Revolution provided a similar impetus for change in the later eighteenth century. Innovations and industrial developments in the production of textiles, the extractions of metals and raw materials, and the revolutionary transformations to machinery and to different modes of transport rapidly increased productivity and, as Adam Smith demonstrated in his immortal *Wealth of Nations* (Smith 1776), provided the potential for its effectivity when organized through the division of labour. However, the social, political and economic transformation planned to maximize the productive potential of these moves did not materialize, for two reasons. The first was that the British economic system was still very much based on mercantilism and protectionism; and the second was that by the end of the eighteenth century Britain had become embroiled in a war with France under Napoleon that sought continental military dominance.

The protectionism that existed in Britain to some extent was a result of the aristocratic flavour that was evident in both the social and political hierarchy in the country in the late eighteenth century. With a sustained period of dominance of Tory rule (the party that tended to maintain the traditional interests of the aristocracy) within Parliament at the time, this status quo would be maintained. In terms of social relations, Britain also had the same Poor Law system that the country had in Elizabethan times, where parishes would provide poor relief to those in their vicinity. This effectively limited the movement of the population and restricted them to their individual parishes. Tentative attempts were made to address this by certain parishes worried that the changes brought about by the Industrial Revolution could no longer sustain adequate relief, but the government at the time was reluctant to alter the situation. This was also reflected in the electoral system of the day, where a combination of bizarre local traditions, landed privilege and uneven constituencies allowed for the aristocratic control of Parliament.

The Napoleonic Wars not only imposed a war economy on Britain for more than 20 years, but more obviously was geared towards preventing another power from controlling the whole of Europe. The variety of military alliances put together by the opponents of Napoleon in order to balance out the French also underlined the British commitment to sovereign self-rule on the continent. The resulting victory did much to ensure that the British could undertake a position to enable them to police the balance of power within the state system in a manner that would ensure it remained intact. The result at the European level was the Treaty of Vienna, which allowed for this arrangement to be realized as it established a peace which was geared towards making sure war would not engulf the continent in a similar manner in the future. What this meant in practice was that the situation would not arise again where one power could attempt to conquer Europe by force.

The Concert of Europe, as it was called, was set up in 1815 and formed a system around the four powers of Austria, Prussia, Britain and the Russian Empire, and it would be these four that would secure Europe in a sort of nineteenth-century version of the United Nations Security Council. It was not geared to provide a universal form of stability, nor did it give Britain a leading role in the relationship among the four. As mentioned by the historian R. B. Mowat, who provided one of the first studies on European foreign relations in the nineteenth century, the congress believed that the 'old system' before the war had provided stability and liberty, so its purpose was not to construct a new system but rather to restore the old (Mowat 1922: 5). While accounts have debated whether the congress was the result of a hegemonic strategy by certain states, or whether it was merely an attempt to put in place a system that would maintain and manage a more formal balance of power on the continent (Gruner 1992; Schroeder 1992), the congress did not allocate one specific state 'special interests' in terms of territory or key strategic interests. Indeed, the treaty seemed rather to provide a forum whereby the great powers, along with their overseas territories, could be managed in an appropriate way (Mowat 1922: 2–5). As far as the British were concerned, the real result of the treaty was that it could stabilize the system within Europe and allow for a period free from war, when they could use the economic advancement achieved by the Industrial Revolution to their advantage.

The Self-Regulating Market and the Pursuit of Free Trade

With the end of the war in 1815, Britain sought to maximize its economic production amid renewed talks of reforming the labour market and the electoral system. While the later years of the formidable Lord Liverpool-led Tory government (which served from 1812 to 1827) brought in certain reforms to the socio-political system, it was the Whig policies of the 1830s and 1840s that transformed society. The collection of acts that were introduced through Parliament between 1830 and 1846 effectively saw power move from the aristocratic class to the manufacturing middle classes. The 1832 Reform Act did much to encourage this shift as it provided the middle classes with the electoral vote, and the growing urban centres with representation for the first time. Yet it was the radical changes to the Poor Law that gave the market a greater role in the determining of the outcome of the economy.

In his landmark study *The Great Transformation*, Karl Polanyi saw the abolition of the Speenhamland System as the main factor behind the consolidation of the British liberal state (Polanyi [1944]/2001: 77–85). The system, named after the parish in which it began, gave relief to the poor, irrespective of their social status. The relief was tied to the price of bread and prevented parishioners from starvation or from absolute poverty. Despite the system never being a universal one, it did bring in some necessary revisions to the outdated Elizabethan Poor Law. However, unless there was an upheaval of the system itself, landowners could continue to undercut their workers in the knowledge that the parish would effectively top-up their weekly allowance. More important, it prevented any form of urbanization or free movement as the workforce became tied to their parish. To address this, the controversial Poor Law Amendment Act was passed by the Whigs in 1834. The Act stripped parishes of their right to provide poor relief and set up 'workhouses' in their place. These institutions later became infamous because of their inhumane conditions and brought in a morality that placed the emphasis on finding work and labour at the core of social stability. As a result there was a radical increase in urban migration as Britain became the first industrial capitalist state.

According to Polanyi, it was the Poor Law Reform Act that set the standard for the logic of the nineteenth-century market system by effectively creating a social structure that saw the state look to retreat from interference in the economy (Polanyi [1944]/2001: 83). The 1840s saw the repeal of the Corn Laws, which had protected the price of bread artificially from market competition, along with the Bank Act, which provided the basis for ensuring the strict application of the gold standard to the international system. This was followed by the Companies Act, which helped to further regulate private business activity, and these reforms allowed the British government to adopt a laissez-faire approach to the economy in the 1850s and 1860s (Bentley 1984: 161–77).

From this base, the British were able to maintain a hold over the international economic system, and competing states looked to engage with the principles of free trade that the British were keen to promote to enable their economies to 'catch up'. By 1850, Britain was the only European nation that had more than 20 per cent of its population living in urban areas with more than 100,000 inhabitants (Hobsbawm 1962: 319–20). Through this urbanization, and by opening up its domestic markets, other states were influenced by the British mode of development and benefited from factors such as the communication networks that arose from its expansion. European powers responded to the British free trade movement by reducing protectionist fortresses of their own and states eagerly looked to industrialize and transform in the same manner that was being seen in Britain (McKeown 1983: 82–90).

Britain obtained an economic position at the height of its supremacy whereby it could undersell its competitors and achieve a unique position where it could alter the structure of the world's economy for its own benefit. Technically, competitors of the British could have contested their domination of the international economy by refusing to trade with them, but the newly emerging bourgeoisie on the continent could see the material riches being harnessed in Britain and looked for a chance to do the same (Hobsbawm 1975: 38). More practically, despite the fact that the expansion of world commerce was making Britain increasingly strong, the beginning of free trade allowed competing nations to industrialize and strengthen their own economies. This was the era when Ricardo's theory of comparative advantage became highly influential as the rhetoric that a greater engagement with untariffed goods provided a common wealth for all involved. The increase in the exports of British railroad iron, steel and machinery in the latter half of the nineteenth century saw Britain not just aiding but also facilitating the industrialization of other European countries (Hobsbawm 1975: 39).

There remain questions, however, over how far the nineteenth century is one that was defined by British power, or one defined through the ideological strength of classical liberal economics. Because, while the success of British economic power might have been evident during the period after 1832, there are wider questions regarding whether this power had a direct effect on shaping the economic and political character of the international system. As will be discussed in Chapter 3, the economic dominance or leadership of Britain provides the first historical example of hegemonic stability. Debates over the extent to which Britain exerted this hegemony are seen in how far it established the gold standard, and how far it was central to the international pursuit of free trade. For example, while the City of London became the recognized centre of the financial world and the place that drove the international economic system, so self-regulated was the market that the state's main contribution was to maintain these liberal conditions (Clark 2011: 109). This, as Polanyi described all too well, became too contradictory because, in order to continue to make the market as free as possible the state was required to intervene by providing forms of regulation (Polanyi [1944]/2001: 136–9).

More significant was the fact that the main principle the British state was trying to retain during the nineteenth century was the liberal ideology of free trade. The period might be associated with the enlightened works of Adam Smith, David Ricardo and John Stuart Mill but the moral consciousness that the British establishment and the then dominant British Liberal Party was trying to promote seem to have more in common with the ideas of Thomas Malthus than anyone else. Malthus's musings on population control and social hierarchy (1798) were geared around the idea that living in poverty and inequality was the natural state of humans, and if the state interfered by preventing a disaster or natural catastrophe then this natural balance would be interfered with artificially. The liberal governments in Britain up to the late 1860s seemed to agree with maintaining this principle by refusing to interfere in any aspects of the economy. Most notoriously, this was seen when such Malthusian ideology prevented the state intervening in a blight famine in western Britain and – most devastating and significant – in Ireland, with catastrophic effects.

'Rival Imperialism' or the Interregnum?

The weakening of the British-inspired era of liberal hegemony can be seen with the rise of labour and democracy movements within Britain. The 'backlash' or 'counter-movement' that marked the whole notion of a self-regulated market appeared prominently in the form of organized union movements and in electoral movements such as the Chartists, which demanded universal suffrage (Polanyi [1944]/2001: 234–5). The resulting Reform Act of 1867 effectively ended the golden era of parliamentary liberalism as the urban working class received the vote and demanded an improvement in working and labour conditions. By the start of the twentieth century, socialist organizations began to emerge that were to contest further liberalism, and moves were made in Britain to place tariffs back on goods to give preferential protection to the British Empire (Cox 1987: 154–7; Hobsbawm 1987: 251). This was compounded in the years before the First World War, when the Edwardian Liberal Party ushered in the beginnings of the welfare state. The roots of this were established with the 1909 People's Budget of David Lloyd George which brought in a super tax for those at the top end of the salary scale.

The regulation of the liberal system and the protection of national empires were what Robert Cox describes as the move away from the liberal state (or from liberal hegemony) to an era where a form of welfare nationalism began to emerge (Cox 1987: 165). What was becoming clear by the end of the nineteenth century was that the laissez-faire belief that the market could regulate itself without state interference was no longer applicable. What accelerated this process was the re-emergence of nationalism from the 1880s onwards, coupled with the imperialist expansion by European powers into new areas of the world. The 'era of flag wavers', to quote Hobsbawm, was reflected in the emergence of new super nations at the heart of Europe and a renewed period of territorial expansion (Hobsbawm 1987: 46). The unification of Germany and Italy prompted a competitive scramble for Africa that led to a more strategic form of colonialism in the form of imperialism (Young 1995). This replaced the idea that one specific state was superior or influential in the world system as a whole (though there were distinct differences in terms of the size of respective European empires), and tested the balance of power mechanism that European powers still relied on over 50 years after Vienna.

Economically, the supremacy of Britain was also challenged significantly by the emergence of Germany in particular. While Germany would never gain a territorial advantage over either the British or the French, its economy led to a challenge, both industrially and militarily. By the 1890s, Germany had surpassed Britain as the main European producer of steel (Hobsbawm 1987: 53–5) and the development of military and naval power put an end to the notion that Britain was an isolated super-power. Ideologically, the model of political economy that Germany preferred in its industrial development was heavily influenced by the work of Friedrich List, and fundamentally contested the liberal one favoured in Britain and beyond. List believed that free trade aided those countries that relied heavily on oversees commerce, while undermining the development of national manufacturing (List 2005c). Following in the spirit of Alexander Hamilton, List believed that, by constructing tariff boundaries to protect national industry from oversees competition, rapid industrialization could be more effective. Indeed, List heaped praise on the British industrialization process for using mercantilist strategies to prepare the environment to allow for the innovation of the Industrial Revolution. The pursuit of liberalism was a similarly strategic attempt by Britain to maintain and strengthen its competitive advantage (List 2005a: 62–70).

The Slow Emergence of the USA

While the hegemonic ideas of classical liberalism might have been eroded by the re-emergence of mercantilism and the scramble for empire, the gold standard remained intact and the banking industry became an increasingly international phenomenon which began to wield significant influence within global affairs. A number of studies have looked at this further and have shown how, from the nineteenth century onwards, a transnational capitalist class began to emerge centred largely on Europe and North America (van der Pijl 1984, 1998; Sklair 2000). As the liberal ideal flourished in London in the nineteenth century, the growth of a financial centre in the USA based around New York had gained significance by the start of the twentieth century. Traditionally, the nineteenth-century development of the USA had been marked by the protectionism of Alexander Hamilton. However the embracing of the gold standard and the signing of the Federal Reserve Act in 1913 had transformed the country into one that was prepared to establish its own form of liberal capitalism.

The post-First World War boom in the 1920s continued the stock of American capitalism and certainly added to the belief that New York and Wall Street were emerging as the central financial capital in the international economy. Yet isolationism remained prominent with American political society when it came to wider international affairs. Indeed, both the establishment of the central federal banking reserve and the US entry into the First World War were faced with considerable opposition across the country, and President Woodrow Wilson's ideas for post-war international institutional stability were met with further hostility. As a result, the League of Nations, which owed a significant debt to the vision of Wilson, ran without the USA on board.

The uneasiness of the American engagement with global finance came to the boil with the Smoot–Hawley Tariff Act (1930), which brought back tariff duties on a number of foreign imports. While this was introduced after the Wall Street crash, there are some accounts that suggest that the preliminary discussions of the bill contributed to the lack of confidence in the market and to the impact of its collapse (Beaudreau 2005). The tariff duties themselves were popular with the public at large and the resulting New Deal in the 1930s saw the USA retreating further from international politics. The resulting troubles in Europe also allowed the USA to isolate themselves even more from global affairs, but as Europe and the rest of the world went into conflict, many financial institutions moved their centres to New York.

The Atlantic Charter and Bretton Woods

If two war-time acts could highlight the importance of American influence on the future international system, it would be the Atlantic Charter and Bretton Woods. The Atlantic Charter was formulated in 1941 prior to the US engaging in the war. Here, President Roosevelt and UK Prime Minister Churchill signed a pledge that would agree to build a United Nations system after the war that would preserve the right of self-determination. This effectively bought to an end the era of the European empire and placed a firm pledge towards a post-war world that would make a commitment towards de-colonialism. In some accounts, it also symbolized the handing over, so to speak, of hegemonic power from the British to the Americans (O'Brien 1999). Alternatively, it can be seen as an attempt to rekindle a liberal ideal in the transnational 'Lockean heartland' (van der Pijl 1998). The upshot was that, unlike the situation at the end of the First World War, the USA made a practical commitment to establish an international institutional structure with its own ideals at the helm.

If the Atlantic Charter set the political ambitions of post-war American power, then Bretton Woods realized the economic ones. The economic conference at Bretton Woods in 1944 was again a predominantly Anglo-American summit, with the USA significantly gaining superiority. In this case, the economist, John Maynard Keynes, whose work on the regulated economy and on demand-side economics was highly significant during the inter-war years, was to provide the influence from the British side. Keynes' idea for an international monetary system was agreed on by the conference, but the American contingent insisted that the new gold standard would be pegged to the dollar. Keynes himself had long favoured an international currency for this purpose, as he feared that a public national currency would not be able to boost its own economy on the one hand and provide stability for the international economic system on the other. Yet the outcome of the Bretton Woods system was that the

American delegation succeeded in getting their way overwhelmingly over the significant role of the dollar and subsequent control of the post-war international financial system. The consequences of these decisions will be discussed in greater depth in the next chapter.

Conclusion

This chapter has outlined the different historical patterns that have emerged when understanding the nature of hegemony at an international level. It has also shown how, when we look at the origins of hegemony in international society, the questions of state leadership and ideology remain complex. In each historical order or historical bloc, a leading region, state or institution has appeared to adopt an influential position which characterizes that specific era. Yet the extent to which this 'hegemon' has managed to assert its authority is more difficult to ascertain. The historical era has also been characterized by a specific hegemony ideology. Again, it is difficult to measure just how prominently and strongly such an ideology marked any given era. However, certain general trends and characteristics have certainly marked eras and distinguished them from others.

What is also noticeable is that the dominant feature, often seen as inspiring a given hegemonic order, does not necessarily have to be a state. The Roman empire might, in the eyes of famous accounts, be seen to have asserted its general hegemony for over 1,500 years. As Edward Gibbons' celebrated account suggests, Rome moved its position from formal empire to informal empire through the moral authority of the Catholic Church (Gibbon 1789). Subsequent eras have seen territories take certain leads with the formation of statehood. The onset of exploration and the transformation of production have tended to coincide, consciously or unconsciously, with the rise or prominence of a specific state.

We have also seen that, contrary to certain arguments, hegemony has not been entirely understood, either through an ideology or via state domination. The arguments laid down by Thucydides and Machiavelli do not see hegemony as something that is fuelled predominately by state power or domination, but by a mixture of coercion and consent. In this way, their understanding of the process of hegemony is actually closer to that of Gramsci in terms of locating how power is wielded. How does this provide us with an insight into how hegemony is played out and understood in contemporary terms? The next chapter will look into the roots of US power after the Second World War, and how this power manifested itself at the global level. We shall also look at the shortcomings of understanding post-war US hegemony, and ways which in which we can move beyond these shortcomings.

3
US Hegemony

Despite the ascension of the USA as the major power in international politics that created a large amount of interest in contemporary accounts of hegemony within international relations (IR), it was the emergence of hegemonic stability in the 1970s that was to dominate debate in the subsequent decades. Hegemonic stability theory became significant in understanding the workings of the international economy, and subsequently world politics as a whole. Yet it was the notion that US power and leadership was being eroded in the 1970s that actually popularized hegemonic stability theory. As I shall explain in this chapter, the power that the American state built up after the Second World War became a feature of the post-war environment in world politics. Yet it was the the fallout from the collapse of the dollar system, which had been constructed through the institutions created at the Bretton Woods conference in 1944, which led to the concern that the international economy would struggle if discussions centred on whether US power was actually now in sharp retreat.

As this chapter will outline, the fallout from the dollar crisis might have led to a conviction that US power was in some form of terminal decline, but the events of the 1980s and 1990s seemed to suggest that the structural power asserted throughout the Cold War put the USA in a stronger position for wider leadership. In the 1970s, the dominant view that emerged in the light of the crisis was that the USA needed to embark on a defensive policy of containment in foreign affairs, in view of both the retreat of the dollar and the continued prominence of the Soviet Union. But the 1980s saw a move by the Reagan administration to make an aggressive challenge to the doctrine and the economic viability of the USSR. The resulting 'victory' of the West and the subsequent collapse of the Soviet Union left the USA as the only official superpower in international politics, and any claims of its demise as being baseless. This chapter will show that, as a result, the term has found greater significance in the decades following the fall of communism to illustrate how the USA has asserted its control over world politics.

As well as looking at the rise of the USA as a form of state hegemon, this chapter also looks at how the concept of hegemony has emerged as a key function within the specific discourse of international political economy (IPE). IPE, or at least the American understanding of this, emerged as a specific response to President Nixon's decision in 1971 to discontinue the link between the dollar and gold, and subsequently end the economic system that had been in place since the Bretton Woods conference in 1944 (Cohen 2008). In the aftermath of the Cold War, however, the term was to become far more universal within the discipline as a whole.

Hegemony began to gain considerable interest from those involved more centrally in international security, and particularly from those of a conservative persuasion. As Niall Ferguson so unapologetically proclaimed, it would appear more acceptable to flaunt the success of empire and hegemony freely if it leads to stability and prosperity (Ferguson 2003: 295–6). Yet perhaps more interesting was whether the form of unipolarity that had emerged since the end of the Cold War could sustain itself for a significant period (Kapstein and Mastanduno 1999). This became even more apparent in the post-9/11 environment, when fears arose alongside the neo-conservative agenda over the future security of the world if the USA (as the hegemon) ignored specific threats (Krauthammer 2002/3). Thus, this chapter will look at the rise of US power, before reviewing the manner in which hegemony has been understood in orthodox IR theory, first through hegemonic stability theory, and second, through post-Cold War understandings of unipolarity.

The Rise of US Power

The rise of the USA was not complete on the international stage until the disappearance of the Soviet threat and the end of bipolarity. The existence of the Soviet threat and the cultivation of state socialism meant that the USA's influence would only extend to the capitalist world. Its military and security organizations would wield significant control, also ultimately extending to the Western world. This was similar to the economic power that emerged from the Bretton Woods agreement. The establishment of the dollar system extended only to those states that had bought into the system. This was reinforced by the onset of conditional loans to Western Europe in the aftermath of the Second World War, effectively steering the American sphere of influence on ideological lines.

The most significant of these loans, the aptly named Marshall Plan (named after Secretary of State George Marshall), was to have the greatest effect in shaping the post-war environment. The Marshall Plan was co-ordinated through the Organisation for European Economic Co-operation (OEEC), and funds were distributed according to the decisions of this agency. The purpose of the plan on paper was merely to use the funds to rebuild war-torn European economies, but the wider connotations were along ideological and strategic lines. For example, in the process of rebuilding, industrial relations were aided by the co-operation of labour unions within Western Europe, which detached themselves from their more left-wing radical elements to endorse the plan (Rupert 1995). In addition, incentives were presented by the USA to make sure that unions with communist or radical left-wing elements in France and Italy were denied consulting access to their respective post-war governments (Cox 1987: 215).

The result of the loans in Europe was mixed. In certain states, such as Britain, the domestic forces of social democracy that were ignited with the Labour landslide election victory in the months after VE Day (Victory in Europe Day) became diluted with the more liberal application of the mixed economy that was favoured on the other side of the Atlantic. As a result, the major political organizations in Britain were quick to form a consensus around the basic undertaking of a welfare system, a mixed economy and a commitment to the international conditions emphasized at Bretton Woods. The extremes from both the left and right that sought to contest this consensus were increasingly marginalized (Beer 1967).

In places such as France and the newly created Federal Republic of Germany (West Germany), American influence was more noticeable. Here, financial support was given to sectoral integration and to unifying key industries within the two countries, to prevent conflict on the one hand and fight the threat of communism on the other. It was from here that the European Coal and Steel Community (ECSC) was formed. Both German Chancellor Adenauer and the German Christian Democrats, and the French statesman Jean Monnet and Robert Schuman, were encouraged and aided by the President Truman-led US administration as an ideal collective foil to stave off the communist threat (Ellwood 1992). Stronger US influence could be seen with the anti-communist stance taken in Italy, where action was potentially strong enough to disrupt the process of parliamentary democracy. In the 1948 Italian election, the USA planned military intervention should the strong Communist Party win. By the 1950s, campaigns against communism had reached such a level that political parties sought a succession of multi-party coalitions at the level of central government to force the communists into opposition. Concern for the withdrawal of funds coupled with the threat of potential military action provided enough incentive for such an action (Cipolla 1970; Hobsbawm 1994). This was also a later characteristic of states that were geographically close to the 'Iron Curtain' (the border in Europe between the Western and communist states). Finland, for example, employed a long-term Cold War tactic of creating large rainbow coalitions merely to exclude the communists.

If the Marshall Plan and the first moves towards European integration provided the platform for US influence in Europe, then the institutional framework built on the Atlantic Charter (see chapter 2) gave it its hegemonic legitimacy (Clark 2011: 140–4). The Bretton Woods agreement not only produced the dollar system, but it also led to the construction of the World Bank, the International Monetary Fund (IMF) and in time the General Agreement on Tariffs and Trade (GATT). The UN system that accompanied it provided institutional support (over time) for the process of decolonialization and for US-backed initiatives. The institutions of the UN were heavily backed by US funds and were met by vetoes issued by the Soviet Union as a result. As many of the institutions linked monetary contributions to voting rights, the US gained considerable influence over the decision-making process. This was highly significant once the post-colonial movements began to emerge. Bodies such as the World Bank and GATT provided a source of income to newly independent states, which in turn provided greater legitimacy to the US-backed Western system. While this did not necessary equate to direct US involvement in post-colonial states, the funds that were made available meant that such states could buy into the system to which the competing USSR was opposed.

The institutions built by the USA allowed for economic power to be generated in different ways. Economically, through the construction of the Bretton Woods organizations, the USA could wield what has often been referred to as 'soft power' (Nye 1990). Here, power is legitimized through the rules laid down by the institutions so that it appears to be universal and democratic. Yet, as the institutions were founded and maintained through an uneven voting and financial system, the USA could still assert its general overriding authority. Security organizations, on the other hand, were more mixed in terms of their own international authority. The North Atlantic Treaty Organization (NATO) did not actually emerge as an American creation, but rather as a European entity initially geared towards maintaining stability within Europe. With the start of the Marshall Plan, and in the aftermath of the Soviet Berlin blockade, NATO turned its attention to, as famously remarked by the first Secretary General, Lord Ismay, 'keep[ing] the Americans in, the Russians out and the Germans down'. As a result, US influence over security seemed to be geared to specific geographical regions to contain the Soviet threat (Gaddis 1987). As stability and containment in Western Europe matured into détente, US influence moved into other parts of the world, prompting the USSR to do the same, thus reinforcing the bipolar world as a result.

Therefore, one could argue that US dominance at the international level was more noticeable at an economic level than it was in terms of security. This certainly seemed to be reflected in the IR literature during the Cold War, where concepts such as the 'balance of terror' were describing the realities of the bipolar world (Porter 1972). In economic terms too, the establishment of the Soviet-led Council for Mutual Economic Assistance (Comecon) did provide an alternative to Bretton Woods, and did include states such as Mexico and Finland as observer states during the 1970s. However, this system never became more than an extended tool of Soviet centralism, and never attracted more members than the countries in the Eastern bloc plus a few notable additions, such as Cuba and Mongolia. Therefore, despite its attraction to underdeveloped post-colonial states, it did not provide the socialist alternative to the wider international economic system (Lane 1996). The Bretton Woods system, in contrast, remained the standard international economic system throughout the 1950s and 1960s. It also firmly established the supremacy of the dollar as the one dominant currency that provided a firm lead for other currencies to value and stabilize. As a result, its effects became a truly international phenomenon, propelling the Federal Reserve and the US Treasury into becoming a key global actor. However, the establishment of Soviet-led defence institutions such as the Warsaw Pact reinforced the post-war condition of bipolarity. Later, collective arrangements such as the Brezhnev doctrine, and the increased attraction of Marxism-Leninism to newly independent developing states certainly suggested that the condition of bipolarity was one that would continue for some time.

Hegemonic Stability Theory

The theory of hegemonic stability theory emerged largely as a conse-quence of the failure of the dollar system and the eagerness to iden-tify what would occur next, or develop out of its ashes. The general understanding of the theory was developed by Charles Kindleberger in his 1973 monograph, *The World in Depression*, and by Robert Gilpin in his later book, *War and Change in World Politics* (1981). Kindleberger attributed the period of depression to a lack of leader-ship at the international level. The era of British leadership had past, and as the USA was reluctant to take up the reins at the time, the world economy, lacking a prominent leader, would be defined through its instability. As he stressed in his monograph, for the world economy to be stable, or at least stabilized, there has to be a stabilizer (Kindleberger 1973: 305).

Gilpin extends this to the wider international picture and shows how conflict at the international level tends to emerge when one power is being challenged by others. Returning to Thucydides (see Chapter 2), Gilpin illustrates that when the leading power is being challenged it will use aggressive retaliatory tactics to reduce the threat while it still has the ascendency (Gilpin 1981: 191). This was seen with the change of hegemons in both ancient Greece and the Roman Empire; in the latter case, imperial over-stretch could not sustain the decline at the centre. More important, however, was the story of the British decline. As Britain began to be challenged by emerging powers such as Germany, it responded by increasing its naval capac-ity and expanding its overseas territorial gains in order to maintain its superiority (Gilpin 1981: 193–7). By doing this, Britain compromised on its liberal principles and the world descended into a new era of state tension that was to descend further into two world wars in the twentieth century.

Gilpin's concerns for the sustainability of US power were to be central to accounts within hegemonic stability theory at the time. As British hegemony began to decline in the latter part of the twentieth century, so the USA had sown the seeds of its decline almost as soon as it reached the position of international hegemon. Just as Germany emerged to challenge the leadership of the British, so the prominence of the Soviet Union did the same to the USA in the years following the Second World War. Gilpin's concluding chapter saw the USA being unable to maintain the economic leadership it had achieved during the dollar system, but willing to accept Soviet cohabitation (ibid.: 239–40). The general hypothesis that emerged from Gilpin and from Kindleberger's subsequent work (1981, 1983) was that the USA was in relative decline, and that a new leader would emerge to challenge the fabric of American hegemony. The fear here seemed to be that states were reluctant to take on the responsibility of leadership, with potential challengers opting to act as 'free riders' rather than make a bid to assume the role (Kindleberger 1981: 252). Kindleberger, with his previous historical studies in mind, feared the development of a similar situation to that of the 1920s and 1930s, where the reluctance of the USA to assume the role encouraged instability (1981: 248–50). At one period, it seemed that Japan might emerge as the more likely candidate to assume leadership (Kindleberger 1983: 7–8; Iriye and Cohen 1989).

The fear of US decline was heightened in the 1970s by the belief that the end of the dollar system would reduce the pursuit of free trade and openness across the international economic system. The link between trade liberalization and a strong hegemon was tentatively suggested by Albert Hirschman in his first notable book *National Power and the Structure of Foreign Trade*, published in 1945. The book is taken to have had a significant influence on those who adhered to hegemonic stability theory (Cohen 2008: 74), but its influence is possibly more understated when looking at contemporary arguments for a hegemonic state (see below). Hirschman suggested that, by aggressively seeking power and superiority, a state should open up to trade. This would lead to prosperity for that state as well as allowing for potential stability across the system as a whole. The retraction of the pursuit of open trade by adopting a 'national-first' form of protectionism produces a zero-sum situation whereby both trading partners miss out (Hirschman 1945: 27–9). As a result, the pursuit of trade is central to national power. Yet if this pursuit is employed in a manner similar to that adopted by Britain in the nineteenth century, and challenged through trading regimes and institutions, a more prosperous result would be achieved. Nazi Germany, insisted Hirschman, did rely on trade in order to expand and maintain its position, but this was done through dubious and unsustainable means, as the official policy was one distinctly against the notion of open trade (ibid.: 33–8).

Hirschman's analysis would lead many to deduce that the pursuit of power by states can lead to open liberal trade regimes which provide stability and prosperity when acted on (Krasner 1976, 1996). His arguments also form a resounding base which would be used in the aftermath of the Cold War in more popular appraisals of aggressive state power (Krauthammer 1990; Ferguson 2004). In the 1970s, however, there was a firm belief that, unless some intervention took place to replace the dollar system, a new era of protectionism and de-internationalization would occur that would leave the world stagnant and unstable. The Reagan administration's pursuit of the USSR showed that the USA would not be willing to stand back as leader of the Western world. At the time, however, hegemonic stability theorists saw the policies as being indicative of a reaction of a hegemon in decline. For example, trying to attack rival contender states in a certain manner, as the Reagan administration was doing, had a remarkable similarity to tactics that the dominant city-states adopted when in decline in ancient Greece (Gilpin 1981: 199–200).

A more tangible response to this came from Robert Keohane. Keohane accepted many of the central assumptions of hegemonic stability theory, but dismissed the idea that the principle holds universal appeal. Instead, he argued that states can co-operate without a leader or a hegemon, providing regimes are forged in a manner that compromises self-serving interests for mutually better outcomes (Keohane 1984: 243–52). Keohane's problems with hegemonic stability include factors that were related more to the US case of post-war hegemony than to any universal principle. Here he cites US dollar protection from emerging currencies and ongoing lack of confidence in the markets as economic factors that hegemonic stability could not include (ibid.: 207–8). However, it was his third point that was more telling, as it questioned the reliance on gross domestic product (GDP) rates as the telling factor of US decline (ibid.: 209–10). This raised deeper questions that were to be thoroughly examined in the latter part of the 1980s.

Two contending accounts could be seen, by Bruce Russett and Susan Strange, that built on the empirical shortcomings of hegemonic stability theory. Russett picked up on the point of empirical concerns in the declinist arguments and suggested that the main indicators used for measuring the strength of a hegemon seemed to be manufacturing production, military expenditure and gross national product (GNP). Yet none of these account for the American-led projects that were seen at a more substantial level, such as decolonialism, the successes of American-led capitalism, and, from a security point of view, the overwhelming dominance of the nuclear industry by the USA (Russett 1985). Russett also points to the fact that hegemonic stability theory used these indicators to measure the strength of a hegemon despite these same measures not being applied vigorously to previous historical periods of hegemony, such as that of the British (McKeown 1983; Russett 1985: 211).

Susan Strange (1987) made a more poignant argument that would form the basis for many who criticized the way that hegemonic stability was being understood at the time. Strange argued that there was absolutely no basis for declaring that the USA had lost any power since the fall of the dollar system: on the contrary, in fact, it was still the clear leader in international affairs in terms of the four key areas of security, production, finance and knowledge that underline the forces of structural power. On this basis, the idea that American power was in any way in decline was both misleading and misunderstood. This added to a wider concern regarding the manner in which hegemonic stability was measured and understood. As we shall see in Chapter 4, much was made of the positivist nature of the way that conclusions were reached. The criticisms developed by Strange show how problematic it can be when certain assumptions are gathered using selective indices. Indeed, if the wider questions on hegemony focus on questions of states versus ideology, then the form of statist hegemony developed here becomes rather crude in terms of its measurement. Furthermore, the assumption of US decline appeared rather sweeping in its conclusions.

This is not to say that hegemonic stability theory at the time was crude in its overall analysis, or in the manner in which hegemony is understood. Contrary to numerous assumptions, many of the accounts of hegemonic stability theory did acknowledge the different accounts

of hegemony and did also suggest that the use of ideological constructions of contest of the sort that Gramsci used were useful in terms of
developing the concept (Keohane 1984: 32; Gilpin 1987: 73). The
main problem was not what it contributed to a theory, but that the
conclusions it developed proved to be flawed. As the 1980s
progressed, it appeared that the grand predictions of US decline of the
preceding decade were indeed correct (Oye *et al.* 1979; Rosecrance
1976). Gilpin stated as late as 1987 that the moves by President
Reagan to further greater market reforms only appeared to reinforce
the belief that the USA was moving away from its international
commitments, and that the liberal world order was in a 'downward
spiral' (Gilpin 1987: 370–88). Yet within five years the Soviet Union
had disintegrated and the USA remained as the only remaining world
superpower.

US Hegemony after the Cold War

Rather than facing new challengers for leadership in the way that
hegemonic stability theorists foresaw, the collapse of the Soviet
Union saw the end of the main ideological challenger to American
ideology. Capitalism found itself in a position to be able to expand
globally without the threat of a rival ideology. For some, history had
reached the end of its traditional struggle with ideology and the super-
state conflict (Fukuyama 1992). What was becoming apparent was
that, as state socialism died with the removal of the Berlin Wall, then
the forms of social and regulated capitalism that became synonymous
with the post-war era began to erode in a similar fashion. The globalization of free market capitalism and the rise of transnational financial
actors have transformed the way that global politics has been
perceived since the end of the Cold War (see Chapter 4). The first indi-
cations of this new and homogenous post-Cold War environment was
seen with the first Gulf War where, after a unanimous UN Security
Council resolution demanding the withdrawal of Iraqi troops from
Kuwait, a coalition of military forces led by the USA but containing
partners from surrounding states such as Syria, Egypt and Saudi
Arabia as well as from Europe, Asia and Africa, forced the Saddam
Hussein-led Iraqi invasion to retreat. Hailed, as George Bush Sr put
it, as the 'The New World', this would set the scene for the new era,
free from ideological division. The idea in this case was that if US

hegemony or leadership had previously been held back by the Soviet threat, it would now be free to take up the role of the global policeman with the backing of the international community.

In the first place, this was to build on what those within hegemonic stability theory had favoured. The USA would be able to provide a stronger basis to legitimize an institutional form of hegemony from the existing UN and international bodies (Keohane 1984; Ikenberry 2001). This legitimization could also provide the basic of policy co-ordination in certain areas that were often restricted during the Cold War era. The 'new world order' was thus an opportunity for the USA to pursue a Wilsonian vision of liberal internationalism of the sort that was never potentially possible before (Slaughter 2008). Yet, during the next two decades, confidence in and popularity of the United Nations (UN) within American political society plummeted and a confrontational attitude became widespread, to the extent that many who favoured intervention believed that the UN hindered the process. In the aftermath of 9/11 and the wars in Afghanistan and Iraq, many went further, arguing that the UN provided an opposition to American intervention in issues of international security (Krauthammer 2004).

As a result, those who feel that the USA should play a hegemonic role in the management of international politics differ in the manner in which they think this should be done. In simplistic political terms, this has often been seen as the difference between the largely liberal insti-tutional position, favoured generally by the centre-left and the US Democrats, and the more anti-institutional interventionist position favoured by the neo-conservative right and the Republicans. In actual terms, this position seemed to change between the 1990s and the post-9/11 world, whereby the 1990s saw the US favour a greater use of intervention through institutional channels – seen with the NATO intervention in the former Yugoslavia and with an increase in UN activity in civil disputes across Africa. This was to change after 9/11, when the US failure to obtain support for intervention in Iraq brought in a new approach to leadership rooted in the belief that reliance on international institutions merely gave greater incentives for potential hegemonic challengers to emerge (Kagan 2003).

The debate over the nature of US power leads us to the wider ques-tion of how we can understand the manner in which it is expressed within international politics. Or, if we are to take the idea seriously that the USA is the only significant power in the international arena, how can we analysis how its power is expressed? Here we have accounts from across the political spectrum that have analysed the exceptionalism of US power in contrasting ways. We can understand them broadly from the premise of (a) US hegemony from the structural confines of unipolarity; (b) US hegemony as some form of liberal empire; and (c) US hegemony as a form of imperialism.

Unipolarity

Certainly the most significant change in structural realism thinking after the Cold War was the emerging unipolar nature of the international system. Structural realist thinking was so influenced by Kenneth Waltz's *Theory of International Politics* (1979) that the reality of the emerging unipolar world was difficult to fathom (Mowle and Sacko 2007: 29–30). Waltz's own suggestions was that international interaction could be ordered only in either a multipolar or a bipolar one, as the specific units (or states) in a system would need to balance each other to maintain stability. For Waltz, the bipolar system represented a much more stable system, as fewer powers were required to stabilize it (1979: 202–8). With this in mind, it was not surprising that the first significant accounts after the demise of the Soviet bloc, including those of Waltz himself, suggested that other powers would inevitably arise to challenge the USA and its position, and a multipolar world would emerge (Mearsheimer 1990; Waltz 1993). However, arguments within conservative and liberal circles alike began to challenge the conviction that it was unsustainable. While the latter might push for a new era of leadership to provide a renewal of Wilsonian liberalism, the former wrote enthusiastically in influential conservative journals such as *Foreign Affairs* and *National Interest* (Krauthammer 1990, 2002/3) about the 'unipolar moment'.

Accounts of the survival of unipolarity have pointed to the idea that a dominant state can prevail in balancing a system if it works strategically around offensive and defensive management (Mastanduno 1997). Some have looked favourably at hegemonic stability theory in IPE and have pursued their understanding on leadership. Most prominent here has been the work of John Ikenberry, who adopted the logic that had been a hallmark of Kindleberger's ideas of leadership in much of his work. Yet Ikenberry did not see 1945 as a watershed moment in the same way as hegemonic stability strategists did in retrospect. Rather than being something that was merely US-created, the post-Second World War order was more protracted in its development. To steer Western Europe away from potential Soviet influence, the USA looked to forge a political environment formed carefully through alliance building (Ikenberry 2006). As a result, and following on in the same spirit as Strange and Russett, the end of the Bretton Woods dollar system did not represent a decline in US power. Instead it was reshaped around a combination of soft economic power and continued military and nuclear dominance. By the time the Soviet Union had collapsed, US power had reached proportions of domination not seen before in the modern state system (Ikenberry 2004). As a result, if ever there was to be a moment for a sustained period of hegemonic leadership, this was it.

Thus for Ikenberry, unipolarity, embodied in the current form, does not have the same balance of power requirements as previous arrangements, because the state appears to be too central and too powerful to attract instability. The USA needs to act against threats to the system as a whole, and in particular against those that aim to undermine its liberal character (Ikenberry 2011). This is a view shared to a certain extent by others, such as Daniel Nexon and Thomas Wright, who have suggested that, under a unipolar arrangement, the inter-state balance of power mechanism is replaced by an inter-systemic balance of power dynamics (Nexon and Wright 2007). The question of stability is extended to the nature of security, with some arguing that one state acting as a so-called 'policeman' in international affairs provides a better basis for maintaining order than systems with more than one power (Wohlforth 1999). The characteristic here is that, as no state is big enough to challenge the dominant hegemon, conflicts never threaten the prevailing order. As the USA provides an overwhelming military advantage over any other states, its supremacy could not realistically be threatened, making any world war or conflict untenable (Posen 2003).

The question posed by many students of unipolarity is how it can be sustainable as a lasting condition within international politics. The question of durability has been a key factor that has often dominated debates over those that ask wider questions as to whether the state of unipolarity makes for a more peaceful world (Monteiro 2011). The main focus here seems to be on whether an offensive or defensive strategy should be pursued by the leading state. As Mowle and Sacko suggest, the two strategies presuppose two contrasting hypotheses on the nature of a unipolar world. One hypothesis assumes that an offensive approach is an advantage and a necessity, as intervention can successfully reduce conflicts, which it would not have been able to do under rival state systems (Mowle and Sacko 2007: 131–2). The other suggests that under unipolarity the leading state should bypass external conflicts if it wishes to maintain its position, as involvement will make it prone to internal weakness and to the threat of emerging powers (2007: 117).

An offensive strategy can be seen as one that can seek to embed universal practices through the liberal principles in which the USA has been traditionally positioned, or as one that pursues a direct military engagement with potential threats. Offensive strategies can therefore be those that are both multilateral and unilateral in their execution. The unilateral approach that became evident after 9/11 might be different from the Wilsonian vision of liberal institutionalists, but both share a commitment to an offensive US strategy on the international stage. Where they do differ is in the method by which an offensive strategy should be applied. While a multilateral focus might stress the importance of liberal co-operation, coalition building on a renewal of the principles of international institutionalism (Posen 2003; Ikenberry 2011), a unilateral focus is one geared towards military action provided by the leading state, preferably with the involvement of allies (Stelzer 2004; Kagan 2008).

An offensive strategy is how one would describe US foreign policy since the start of the unipolar era, with successive US governments pursuing different offensive agendas to stabilize the system and eradicate potential opposition. However, many of the Walzian-inspired neorealists maintain the view that if the USA pursued an offensive stabilizing strategy, it would lead to a process of over-stretch and of distrust among the international community (Coulon 2003). Perhaps the most noteworthy of all such accounts here is from some of the most conventional of all neorealists, who provided a scathing criticism of the Iraq War from the viewpoint of systemic defence (Mearsheimer and Walt 2003). The rise of China is a factor that has long been central to the defensive form of understanding unipolarity, with its prominence largely being one that would precipitate a multipolar world, as other rising and resurgent powers or regions would respond in turn to its rise and assert their own power (Waltz 2000). Unipolarity is thus seen here not as a system that provides overriding stability, but as one that attracts more forms of conflict (Monteiro 2011). By attempting to deal with and intervene in such conflicts in order to stabilize the international environment, the leading state eventually puts the system at terminal risk (Layne 2006).

Empire

One of the more notable consequences of previous periods of unipolarity is that they have established empires under their jurisdiction. Regional empires, such as the Roman Empire in Europe, the Mongol Empire in Asia – and the Persian Empire in the Middle East that pre-dates both of these – have sought to extend their influence by assuming sovereign control over their respective regions. In the modern state system, this would effectively mean that an empire would not recognize the sovereignty of a specific area and would intervene, presiding over that area when necessary. The difference between forms of unipolarity within a state system and empire would be that the former takes into account statism and assumes influence through formal practices within IR, while the latter intervenes within its own hierarchal power structure (Nexon and Wright 2007). If a permanent process of offensive intervention is practised by a dominant state, then the principles that govern the international system (sovereignty, international agreements, law and so on) are increasingly ignored.

The Iraq and Afghanistan Wars (and before that, conflict in Kosovo and Bosnia) could be perceived in some quarters as being indicative of empire building, as central elements of due process were ignored in intervening (Ignatieff 2003; Mann 2004). Yet if US hegemony can be understood as a form of empire, then it is of a specific type not witnessed previously in the confines of international history. In addition, an empire is generally regarded as an entity that relies on the annexation and seizure of land in order to assume rule. The USA might have annexed lands in its expansion as a nation, but it has not attempted to apply any formal rule over lands that have been rife with American influence (MacDonald 2009). However, 'influence' or 'informal domination' in places such as Liberia, the Caribbean and the Pacific underlined the emergence of the USA as a key power. This, as Michael Cox notes, still leaves the fact that one of the primary objectives of the USA as soon as it assumed hegemonic influence was to promote the concept and the right of self-determination. However, it could be seen that this self-determination was in the US strategic interest in the emerging post-war environment (Cox 2004: 600–1).

Any account that takes seriously the concept of a US empire would also need to stress that its chief attributes are based on the principles of liberalism and – to quote Thomas Jefferson – an 'empire of liberty'. This was endorsed enthusiastically by Niall Ferguson, whose main criticism of US empire building was that it should have positively embraced the idea of empire, and been less supportive in its commitment to a decolonization process that often led to a retraction of liberty in newly independent states (Ferguson 2004). This is a view extended by William Odom and Robert Dujarric. They believe that the USA has aimed to retain the sovereign norms of the state system, but is compelled to act when instabilities and multilateral deadlock become apparent (Odom and Dujarric 2004). As a result, it appears as an empire. The notion of a US empire is an appropriate term because its influence extends to the far reaches of the world, and American intervention is sometimes demanded by wider civil society, demonstrating certain elements of acceptance.

The question of empire is also one that has attracted the interest of the Russian scholar and activist, Boris Kagarlitsky. He suggests that an empire that takes on the role of a hegemon has the difficult job of balancing a range of disputes in the world, because it needs to stabilize a system on the one hand and to maintain its unique policing role on the other. More 'formal' empires such as the British one managed this better. The era of Britain's 'bourgeois empire' was one that appeared at the end of the Napoleonic Wars and was built on the Industrial Revolution and on its colonial expansions in India that had been established in the previous century (Kagarlitsky 2014: 258–67). This provided a leverage where Britain could assert a form of economic hegemony over the rest of Europe, while maintaining a position of 'splendid isolation' in its foreign policy. Lacking this physical empire, the USA has sought to police the international system, either through providing conditional aid or by using force to contain potentially threatening regimes (Kagarlitsky 2014: 334–6). By doing so, they have left themselves economically and militarily vulnerable.

However, it is perhaps the more original accounts of empire that have attracted the most attention. Justin Rosenberg's notion of the 'empire of civil society' suggests that it is the fashioning of class relations that forge international systems, and these have always been driven by forms of empire. The US Empire is just an extension of other empires, such as the Spanish, Roman, British Empires and so on, which had a strongly hierarchal structure shaped through a class system (Rosenberg 1994). Therefore the systemic forms of analysis used by realist IR theorists to explain the international system are missing the wider social dimension. Sovereignty and anarchy do not remain independent of the ruling principles of international politics when understood at this wider level. Michael Hardt's and Antonio Negri's understanding of empire is as a liberal one, but also as one that moves beyond the confines of the traditional state system. It appears as a myriad forms of governance, where international institutions, leading states (of which the USA is the overwhelming leading player) and leading business classes combine to forge an 'empire' of liberal democracy (Hardt and Negri 2000).

Such commentaries show that the concept of empire is a contested one, and not based exclusively around the primacy of American power. Modern accounts of the term maintain the spatial dimension of 'empire', but believe that this does not have to be in a physical or a legal manner through the expansion of territory; it can be understood through other means, such as through the global economy, the globalization of culture, and the emergence of non-state actors across global society. The base for a US Empire thus moves beyond traditional understandings of the formal empires of the past and towards the more informal dynamics of soft and ideological power.

Imperialism

Empire is often coupled in the understanding of state power with the concept of imperialism (Cox 2004; Ferguson 2004). Indeed, it was through the Roman Empire that the term imperialism (via the term *imperium*) emerged, as noted in Chapter 1, and it was through the establishment of empires during the notorious 'scramble for Africa' in the late nineteenth century that the term was most used. While the concept has attracted much debate in terms of its exact meaning, its general implication is that it refers to the economic exploitation of a certain area by a specific state (Kiely 2010). Thus any understanding of US hegemony in terms of imperialism would have to demonstrate ways in which the USA and its interests have sought to exploit certain areas and resources for their own gain. While any application of neo-imperialism would need to distinguish itself from classical imperialism, there are certain characteristics that are remarkably similar in nature.

Writing before the start of the First World War, Rosa Luxemburg suggested that capitalism rests on the need to pursue new markets in order to accumulate wealth. One form of doing this is through 'accumulation by dispossession', where lands and territories become capitalized by states and companies seeking to increase economic growth and profit margins (Luxemburg [1913]/2003). For the influential Marxist scholar, David Harvey, accumulation by dispossession becomes a central theme of US imperialism as key US companies have looked to purchase land and labour for their own gain (Harvey 2003: 157–200). The crux of this has been through the privatization measures taken by US-dominated economic structures such as the World Bank and the IMF in the wake of the debt crisis of the 1970s and 1980s. The restructuring of developing economies to cover the conditions of the loans that were given by the organizations to cover debt repayments, were thus made for the benefit of US and Western corporations, which took advantage through the purchase and developing of land within these countries.

Recent forms of militarism in the oil-rich parts of the world have also added to arguments that the USA has looked to secure contracts with allied oil-rich regimes. The conflicts with regimes in Iraq and Venezuela have led many to suggest that the war (in the case of Iraq) and hostilities (Venezuela) are exclusively about the management of oil reserves (Klare 2004). Many have been at pains to suggest that US imperialism is far from being just an economic procedure, however. The success of economic neoliberalism, the globalization of American values and the increase in military intervention are all examples of contemporary imperialism (Panitch and Gindin 2003). The notion of cultural imperialism has long been a factor in some areas of the social sciences, and the idea that the globalization of US entertainment, media, consumerism and the spread of the English language has been central to major debates in recent decades regarding the content of imperialism (Tomlinson 1991; Said 1993). As a result, this idea of US imperialism stretches across the boundaries of the economic and into cultural and forms of soft power that are often overlooked when attempting to measure power.

Other accounts see imperialism as being an inevitable result of the USA taking a hegemonic role within a wider capitalist world system. World systems theorists, for example, understand modern capitalism as a structure organized though a state system that becomes ordered through core, peripheral and semi-peripheral states (Wallerstein 1979). Production centres on a financial core that includes the European and North American states as well as some parts of East Asia, and peripheral and semi-peripheral worlds that provide a source of raw materials and cheap manufacturing labour to facilitate the system of international capitalism. Some world systems theorists understand hegemony as being the product of the most powerful of the core states that lead imperialist desires (Arrighi and Silver 1999).

The role of the hegemon in world systems research is thus to 'lead the system of states in a desired direction, and, in so doing, is widely perceived as pursuing a general interest' (Arrighi and Silver 1999: 27). American hegemony has assumed a position that enforces a system of imperialism around the key core financial centres of the world (Reifer 2004). As such transnational elites are formed in the core economic heartlands to facilitate the contemporary form of imperialism, which, as others have been quick to point out, has often been under-theorized as a wider explanation for free market capitalism (Callinicos 2009). Yet the structural configuration of a world system is such that it requires a state hegemon to lead and direct its function. The US facilitates this role in the contemporary world. For world systems analysts, the longevity of a system depends on the strength of the hegemon to maintain its leadership. Debates have thus been centred on whether US hegemony appears to be in decline, and if it is, the world might be on the verge of a transformation (Wallerstein 2004), or whether it appears able to sustain its longevity (Saull 2012).

While imperialism is generally understood as a derogatory term, which is used within a wider framework of critique, some authors have been quick to praise the idea of US imperialism. Again, the most obvious critiques here are in the writings of Niall Ferguson, who offers a traditional modernist view that imperialism has provided a progressive and civilizing influence on the development of the world (Ferguson 2003, 2004). Conversely, this is not far away from certain Marxist arguments that stressed the necessity for imperialism to develop working-class forms of consciousness and struggle (Warren 1980). More prominently, influential individuals close to previous US administrations have defended the use and application of imperialism. David Rothkopf, a current editor of *Foreign Policy*, who previously worked for the Clinton administration in the area of overseas trade, defended the cultural and economic combination of US imperialism. Citing examples such as the consumption of mass media and globalization, he argues that imperialism can provide a beneficial and productive role in world politics, provided it is rooted in liberal and humanitarian principles (Rothkopf 1997).

The idea of US imperialism is thus seen from different perspectives as an explanation for American power at the global level. It is generally rejected, however, as the official line from the centre of power, and was vehemently rejected by the large majority of neoconservatives during the Bush administration. For example, Donald Rumsfeld, former US Secretary of Defense, stressed the point that USA was not an imperialist country and did not seek an empire, and Krauthammer similarly insisted 'we are not an imperial power', but a 'commercial republic' (Krauthammer 2004: 3). While these rejections do not account for the different interpretations of imperialism that have emerged in recent years, they do reiterate the view that imperialism is based on the physical procurement of land and territory, a premise that the US state does not seek to follow, and which it has made it its policy to rally against.

The Problems with US Hegemony

There seems to be no doubt that the USA has played a hugely significant role in determining the form of global affairs since the Second World War. What is less evident, however, is the assumption that hegemony in IR can only be applied to the USA. As we have seen, hegemonic stability theory went so far in explaining how the international economic order could prosper. Furthermore, it relied on certain factors that were highly state-centric in their orientation. The declinist school – those who believed that US power was in decline after the collapse of the dollar system – placed far too much emphasis on data such as GDP and military expenditure to reach their conclusions. Yet this points to a wider problem with the state-centric understanding of hegemony. How, for example, can we rely on certain measurements of indicators to assess the strength of a particular hegemon? The follies of the declinists should serve as warnings to contemporary accounts of hegemonic stability. While they do acknowledge the forms of structural power that Strange and Russett supported (see above) and the declinists ignored, accounts of unipolarity tend to simplify the rigours of the international system. They also tend to provide legitimacy for selective unilateral intervention; a trend that was especially apparent in the aftermath of 9/11, with the wars in Afghanistan and Iraq. Or, to borrow from Robert Cox in his wider critique of realism, it appears as a theory that is used to 'serve the interests of someone and something' (Cox 1981).

The problems with measuring state indicators of hegemony can also be extended to those that refer to the notion of liberal or imperialist forms of US hegemony. The question here is how do we know that the prescribed form of liberalism that has emerged within the international system is necessarily indicative of US hegemony or US leadership? And a similar point can be made about the idea of imperialism. Are the economic activities of US and Western companies indicative of the imperialist advancement of the American state? Or are they the result of a wider class configuration, where a larger transnational capitalist class pursues their collective interest in an increasing globalized world (van der Pijl 1998; Sklair 2000)? Following from this, can we similarly argue that cultural imperialism is actually the product of the USA or of American power, or is it the result of a hybrid collection of cultures that have resulted from mass consumerism (Tomlinson 1991)? As Hardt and Negri demonstrated (see above), the concept of empire does not have to focus around one specific state, but rather around certain dominant conditions organized within institutions that do not have to be at the state level.

These point to the wider concerns with the notion of structural power. Susan Strange's argument that American power could not be measured by comparing state figures on GDP and military capability proved to be a well-founded one (Strange 1987, 1988). The expansion of US-orientated capital and consumerism has reinforced the idea that American power was alive and kicking and was particularly prominent in the 1980s during Reagan's attacks on the Soviet Union. Yet in the post-Cold War era, the battle for East–West influence made way for an era where the conflict over ideology was no longer evident. Even if it was far too premature and presumptuous to assume that 'history was ending', the era of communist/capitalist rivalry was over in terms of how states organized production. It is, however, the precise notion of ideology that makes up a wider understanding of how hegemony is understood.

As processes such as globalization became a reality and world leaders increasingly suggested that there was no alternative to market economics, and that engaging with the emerging globalized market was the only viable way of pursuing economic growth and prosperity. In this environment, it was not necessarily the state that sought to dominate the way an international regime should be run, but the ideology of market economics (see Chapter 5). While hegemonic stability theorists could easily demonstrate that it is, first and foremost, the leading state that lays down and absorbs an ideological system into practice (Krasner 1983), it is not able to account for the many actors that have emerged who contribute to the governance and the consolidation of this new economic order. Before we examine how the post-Cold War era has developed, and how it has produced certain practices that we might consider hegemonic, we need to look at how we can move theoretically beyond the state-centric notion of hegemony primarily as a medium of US power. The concept of hegemony as a social process as opposed to one formed through states within a state system is developed in Chapter 4. Some of this is derived from the notion of hegemony that Gramsci and other Marxists were discussing and developing in the early part of the twentieth century. Many of these accounts also still rely extensively on leading states, and in particularly on the USA as the main source or departure point for hegemonic power in international politics. Yet, as we shall see, it is the way this power is exercised that differs from the more conventional accounts outlined in this chapter.

4
Hegemony, Gramsci and World Politics

If the traditional concept of hegemony within a state system is based around the idea that one leading and dominant state provides a source for its stability, then its evolution as a process that explains an ideological order takes a contrasting form and emerges from a different departure point. Largely coming from the Marxist tradition that was emerging at the start of the twentieth century, the concept has become associated with Antonio Gramsci. In international relations (IR), the growth of the 'neo-Gramscian' approach has applied different versions of Gramsci's notion of hegemony. In this chapter, I shall outline the understanding of hegemony that Gramsci developed, show how this has been applied in different ways and outline its shortcomings. I shall also look at how the development of its application in other fields across the social sciences can add to new studies of hegemonic consent in international politics.

Hegemony and Marxism before Gramsci

The concept of hegemony was discussed in depth by a number of key figures in the socialist movement. In particular, it became debated with the experiences of the Russian and German social democracy and later with the emergence and the significance of the Bolshevik Party in Russia. Many of these debates took place in the 'Second International', which was a forum that took place between 1889 and 1916, where socialist and labour organizations across Europe and the Americas discussed key developments of the day. As the Second

International gained momentum in the first 15 years of the twentieth century, influential figures such as Karl Kautsky, Georgi Plekhanov, Rosa Luxemburg, Leon Trotsky and V. I. Lenin all discussed the nature of hegemony. Hegemony came to be seen as a term that explained the revolutionary process required for socialist transformation. Hegemony therefore became both a strategy and a form of consciousness within the wider process of socialism. The development and form of hegemony differed and was debated by key figures that were prominent in early-twentieth-century socialism. In their classic study of the development of the term, Ernesto Laclau and Chantal Mouffe showed how the term was used by such figures to reflect their specific socialist strategy. From Luxemburg's notion of spontaneity to Kautsky's 'war of attrition', hegemony served as a process within which the working class could form a revolutionary spirit and consciousness that would serve as the basis for the construction of the proletariat state and its political society (Laclau and Mouffe 1985: 8–29).

Yet, it was with Lenin that the term hegemony was initiated in a manner that would allow for others, in particular Gramsci, to develop later. For Lenin, hegemony, or *gegemoniya* in Russian, was a strategy where the urban proletariat, represented by trade unions, could forge a partnership with the rural peasantry, creating an alliance where revolutionary change could occur (Lenin 1965). Lenin's use of the term was to become synonymous with the notion of dictatorship of the proletariat, which dominated Marxist-Leninist thinking during the era of state socialism that was to follow the Bolshevik Revolution. The 'dictatorship of the proletariat' was the phase of transition required to enable the state and its capitalist apparatus to wither away and a communist society to develop. In his critique of the Gotha programme, Karl Marx commented that 'between capitalist and communist society lies the period of the revolutionary transportation of one into the other', and that this transitional period must be facilitated by a 'revolutionary dictatorship of the proletariat' (Marx 1977: 565). Lenin understood this process to be one where the proletariat gains control and aims to suppress the old system. In his landmark *State and Revolution*, written on the eve of the Bolshevik Revolution, Lenin commented in depth on the main revolutionary purpose of the historical phrase, which he believed needed to be disciplined and supplemented with force:

In the transition from capitalism to communism suppression is still necessary; but it is now the suppression of the minority by the exploited majority. A special apparatus, a special machine for suppression, the 'state' is still necessary; but this is now a transitional state, it is no longer a state in the proper sense; for the suppression of the minority of exploiters by the majority of *yesterday's* wage slaves is comparatively easy … The exploiters are naturally in no position to suppress the people without a most complex machine for performing such a task, whereas *the people* can suppress the exploiters almost without a 'machine', without a special apparatus: by means of the simple *organization of the armed masses*. [Original emphasis] (Lenin 1992: 81)

Yet, as many have suggested, the process of dictatorship of the proletariat should not be seen as being synonymous with Lenin's theory of hegemony. Christine Buci-Glucksmann and Jonathan Joseph, for example, both stress the point that Lenin understood hegemony not in terms of being only a political strategy but rather as the function and appearance of the working class as a whole (Buci-Glucksmann 1980; Joseph 2002). Here, Lenin's understanding included the sum of political and social agents that made up the working classes. The vanguard party, trade unions, rural and peasant representatives and key intellectual figures in the wider education of the proletariat combine to make up the sum of hegemony and so, for a socialist revolution to succeed, these parts need to revolutionize the capitalist system dialectically.

Lenin's main concern was that the parliamentary route to socialism favoured by Kautsky and later by social democratic Western European political parties, would be rejected as it favoured an alliance with bourgeois political parties as opposed to building an alternative socialist hegemony. Indeed, the bulk of *State and Revolution* appears to be an angry attack on Kautsky, amid accusations of revisionism and treachery (Lenin 1992). Yet it should be added that Lenin's own understanding of how the dictatorship of the proletariat should be forged was fuelled by his own experiences in Russia. Trotsky would later stress the differences between working-class movements in his native Russia and in the more developed capitalist nations in the West in his theory of combined and uneven development. Here, the stress was placed on how different nations and regions appear at different stages of respective human, social and economic capitalist development. The character of hegemony was far more advanced in the West, where the bourgeoisie had developed more sophisticated forms of state apparatus and civil society than was the case in Russia (Trotsky 1977). This was an observation shared by Gramsci when he noted that, in Russia, the state was 'everything' and civil society was 'primordial and gelatinous', while in the West there was a 'proper relation between State and civil society' whereby the state was 'only an outer ditch, behind which there stood a powerful system of fortresses and earthworks' (Gramsci 1971: 238). It was on this complex relationship that Gramsci's understanding of hegemony focused.

Gramsci and Hegemony

From the discussions that originated at the Second International, Gramsci built a theory of hegemony that unravelled the fortresses within civil society that he had observed were strong in Western forms of capitalism. Having been imprisoned by the fascist Italian state in 1926, as noted earlier, he embarked on writing the well-known series of notebooks that sought to map out the many forms of social, cultural and political agents that contribute to form a hegemonic relationship between different classes in society. What we are left with is a wide kaleidoscope of material Gramsci collected in order to illustrate the strength, the nature and the fashioning of hegemony. For Gramsci, hegemony represents the ruling totality of society, which is saturated in a way that even 'constitutes the limits of common sense for most people under its sway' (Williams 1980: 37). In his notebooks, he highlights that the complexities of the super-structural form Marx illustrated were born out of the economic materialist condition of class struggle. Yet, while Marx showed how political institutions and practices are born from the bourgeoisie in capitalist society to govern and legitimate its workings, Gramsci showed us that the relationship between super-structure and base is far more layered and complex in nature.

In Gramsci's terms, hegemony appears as the result of a class struggle between the dominant and the 'subaltern' classes in society, whereby the former win over the 'hearts and minds' of the latter through the pursuit of consent (Gramsci 1971: 333). While Gramsci is quick to recognize the role that coercion plays in class relations, he follows Machiavelli ([1533]/1984) in arguing that a successful and stable hegemony is based on consent. More prominently, the hegemonic process consists of an intellectual, moral, political and economic order towards which the majority of the popular masses subscribe (Gramsci 1971, 1992). In identifying the way in which such consent is shaped, Gramsci places great emphasis on the role of intellectuals (for a wide overview, see Gramsci 1971: 5–23). Here he distinguishes between traditional and organic intellectuals. The former represents the formal leaders of institutions such as the church, schools, universities, lawyers, politicians and so on that have traditional roles of influence. Organic intellectuals appear as significant inspirational leaders across social groups, who might appear within local communities (such as union leaders, shop stewards, preachers and so on), or they can appear as figures within popular culture. It is these organic intellectuals who add significantly to and embed the key principles of a hegemonic order, which their traditional counterparts formally endorsed.

Gramsci's interest in the fashioning of hegemony extended to areas such as national folklore, popular literature and culture, different forms of religion and popular pastimes as well as the more renowned super-structural forms of agency such as media, political parties and education. Through this, Gramsci's model of hegemony was far deeper in its analysis of civil society than those that had been discussed before. Two departure points of analysis for understanding the process of hegemony in his notebooks were Gramsci's understanding of Machiavelli's ([1532]/1984) *The Prince*, and how this could be understood through the birth of the modern bourgeois state. Machiavelli caused great controversy by arguing that, for leaders to gain support and esteem from their subjects, they need to forge a popular bond. Thucydides had argued that the seeking of consent between the ruler and the ruled was favourable for stability in a similar way to Machiavelli, when the latter suggested that a successful prince requires popular support in order to secure a stable reign (Machiavelli 1984: 60–9). By the time the bourgeois state was created from the ashes of feudalism, the prince could be understood not as a sole leader, but as an 'organism, a complex element of society in which a collective will, which has already been recognized and has to some extent asserted itself in action, begins to take a concrete form' (Gramsci 1971: 129). By establishing the post-feudalist state, the spirit of 'Jacobinism' that embroiled the new revolutionary class, was to lead to a complex set of layers that embodied the modern state, and underlined its historical hegemonic development (Gramsci 1971: 79).

By understanding hegemony as a process akin to that of a modern prince, the socialist movement needed to rekindle that Jacobin revolutionary spirit inherent in the establishment of the modern capitalist state when looking to build an alternative to it. Thus the modern socialist prince was to serve as a wide project capable of contesting the character of the capitalist state at every level of political and civil society to encourage successful revolutionary change. It was only on this wider terrain that the battle for hegemony could be won. Putting it more mundanely, Gramsci argued that there were two ways in which the nature and character of hegemony could be challenged. The first can be seen as a war of movement or manoeuvre that represented a frontal ideological assault on the state. It is here that the main fabric of the ruling order is confronted. As the war of movement is best employed through times that are strategically effective, then it appears to be more successful during times of economic and/or political crisis (Gramsci 1971: 233). Tactics such as mass protests or strike action can be seen as being indicative of a war of movement as they are geared towards challenging the very socio-economic fabric of the political order. The second, and more poignant, form of contestation can be seen with the war of position. It is through the war of position that all forms of implicit power are contested and constructed. It is here where civil society is reconstructed and reorganized so that it is consistent with the form of production and the general character of the emerging ideological order.

Of particular interest to Gramsci was the manner in which strong forms of civil agency were used to strengthen the character of a hegemonic order. The role of religion and the Catholic Church obviously played a very important part in Italy's historical development, and Gramsci was especially interested in how religion was used in order to complement specific orders (Gramsci 1992: 162–3). The role the church played in the emergence of the modern state, in Italy's turn to fascism, and the role that faith played in the origins of the socialist movement and the Protestant pan-Christian movement were all of interest to Gramsci (Gramsci 1992, 1996, 2007). They showed that religion appeared as a sort of a neutral agent, in that it could adapt towards a process that could either reinforce the existing order or could act as a key component in either a progressive or a reactionary form of alternative hegemonic project (Gramsci 1995: 1–137). Unlike conventional Marxist readings of the time, Gramsci argued that factors such as religion, as well as forms of popular culture, popular folklore and national mythology, should be engaged with to build a successful hegemonic project. This differed from dominant Soviet views at the time, epitomized by Nikolai Bukharin's understanding of historical materialism, which believed that such practices were prominently used by ruling class elites as tools of oppression and would subsequently be transcended under conditions of socialism (Bukharin 1925).

Gramsci and World Politics

From the time the 'Prison Notebooks' became readily available in the Western world, new understandings arose on varying subject areas that looked at the ways that power and consent are forged in political and civil society. Studies in politics and culture have in particular thrived on Gramsci's understanding of hegemony, with many innovations being made to explain how class and power are configured in liberal democratic societies (Miliband 1969; Mouffe 1979; Poulantzas 1980; Williams 1980; Hall 1988). Yet, in international politics, hegemony has – as we have seen – been defined and shaped by the structures of the state system. Therefore, if one is to understand hegemony at the international or the global level, this would have to be taken into account. This was a point very well made by Randall Germain and Michael Kenny, when they argued that Gramsci's prescription of hegemony relied on an equation of state = political and civil society. As there is no hierarchal structure of governance within international politics, some mechanism must be put in place instead to understand how hegemony is wielded (Germain and Kenny 1997).

There have been a number of ways in which Gramsci's concept of hegemony has been applied to world politics to circumvent this. The large majority owe a debt to the work of Robert W. Cox. The two *Millennium* articles written by Cox in the early 1980s developed the way in which Gramsci's understanding of hegemony could be of use to students of IR when considering what he defined as 'world order'. Cox argued that, at the international level, power structures are determined by a number of interrelated factors. These include (i) the organization of production; (ii) state formations; and (iii) the nature and form of social forces (Cox 1981: 137–42). These three factors define the character of world order at any given historical time. In looking at these separately: production defines which form of political economy is dominant at the international level; state formation defines what type of states make up a specific order and whether a diversity of state formation might provide a clash leading to potential instability; and social forces make up the form of political and civil movements within respective states.

Taken abstractly, one way of understanding hegemony at the international level would be to suggest that it appears to be the sum of these different factors. However, for Cox, these make up the character and historical form of the world order. For example, if the general form of production internationally was of a capitalist nature, then different states might still choose to adopt an alternative form or be at a different stage of development than others. This would also carry over to the character of social forces that make up the world order. For example, during the Cold War, two dominant forms of social forces emerged that shaped the overriding character of both the form that states might take and wider international production. Prior to that, in a multipolar world (see Chapter 3), a combination of competing social forces results in a world order that is more unstable and retracted in character. Cox made a wider historical study of the changing nature of world order in his book *Power, Production and World Order* (Cox, 1987). Here he provided an alternative historical framework for the changing patterns of power and order to the one offered by hegemonic stability theorists. Here, historical periods were understood as different forms of world order, which were distinguished upon their respective characters, as opposed to basing them just solely on the wishes of one dominant state.

What, though, can we say of Cox's use of hegemony? Here, he came to similar conclusions, at least in his earlier work, as did the hegemonic stability theorists. In constructing his different world orders, Cox suggested that there are world orders which appear to be hegemonic in nature, and those that appear to be non-hegemonic. In understanding this, he used a remarkably similar observation in terms of historical lineage to the former, more state-centric accounts used earlier by Robert Keohane and Charles Kindleberger. He argues, for example, that as the UK and the USA in the nineteenth century and the post-1945 years respectively were clearly dominant in terms of their influence, then the form of world order they favoured became hegemonic. So, for example, the British constructed a liberal world order on the international stage by introducing the gold standard and free trade. This in turn became hegemonic, as no other state emerged at the time to provide an ideological challenge to contest it (Cox 1987: 131–5). When this was contested by the end of the nineteenth century, a new world order emerged, based on competing forms of nationalism, but no hegemonic principles existed at the international level. After the Second World War, the USA followed a similar liberal path to that of Britain a century earlier and presided over a liberal order (Cox 1987: 211–73) that was to flourish globally at the end of the Cold War (Gill 1994).

Gramsci's form of hegemony is thus understood as the leader or the inspiration for a specific form of world order (Robinson 2005; Worth 2011; Gill 2012). At the international level, the main source of this is from the leading state. Yet Cox's framework has allowed many developments of hegemony to be used and developed at the international level. As I shall explain here, the term, however, often becomes clouded in the manner in which it is used. While many are quick to attach the Gramscian label to their different applications of hegemony, the actual manner in which hegemony is understood becomes less clear. Nevertheless, there are three general ways in which hegemony has been applied in a Gramscian or 'neo-Gramscian' manner within the area of world politics: world order; transnational capitalist class; and hegemony as passive revolution. We look at these three now.

World Order

Following from Cox's notion of world orders, many studies in world politics have been keen to look at the various forms of agency that contribute to a specific order. In this manner, they look at how the hegemonic form of the contemporary post-Cold War neoliberal world order is constructed. To a degree, most have built on where Cox left off in his 1987 book, but have shown how neoliberal social forces emerged in the light of the end of the Cold War by constructing a more 'globalized' order. Studies, particular by eminent scholars such as Stephen Gill and Craig Murphy, have shown how financial institutions and international organizations have added to and consolidated this neoliberal order (Gill 1990, 1993; Murphy 1994, 2008). Since then there have been numerous dissertations, articles and books, all seeking to add to the empirical work on world order by accounting for the development of regional blocs, of trading systems and of the way that neoliberal agendas have been fashioned in the developing world. The central tenet in these accounts is that the USA emerged as the leading state after the end of the Cold War as it was able to pursue the free market doctrine popularized in the preceding decade by Margaret Thatcher and Ronald Reagan in their respective countries.

To address the concerns that Germain and Kenny had in pointing to the lack of an international state, organizations such as the World Bank and the IMF can be understood as facilitating hegemony in the lack of an international state. Both institutions were US-controlled through majority funds and voting, and used forms of neoliberal governance through initiatives such as the Washington Consensus. This facilitated both an institutional form of economic hegemony and, through civil incentives, looked to forge consent at the civil level. Yet the actual form of hegemony is often confusing within studies of world order. It remains unclear whether the departure point of neoliberal hegemony is the USA, or a collection of intellectuals working in some way at an international level. As mentioned above, Gramsci argued that traditional and organic intellectuals played a leading role in fashioning consent around a specific order. While the part played by intellectuals has certainly been discussed in terms of their wider role (Gill 2012), it is not entirely clear whether they emerged as a result of US supremacy in the first place, or as a more generic transnational manner from those who aspire to the neoliberal ideology.

Stephen Gill was keen to clarify this by developing what he terms 'constitutionalism'. He suggested that neoliberalism and market ideology have formed the basis of governance within key governmental structures that have developed since the end of the Cold War (Gill 1995, 2003). This has seen the emergence of studies of regionalism, where regional organizations such as the EU and the North American Free Trade Agreement (NAFTA) have been constructed to reflect the nature of the contemporary world order (Gamble and Payne 1996). While these new regional forms of governance reflect the neoliberal nature of the post-Cold War world order, they also provided a potential for social forces to contest the overriding framework of neoliberalism (Strange 2006). Yet, despite these contributions, it still often remains confusing, at least empirically, to decide where the forging of such a world order begins, and just what the composition of social forces looks like.

Transnational Capitalist Class

One way that hegemony could be seen to be forged is through what has been termed a transnational capitalist class. This is a historical development that emerged from the beginnings of liberal capitalism and a notion that has been developed by writers such as Leslie Sklair, and more prominently for the study of IR by Kees van der Pijl (Sklair 1990; van der Pijl 1984, 1998). Here, great emphasis is placed on how transnational elites from North America and Europe created financial linkages and networks that effectively set up a transnational capitalist class. International banking institutions, international financial organizations and business ventures were set up through transatlantic partnership by the end of the nineteenth century and looked to cement a Lockean heartland within civil society. In doing so, the elites created elitist organizations ranging from the Freemasons to organizations such as the Bilderberg Group. In doing so, the transnational capitalist class could formulize a system of international capitalism by ensuring that such groups were free from government control and appeared as key actors in maintaining, governing and developing international capitalism.

How do proponents of the transnational capitalist class thesis understand the process and fashioning of hegemony? Hegemony is understood as a 'form of class rule based on consent rather than coercion and on accommodation of subordinate interests rather than on their repression' (Overbeek 2000: 175). The forming of consent appears at the national level, whereby various national subordinate classes forge different types of relationship with the capitalist class. This allows for differences in national identity and mythology. There have been a number of empirical works associated in particular with what became known as the 'Amsterdam School' of IR. This school of thought focused on studies showing different ways in which class interests are constructed across borders in order to establish a specific order. In the post-Cold War environment, great attention is placed on how classes have emerged at the international level to forge institutional practices that favour them. As a result, institutions such as the EU, the World Trade Organization (WTO), the World Bank/IMF and the management of finance for post-socialist states have all been understood through the realization of the construction of a globalized class (Bohle 2006; Overbeek *et al.* 2007; van Apeldoorn *et al.* 2008; Shields 2012).

There are some concerns with the manner in which the transnational capitalist class is understood, with some pointing to the problem that the historical development of transnational classes seems to be based on meta-narrative assumptions rather than on any substantial understanding of how the elite classes have been created empirically, and how they interact across respective national borders (Germain and Kenny 1997). One way of understanding this has been through what William Robinson termed 'the transnational state'. Robinson believes that as nation states have deregulated their economies in a manner that allows for global norms and practices, they have allowed for the construction of a type of transnational state. This explains how the new legitimacy of economic global governance has developed to a level where states manage their own economies within the wider confines of the international economic market (Robinson 2005). In these terms we can understand global class formation in the manner of a wider transnational state, where economic globalization is played out to maximize the interest of this global transnational class.

Perhaps more significant is the fact that while those who use the notion of the transnational class to explain the processes of global politics might be able to explain forms of elite building, they often fail to explain thoroughly how consent is reached with respective national subaltern classes. In other words, if hegemony is understood via the relationship created between the ruling and subaltern classes, there is little detailed emphasis given to ways in which the various forms of ideology, common sense, religion, folklore and so on are articulated for a hegemonic relationship between classes to be reached. Instead, hegemony is perceived as a process that seems to be quite mechanical and top-down in its working, with emphasis placed on building elite classes rather than on forging class relations.

Hegemony as Passive Revolution

A more recent application of Gramsci within international politics has been to look at another of Gramsci's theories on the development of the state and to use that as a way into understanding the wider development of international capitalism. Much of this has stemmed from some recent work by Adam Morton (2007, 2011) and in a collection edited by Morton, *Capital & Class* (2010). The notion of passive revolution is one used in depth by Gramsci, largely to explain the development of modern Italy. Borrowing from the Italian conservative philosopher

Vincenzo Cuoco, Gramsci argued that states go through a molecular transformation during historical development, whereby the leading classes seek to forge change through passivity aided by the institutions of civil society. In capitalist development this process explains how both the revolutionary bourgeoisie (in the case of France) and the passive bourgeoisie (in the cases of England and Italy) initiated social and economic change. In both cases, the transformation from feudal aristocratic rule to capitalism took on a lengthy historical change that was passive in character (Gramsci 1971: 376–8).

The way in which Morton looks to provide a wider research project on passive revolution(s) provides a different approach to understanding hegemony at the international level. Pointing to the uneven development of capitalism, he has been quick to show how different states have experienced very different processes of passive revolution in their development of capitalism (Morton 2010). In doing this, a collection of comparative accounts of passive revolutions can be shown to illustrate the development of capitalism in different countries. What this does is to show that Gramsci need not necessarily be applied in a global manner, which attracts many problems, but as a collection of 'inter-' national experiences that bring the state back to prominence. Following Trotsky's explanation that capitalism develops in an uneven manner, the study of passive revolution can provide a wider survey of the different developmental stages of respective states at the international level (Morton 2010).

While an interesting, novel and, it should be noted, more textual account of Gramsci, it does not provide us with much of an insight into how his form of hegemony can be understood at the global level. Indeed, while the majority of those who use Gramsci would argue that hegemony remains the central concept within his work, this would suggest that passive revolution is equally useful. It would also suggest that the process of hegemony is best understood from within separate state forms of development. Furthermore, this could be supported by some textual readings looking at what Gramsci himself wrote about the international system (Ives and Short 2013). While these disagree with the charge that Gramsci wrote predominately about the Italian or the European state and tended to ignore international or global developments (as suggested by Germain and Kenny 1997; and Worth 2008), they do suggest that much of the writing Gramsci did on international politics was on the spread of international organizations such as the Freemasons or the Catholic Church. The main conclusions from this are that, while Gramsci did not talk of 'global' phenomena, he nevertheless did discuss common trends that occurred within states and could be considered as 'international' (Ives and Short 2013).

This again would tend to negate the idea of 'global' hegemony and confirm the notion that studies at national or intra-state levels are more consistent with Gramsci's own writing. However, this does not account for the fact that Gramsci himself was writing in an era where the national was far more prominent in wider international affairs, and any form of global coherence was lacking. The idea of hegemony in terms of its wider process of consent and coercion between classes remains far too rich in terms of its potential when turning attention to the workings of power within global politics. The wider processes and practices of globalization and the global spread of neoliberal ideology allow us to examine the workings of hegemony far beyond the territorial national politics that were prevalent in Gramsci's time (see Chapter 5). The idea of a world order provides at least one route through which we can break the shackles and understand hegemony from beyond the confines of the nation state.

Gramsci and the Idea of Global Hegemony

As we have seen, world order provides one route into understanding how a Gramscian-inspired form of hegemony can be understood at the global level. Yet confusion exists over the way that hegemony is played out within the confines of world order in terms of the role of a wider ideology *vis-à-vis* the role of the USA. Both the concept of the transnational capitalist class and the idea of passive revolution provide a way to apply hegemony further to international politics, yet both, for different reasons, do not get the best out of the concept. As we have seen, one way that this has been developed is through the transnational state model provided by Robinson. As we have seen, the shortcomings of understanding world order and hegemony through a transnational state is that they fail to account for the vast spatial diversities that exist at the different levels of global society spanning international politics. In addition, as was also mentioned earlier, many of those who adhere to both understandings of world order and transnational class formation avoid looking at the complexities that exist for hegemony to be formed. As the primary focus is on elite class construction, they avoid detailed studies of the ways that subordinate classes have formed relationships with such transnational classes (Worth 2008). To expand on these shortcomings, it is useful to look at studies that have developed in other areas. Four thinkers and their accompanying traditions provide us with ways and avenues in which to do this.

Henri Lefebvre and Geography

One way of addressing the problems that have aired over the idea of international or global hegemony is to look at works in human geography. Central to this has been the work of Henri Lefebvre on the social production of space. Compared with understanding the world in the form of separate territorial units, Lefebvre argues that it should be distinguished through different areas of socially produced space. It is within these spaces where contrasting types of hegemony are fashioned (Lefebvre 1991: 10–11). Lefebvre was particularly interested in how the bourgeoisie in urban areas forged social control to enable the city to flourish under capitalism. Politics, culture and knowledge are all used by the bourgeoisie to forge class control and consolidate the practices of capitalism. These practices differ from place to place and from region to region. As Lefebvre notes, in his native France great diversity exists where some parts are urbanized and commercialized, others rural and authentically 'underdeveloped', and other parts militarized for the purposes of the armed forces. These differ not just in size but also in terms of the way they are produced, and as a result in the way in which hegemony is exercised and maintained (Lefebvre 1991: 84–6). The extent of this is seen at the different levels of social and cultural reproduction, which facilitates themselves in the manner in which everyday life is experienced and how communities are managed and represented (Lefebvre 2008).

In terms of the modern state system, Lefebvre distinguishes between the absolute space that constituted the centralized state that emerged from the Roman and Greek empires and was legitimized hundreds of years later through the Treaties of Westphalia and the abstract state that perpetrated modern capitalism and took an international form (Lefebvre 1991: 169–92). Modern representation of global capitalism continues to be understood through this diversity, whereby space is produced both through open forms of economy liberalization and through space that is more regulated by the state. As a result, differences at the different spatial levels of production are not necessarily territorialized through state formations but by the uneven distribution of capitalism apparent at the sub-national, national and international levels.

Lefebvre's understanding of space allows us to use hegemony in a manner that addresses the concerns that many have had in the applicability of Gramsci to the international or the global. If we understand neoliberalism as a global phenomenon, and one where its hegemonic representation is constructed in contrasting ways, often dependent on its spatial form of production, then we find a way in which Gramsci's concept of hegemony can be understood at the global level. In human geography, this has been recognized by a number of scholars, who have argued that neoliberalism has emerged at an uneven level and has been applied through different levels or through different scales of production (Peck and Tickell 2002; Brenner 2004; Gough 2004; Harvey 2005). Increasingly, accounts have emerged in IR/IPE that are borrowing from this spatial dimension and looking to use this as a route into approaching and understanding the diversities inherent in neoliberal hegemony (Macartney and Shields, 2011) The pluralization of IR with human geography seems an obviously one. As both have aimed to look into the increasing globalization of space and politics it seems logical to suggest that the two can provide mutual understandings of global society (Kofman and Youngs 2003).

As a result of such engagements, concepts such as 'variegated neoliberalism' – a term that is also borrowed from human geography – have emerged. This is a belief that the development of neoliberalism has taken a form that is historically specific, uneven, hybrid in nature, and different in the way it is regulated (Brenner *et al.* 2010). Hegemony can be understood in a similar manner, with its hegemonic character differing at contrasting levels across global space rather than through bounded national communities. This addresses concerns regarding at what level hegemony can be applied, and provides us with ways in which hegemony can be understood beyond the national state.

Stuart Hall and Cultural Studies

If human geography provides us with a way into understanding the different levels of hegemony, then the work of cultural studies theorists such as Richard Johnson, and in particular Stuart Hall, allows us to develop studies that look at other areas of world politics that have often been overlooked within neo-Gramscian studies. So who was

Stuart Hall, and how can he help us to understand hegemony at the global level in a manner that is less structured than many statist accounts. Famed for his work on race, culture and identity, Hall grew in prominence in the 1980s during the rise of Thatcherism. He identified Thatcher's campaigns of tax reductions and home ownership as ones that appealed to the British working classes, who, to use Thatcher's own understanding, were keen to advance themselves from the immobility of the British class system. Thatcher's popular appeal was to extend this to consumerism, a greater potential to invest into the economy and a greater freedom of choice. The latter two were used to demonstrate the social benefits of privatization. All these campaigns were seen by Hall as a classic attempt at a hegemonic strategy (Hall 1988). Emerging from the breakdown of Keynesian social democracy within Britain, Thatcherism unleashed a fresh set of principles that established a war of position along the whole terrain of civil and political society. When resistance to this strategy began to emerge through protests and strikes, Thatcher reverted to coercive tactics by using state force to put down such discontent. What this did, however, was effectively to create a 'divide and rule' mentality within Thatcher's Britain.

Such a mentality was not one that would be successful in forging hegemony, so Hall was quick to point out in his commentary that Thatcherism did not succeed in creating a stable hegemonic order, but instead formed a hegemonic strategy that was successful in providing a coherent ideology, backed by an equally coherent set of principles. In responding to this, Hall argued that a similar strategy was needed by the left to counter its advance. Hall joined others at the time who were working for the British Communist Party's magazine *Marxism Today*, which later became synonymous with the *New Times* project, and was to have a significant influence on New Labour in the UK. Ironically, as Hall stated recently, it was only until New Labour accepted much of the rhetoric implicit within Thatcherism that the hegemonic process could be seen to be complete (Hall 2011). This was a development that Hall stressed needed to be avoided, as a competing hegemonic strategy required it to distinguish itself firmly from what it was attempting to challenge.

Hall's understanding of hegemony is one that should not be seen as being structured or determined by a strict equation or through statist lines. He suggests that hegemony should be seen as a process forged on the open and complex terrain of civil, political and social society.

It is here that institutions, structures, cultures and ideologies are formed, constructed and contested. In this way, Hall suggests an 'open' or 'loose' approach to understanding the complexities of civil society. This 'openness' is central to Hall's own understanding of Marxism, which he calls 'Marxism without Guarantees'. In this he argues that, just because economic condition might determine the nature of a specific historical order in the first place, the depth of social and civil practices that emerge at the same time provide the potential for different relationships and outcomes to appear (Hall 1988: 45). So, we can see that social forms of agency can find different ways of organizing and expressing themselves within the confines of an economic order, which in turn might lead them to challenge its central tenets. This is very much in line with Gramsci's spirit of mobilization, where the success of a political strategy depends on winning the hearts and minds of such complex forms of social expression (Gramsci 1992).

What does this mean for the way that we understand hegemony at the global level? By taking an 'open' approach to hegemony, we are freed to some extent from both the statist and the traditional 'class' approach to its study. States appear as forms of agencies in the same way as international institutions, the transnational cultural and social practices of globalization, as well as transnational social and religious movements. Yet, as I shall show in Chapter 5, all are shaped at the outset by neoliberal economic production, but all act in differently ways, which can both contest and consent to its overriding principles. In viewing these as agents, rather than larger structures, a more nuanced approach to hegemony within all aspects of global politics as a whole can be employed.

Raymond Williams

Raymond Williams, who became central to the field of literary criticism, made significant contributions to the theory of hegemony. Williams' interest was the manner in which national cultures were constructed, and how their meanings were articulated. He was quick to show that identities can be constructed in a manner that can provide multiple meanings, but still reproduce itself in a way that allows for the reinforcement of production and of wider class relations (Williams 1980). His understanding of hegemony reflected this position as he stated that, to account for all the contrasting meanings that emerge from civil society practices, hegemony cannot be thought of in a simplistic manner, or even as a singular process. In addition, it is a process that is highly complex in its appearance, and contains a multitude of different social agents that often contradict themselves. Williams states that:

> We have to emphasise that hegemony is not singular; indeed that its own internal structures are highly complex, and have continually to be renewed, recreated and defended; and by the same token, that they can be continually challenged and in certain respects modi-fied. That is why instead of speaking simply of 'the hegemony', 'a hegemony', I would propose a model which allows for this kind of variation and contradiction, its sets of alternatives and its processes of change. (Williams 1980: 38)

Following a similar manner to Hall of looking at hegemony, the Williams model of hegemony allows us to understand international politics as being a wide terrain where these struggles are played out in their entirety. The many conflicting forms of identity, race, nation-alism, religion and war can all be seen as forms of agency which shape or contest the overriding character of a world order. And in the same way that Hall initiated the phrase 'determinism in the first instance', Williams also stressed the central importance of capital-ism in the outcomes, and indeed the nature of, such struggles (Williams 1980), a central tenet which was seminal in the field of literary criticism.

Perhaps this could best be illustrated by Williams' work on his native Wales, published posthumously in 2003. Drawing from litera-ture, culture, politics and history, Williams looked at the contradictions inherent within nationhood and mythology. By looking at how these are formed in Wales he provides useful answers to help us to under-stand international politics and hegemony. As Wales has established its national identity within a wider sovereign entity (the United Kingdom), it has done so by constructing a form of common sense and national identity that accounts historically for 'a nation without a voice functioning in a larger non-national state'(Williams 2003: 191–2). This is a feature he comes back to in the section 'Culture of Nations', which makes up part of the collection (2003: 191–204). Here, he looks at how the fabric and mythology of the nation is maintained, while external material conditions shape the very real political and economic policies of the nation state itself. In this way he can see how the wider global material conditions shape the forms of agency that contribute to the nation. Yet, unlike world order theorists, Williams' departure point is not from a powerful leading state, but from culture, identity and nationhood acting in the light of external productive forces. By doing so, it allows us a way of understanding the various actors in global politics that shape meaning and identity within the process of hegemony. It also allows us to look at areas that are often neglected in the IPE-dominated fields of Gramscian studies. In particular, identity politics and conflict studies, and the politics of globalization and cultural imperialism, can all make significant contributions to the wider study of hegemony.

Ernesto Laclau and Chantal Mouffe

The final and perhaps most controversial writer who looked to open up the approach of hegemony to wider studies in global politics is Ernesto Laclau. Laclau, an Argentinian activist turned scholar, was originally influenced by the structural Marxist tradition of Louis Althusser and Nicos Poulantzas. By the time he wrote *Politics and Ideology in Marxist Theory* in late 1977 (a collection of his own work), he had suggested that 'articulation' of ideology was a more useful way of understanding social formation than the traditional Marxist analysis of class. He suggested that the study of class analysis that had traditionally dominated the Marxist understanding of social life had led to a form of 'sectarian reductionism' whereby all types of political behaviour are determined through the class in which they appear. In response, Laclau suggested that ideology is more profound in arranging how social and political life is ordered. More important, the process of hegemony is formed when a specific ideology is articulated in a certain way within forms of social agency. Like Hall and Williams earlier, this allowed for the consideration of a wide variety of practices in world politics as contrasting forms of nationhood, state relations and economic practice are articulated through a specific ideology. In this case, as Laclau notes, the ideology accounts for the period of market economics since the 1980s that has become known for the reduction of the nation state, the globalization of the economy and the proliferation of international quasi organizations (Laclau 2000: 53). What he discusses here, of course, is the ideology of neoliberalism.

The study with Chantal Mouffe, *Hegemony and Socialist Strategy*, takes Laclau ever further from the Marxist primacy of Marx and a greater distance into the realm of ideas. For many, these authors' reading of hegemony slips away from their Gramscian departure point towards one that is idealist in nature (Joseph 2002: 110). *Hegemony and Socialist Strategy* argued that hegemony does not necessary have a centre of origin as such, and so can be understood through separate discourses. This takes Laclau and Mouffe far beyond Hall and Williams as they understand the construction of hegemony free from any form of productive or materialist influence. In addition, they suggest that hegemony can produce a devolved discourse of narratives, whereby entirely different hegemonic realities are constructed and there is no universal condition in its overriding character (Laclau and Mouffe 1985: 108–14). This provides us with a genuine problem when attempting to examine how global hegemony might be structured, as it becomes relative to separate locations within the wider social sphere.

So, do Laclau and Mouffe ultimately provide more obstacles than answers in their understanding of hegemony? Certainly, they would suggest that, by having no material or productive reference point on which to base a specific hegemonic order, any way of attempting to locate its overriding character would be useless. Yet (as mentioned above) Laclau himself does point to the specificity of neoliberalism when understanding the contemporary world, and a large chapter of Laclau's and Mouffe's book focuses on a new form of radical democracy capable of contesting the advances made by the right in the 1980s. In a similar fashion to Hall and *Marxism Today*, they favoured an approach to politics that could engage with the neoliberal and transform it. Without a central focal point that traditional socialism provided through its class analysis, they favoured a project that would converge the complex discourses which they believed would combine to radicalize society (Laclau and Mouffe 1985: 174–5). Again, while this might appear to be idealist and rather woolly in ambition, something I shall come back to in Chapter 8, it does allow us to investigate the various forms of discourses identified by Laclau, and assess their meaning in a wider context. Therefore it is possible to draw on Laclau's understanding of identity and articulation when trying to unravel the complexities of hegemony, without accepting his rejection of the overall importance of production.

Rethinking Neo-Gramscian Hegemony?

The legacy of Gramsci has been a contested one. I have outlined the different ways in which Gramsci's form of hegemony has been applied within global politics, and have suggested further ways in which a Gramscian approach might be used so that hegemony at a global level can be understood. What is certainly apparent is that Gramsci himself was not merely, solely or arguably in anyway a political economist. Yet, his work in the realms of the study of global politics has largely been restricted to the areas of IPE. To a degree this is what we should expect. It was after all the widespread use of hegemonic stability that led Cox and Gill to offer a Gramscian alternative. First and foremost it was in looking at the primacy of the concept in the workings of the international economy that the alternative interpretation was originally offered. It is also the main reason why many neo-Gramscians locate themselves within the field of IPE. Yet that does not mean that the use of Gramsci's hegemony should be located firmly within this sub-field of the study of global politics. Gramsci's own writings were centrally concerned with how classes in society forge passive relationships across political and civil society. Therefore, the manner in which this has been done should be the main attraction for those studying the construction and fashioning of hegemony. While world order theory and those that see the hegemony through the lens of transnational capitalist class construction, provide a useful departure point for understanding the general framework of the functioning of a hegemonic order, its complexities are less well developed.

Part of this has been a result of the occupation that neo-Gramscians have had when considering the importance of the US state when understanding hegemony. In particular, where the US state fits alongside the wider questions of class and ideology. In understanding the formation of neoliberalism, this has become even more unclear. Despite the work by such as Germain and Kenny, there has often been a lack of clarity over just how a hegemonic order is conceived, contested and maintained globally. As we have suggested, Cox's conception of 'world order' and van der Pijl's conception of 'transnational capitalist classes' have been aided to some extent by Robinson's work on the transnational state, but shortcomings are still evident when looking at the different ways hegemony is fashioned in the many layers within world politics. To advance this, I have suggested that the works of Henri Lefebvre, Stuart Hall, Raymond Williams and Ernesto Laclau can be useful. Each of these provides us with a way in which to understand global hegemony that avoids the problems associated with these criticisms. Rather than being tied to locating hegemony through the structures of state systems, each of these sees hegemony as an open terrain, where states and sovereign bodies can be seen to play off each other alongside factors such as nationalism, economic globalization, and forms of identity that are evident at every level of global politics. Each of these seeks to comply and/or contest the very nature of neoliberalism. While, the importance of each actor differs in terms of how it can contribute to the outcome of hegemony, the consent of each is required for the successful stability of a specific order.

As I shall show in Chapter 5, the fashioning of neoliberalism has never produced total consent, nor could any order realistically expect to do so. The principles of neoliberalism are such that consent has to be constantly re-negotiated for it to succeed. At the same time, the diverse ways in which an agency articulates its meaning under neoliberalism also changes and evolves over time. It is this form of articulation that has enabled neoliberal hegemony to change its overriding direction and character. It has also allowed certain forms of resistance to neoliberalism to be kept at bay. In understanding how hegemony is articulated at different levels of global society and through different agents, a Gramscian approach can be used to understand the dispersion of power in international politics in a way that does not have to rely solely on a dominant state.

5
Neoliberal Hegemony

As suggested in Chapter 4, the riddle of hegemony in global politics can partly be solved by using a Gramscian analysis accounting for the problems that a lack of an international state might cause. Another problem is to demonstrate adequately the form and character that hegemony might take. This is particularly important at the global level, where diversities appear across a national, regional and cultural divide. Therefore, one of the more obvious problems of understanding contemporary neoliberalism is to explore and account for the different ways in which it is articulated across the world. This in itself raises more problems. How, for example, can neoliberalism adequately explain a range of diversities that are undeniable within global political and economic affairs? To try to understand these, a definition of neoliberalism is required that accounts for the diverse forms of consent produced at different levels of global political and civil society. This in itself appears to be a difficult task, as the word 'neoliberalism' itself, and the ideology associated with it can provide a number of different assumptions when establishing a definition for it.

As we shall see, one of the problems with the meaning of neoliberalism is that it appears as both a hugely contested concept and one that has often been used in a general manner. One could conduct a study on the nature of neoliberalism itself: on what it means and entails, and what it does not. Therefore, any discussion of it as the basis of a hegemonic project must define clearly what its overriding principles are at the global level. In addition, it needs to show how such principles have gained consent, and what forms of agency have been mobilized to allow a hegemonic order to flourish and stabilize itself. To do that it seems best to look at the intellectual roots of the neoliberal project and how it emerged, adapted, developed and transformed over time. This will also show whether neoliberalism has any chance of long-term survival in the light of the financial situation at the time of writing, or whether it appears to be in terminal decline and unable to wield legitimacy.

The Roots of Neoliberalism

It is difficult to ascertain precisely when the founding ideas of neoliberalism emerged. To some extent, the inspiration for the new form of liberal capitalism was the laissez-faire model of capitalism that was prominent in nineteenth-century Victorian Britain, often referred to as 'the Golden Age of liberalism'. This might itself have been influenced by the classical liberal tradition, but became synonymous with the Liberal Party's market reforms in Britain. Perhaps the best illustration of this is found in Karl Polanyi's 1944 critique of the self-regulated market society in his text *The Great Transformation*. Here, Polanyi argued that a truly liberal society, where the state retreats to a level such that the market can dictate not only economic productivity but also the fabric of wider society, is ultimately flawed. By deregulating all forms of economic activity, the state and wider society looks to shield itself from the potential barbarity of market rule. As a result, the growth of regulatory bodies, as well as labour unions, universal suffrage and the influx of social welfare appeared to temper the excesses of the market. This succession of 'counter-movements' continued well into the twentieth century, when fascism emerged in the light of market failure (Polanyi [1944]/2001).

Despite many accounts drawing on Polanyi's understanding of the counter-movement, the nineteenth-century form of liberalism differed from the new form of liberal economic reasoning on which neoliberalism was based. Jamie Peck's study on the essence of neoliberal reasoning suggests that the role of the state was not intended to be one that withered away in the light of market forces. Instead, it should play a substantial role in ensuring that the general frameworks of 'individual liberty' and 'market innovation' are maintained. In this sense, the main role of the state is to police a form of working ideology and look to maintain the general economic system (Peck 2010: 4–5). This was precisely the point made by the main body of free market intellectuals that emerged in the light of the growth of social democracy after the Second World War. As both Milton Friedman and Friedrich von Hayek argued in different ways, the problem with the nineteenth-century liberals was that they were too idealistic in their understanding of the market and the state's role in its functioning. The project of neoliberalism would be one whereby state and society would be able to uphold its general liberal principles. Or one that would provide a firm base for hegemonic development.

Many have placed the birth of the neoliberal project with the founding of the Mont Pelerin Society in 1947. This was an organization that aimed to establish a transnational network of neoliberal thinkers looking to critique the mixed-economic Keynesian consensus emerging at that time. They were initially heavily influenced by Hayek's *Road to Serfdom* (1944) that was written during the last stages of the war, coincidentally the same year as Polanyi's *The Great Transformation*. Hayek argued that any form of state intervention in the economy would inevitably lead to a restriction of individual liberty. No matter how well-intentioned social intervention in the economy might be, it would ultimately lead not just to an increasingly unproductive economy, but also to the state increasing its influence over all forms of society. This, as Hayek concludes, ultimately produces measures of authoritarianism, which increase every time intervention is employed (Hayek [1944]/2001: 190–9).

It was on this basis that the Mont Pelerin Society was founded, and the debates and traditions that followed within the group looked at extending the intellectual dynamic of liberal political economy. In the Gramscian sense, these initial debates saw the role of traditional intellectuals in action as they sought to forge the intellectual basis of a new hegemonic society. Yet, as historians have pointed out, many of the ideas at the time were to fall on deaf ears (Mirowski and Plehwe 2009). It was not until problems emerged with post-war forms of Keynesianism and state socialism many decades later that the ideas were to find coherence in the 'real' world. What did emerge, however, were the competing models of liberalism that had been put forward by the many contributors to the society. For example, the 'Austrian School', which contained highly influential figures such as Ludwig von Mises, maintained the belief that the state should largely adopt the classical laissez-faire position and withdraw from interfering in market forces. This differed from those who adopted what was once described as an ordoliberalism position during 1920s Germany. This argued that the state needed to be far more involved as an actor in reinforcing liberal traditions. Later, the emergence of the Chicago School provided a more technical method of ensuring that market principles are adhered to by suggesting monetarist strategies on economies.

The three traditions that emerged were comprised of different visions of how a new liberal society could be built. Each was committed to core beliefs around the principles of market rule and individualism, with arguments based primarily around how such a society could be managed so that these principles could be maximized. In light of the financial crisis that began in 2007/8, the debates that were initially covered in these narrow theoretical and elitist circles have been revisited. This would suggest that the general hegemonic framework these traditional intellectuals envisaged has indeed been successful. The fact that these debates are being taken up in the real world of contemporary politics shows us just how dominant the neoliberal tradition has become.

The Austrian School tradition maintained the conviction that the market would have to create both winners and losers, and as such the state should minimize its role when ensuring that liberal principles are maintained. Policies such as the state bailouts of failing financial institutions and the intervention in interest rates should be avoided. One of the more free market criticisms of post-crisis policy is that it has reinforced the reliance on intervention when key financial institutions are under threat. Certainly, von Mises and later economists on the anarcho-capitalism side of neoliberal doctrine (such as Murray Rothbard) argued strongly that it should be the market and the market alone that dictated success or failure in the financial sphere (von Mises 1934; Rothbard 1994). They also suggested that any moves to expand credit artificially by lowering interest rates from their market value would ultimately lead to instability. As we shall see below, many libertarian accounts of the recent financial crisis have been quick to draw parallels from this argument, and have maintained that it was state interference that ultimately allowed the economy to rely on an unsustainable credit bubble. Without the interference of central bank regulation, the market would be allowed to function as a true equalizer of the economy. For these accounts, therefore, neoliberalism would work more effectively if it allowed the market to play the full role that it should. Intervention that might seem to enforce market rules ultimately restricts its very real potential as an enforcer of rules and norms.

At the other end of the spectrum, the ordoliberal tradition can be seen not only in responses to the financial crisis but also with strategies that certain states have used to try to direct the global market for their own competitive gain. Here, for neoliberalism to be sustained, it needs to maintain the solvency of key financial institutions to allow it to survive. Therefore, the bailing out of banks with state funds is paramount to protect the assets of individuals. It also allows for a reassessment of public state spending and puts the emphasis back on the private sector to re-stimulate the economy. This has been the logic developed in many Western countries since the financial crisis, whereby what appeared as a Keynesian form of intervention in the form of state bailouts has emerged as a policy of state spending moving away from the public sector to facilitate these bailouts. As a result, austerity measures have been brought in, so that the emphasis of policy remains firmly within the private sector.

These were the sorts of debates that were being aired in intellectual circles in the post-war debates of the 1940s and 1950s, but at the time were deemed to be rather irrelevant. What these debates show is that neoliberalism is not a singular ideology, but is made up of a collection of competing models that differ in theory and, as we shall see below, practice. The main tenets, however, remain the conviction that economic activity and production should be stimulated through the private sector. The role of the state might vary in terms of its exact activity, but its central goal is to uphold the principle of the free market and the deregulation of the private sector. Or to put it more clearly, it should facilitate the free market through the rule of law and provide for the upkeep of this relationship. As the traditions that emerged from the Mont Pelerin Society looked to contest and challenge the hegemonic 'common sense' of the post-war consensus, then the alternatives they put forward were intended to produce significant challenges. The ideas and debates flourished over the next three decades but, despite containing very real solutions, they did not make any inroads into the Keynesian dominated society of the Cold War era. As Peck continues in his study, while Hayek's *Road to Serfdom* was a best seller at the time, stimulating great debate and a following within economic thought, it was the relatively unknown *Great Transformation* that reflected the feelings of the time (Peck 2010: 41–2). More prominently, while the neoliberal intellectuals were building up networks of like-minded critics, post-war society had become so committed to different forms of planned economics, that any thought of returning to a self-regulated market system was considered irrational and unfeasible (Kynaston 2007: 22–41). This was largely how it would stay until the collapse of the post-war dollar system set up by the USA with the assistance of John Maynard Keynes, brought in a new era of instability; one in which alternative hegemonic projects could thrive.

Breaking the Mould: Pinochet, Thatcher and Reagan

When US President Nixon suspended the convertibility of the dollar to gold in 1971 – the form of international economic governance that had held together the post-war system since Bretton Woods collapsed. Not only did the era of fixed exchange rates, whereby foreign currencies were pegged to the dollar, make way for a new era of floating exchange rates, but the overall mixed-economy model of economic growth came under threat. The problems were multiplied by the oil crisis in 1973, when the Organization of the Petroleum Exporting Countries (OPEC) states drastically increased the price of crude oil, leading to serious economic consequences internationally. It was against this backdrop that neoliberalism began to mobilize. As the 1970s became marked by instability, turmoil and economic stagflation, a hegemonic crisis began to arise as the Keynesian-inspired order failed to address its problems convincingly. The election at the end of the decade of Prime Minister Margaret Thatcher in the UK and President Ronald Reagan in the USA might have been seen as a significant breakthrough in terms of electoral success for a form of politics based upon the principles of neoliberalism, but a more profound development had occurred earlier in Chile.

On 11 September 1973, Chile's left-wing government was overthrown by a small, military-led group backed by international business actors, US security forces and economists rooted in neoliberal reasoning. The coup, led by the ardent anti-communist General Augustine Pinochet, embarked on a process of privatization, a strategy centred on attracting oversees investment and tax reforms. At the same time, the new regime engaged with the repression of political opposition, the establishment of a military dictatorship and the internment, expulsion and in many cases the liquidation of individuals involved in the previous administration. Through the suppression of any opposition and a tight control on security forces, Pinochet radicalized the fabric of

Chile's economy along market reform lines. As many neoliberals had argued within the circles of the Mont Pelerin Society, the state needed a central role in the fashioning of a market society. In this case, it was the state that acted as a repressive apparatus, enforcing market-led reform without the consenting will of the public. The move was welcomed by the many traditional intellectuals central to neoliberal economic thought. Milton Freedman was brought in as a permanent adviser to the Pinochet regime, and the group of young economists who were at the forefront of Chile's economic revolution in the years following the coup were trained by Freedman and his associates. Hayek was also highly supportive of the new regime, stating that he preferred a 'liberal dictatorship to a democratic government lacking liberalism' (Grandin 2006: 171).

It was the Chilean experiment that allowed neoliberal economists and political strategists to turn their attention to the core developed world. The elections of Thatcher and Reagan saw different experiences with the principles of neoliberalism. What became apparent with both was that they engaged with a form of populism that provided a basis for a new form of common sense. The populism formed around the rejection of 'big government' was a key promotion in the Reagan campaign. The main principles around what became known as 'Reaganomics' was based firmly around supply-side economics, applied via federal tax cuts and the reduction of capital gains tax. Yet, the pledge to cut federal spending was compromised by the renewal of the arms race with the Soviet Union and a greater commitment towards the 'fight against communism' abroad. At home, while Reagan's policies of tax cuts remained popular, his increasing fiscal spending on defence led to a record increase in the national debt. Despite this, the two virtues of tax reductions and anti-communism created a mindset that was to form a successful hegemonic base.

In the UK, Thatcher's pursuit of neoliberalism was rather more turbulent, as she embarked on dismantling the influence of the solid tradition of trade unionism within British post-war industry. In doing so, the economy could be revolutionized from one that had become increasingly stagnated and dominated by uncompetitive state-subsidized manufacturing, to one that would be conditioned through market competition. Taking what could only be described as a 'divide and rule' tactic, Thatcher sort to restrict trade union power, privatize core industries which had been kept in public hands and – taking a leaf out of Pinochet's book – centralize her governmental position by restricting the power of potential local government that might be seen as oppositional. By the end of the 1980s, the UK's economy had indeed been transformed as the City of London developed greater prominence as a global financial centre, and the manufacturing sector went into decline. The transformation took place against a backdrop of instability, however, as inequality rose dramatically and a process of de-industrialization brought high unemployment and social fragmentation to large parts of the country's former industrial heartlands. As a result, Thatcherism emerged as an ideology that had pretensions to become hegemonic, but because of its divisionary nature this did not happen (Hall 1988).

- In all three cases, neoliberalism appeared more as a mindset than as a universal hegemonic project. As the world was still defined by its bipolar character, it did not seem that it could emerge as one that might gain global influence, despite its prominence in the leading states in (what was then) the Western world. However, the impact of Thatcher and Reagan had a profound effect on the future direction of the neoliberal project. First, the perception of its successes by its supporters made significant strides to change the belief that the state should have a central role in stimulating economic growth. Supporters of both governments pointed to economic advances made in the USA and the UK. In particular, they argued that the deregulation measures brought in had created a new-found spirit of innovation and entrepreneurship within business and financial circles. The emphasis on fiscal responsibility and supply-side economics was to also attract an increasing audience. As the 1980s drew to a close, it was increasingly being put forward as a method to reduce the amount of debt that had seen a dramatic increase in developing countries since the oil crisis, while at the same time increasing the flow of private investment.

The parameters of neoliberal ideas were extended during the 1970s and 1980s into the areas of free trade, regionalism and international business. What turned out to be the last GATT round of multilateral trade negotiations began in 1986, amid a fresh impetus for free trade following the emergence of the neoliberal agenda. The 1980s also saw the move in Europe towards establishing a single economic market and put firm foundations in place for a single currency that would emerge from it. These moves saw a battle of ideas within Europe between a neoliberal form of Europe endorsed by Thatcher, and with which Helmut Kohl of Germany certainly flirted, and the form of a social Europe supported by Jacques Delors and backed by the bulk of social democratic parties throughout the continent (Strange 2006). In business, the growth and significance of multinational corporations had already attracted a great deal of attention in terms of the amount of power they were wielding in international politics by the 1970s (Said and Simmons 1975; Keohane and Nye 1977; Madsen 1980). Yet the policies of Thatcher and Reagan saw the influence of such actors increase, and allowed them to put pressure on other governments and institutions to follow similar policies. This added to the renewed logic that it was the private sector as opposed to the state that ultimately provided the stimulus for economic growth.

Neoliberalism on the Offensive: Globalization and the Decline of Socialism

If the experiences of Pinochet, Thatcher and Reagan put down the hegemonic principles of neoliberalism, it was the fall of the Soviet Union that allowed it to flourish. The end of state socialism saw the transition of former Eastern European states as well as Russia itself from managed to market economies, and with the end of ideological hostilities it provided a global market to which the state had to adapt. The new market realities meant that there was a move to what has been termed the 'competition state', where states engage with the global economy and seek to attract investment in order to succeed (Cerny 1997). Through this, a new reality emerged that was rooted in one of the fabrics of neoliberal logic: that a state's main purpose was to make its conditions favourable enough for private investment to thrive and for the market to provide the basis for this to develop. More telling was the reality that economic growth was to stem more from the acquisition of private investment than from state intervention. The extent of such growth would also depend on the health of the global economy itself.

The globalization of the economy would also bring with it a number of further transformations. Technological innovation and the emergence of the so-called 'knowledge' or 'network' society trans-formed the global economy and society in the 1990s, as production became less territorial, and work and skill in the labour force became more flexible in nature (Castells 1996; Moore 2010). This has been coupled with a more profound global division of labour, whereby multinational corporations increasingly became more mobile, moving their operations into different parts of the world to maximize their profits and assets. This transformation during the 1990s allowed the neoliberal project to gain a true hegemonic character, as states and societies moved to accept its general working formula, and as a result embed its general principles as common sense. This was enhanced by a number of political developments, such as the Washington Consensus and the Third Way, discussed below, that supported general global governance.

The Washington Consensus

The conviction that the market economy could provide a solution to the growing debt problem was one that was being aired during the Thatcher–Reagan period. To an extent it also gained inspiration from the Chilean experiment, where privatization and a reduction in state spending, coupled with support from international businesses, banks and economists, led to a reduction in government debt (Valdes 1995). The 'Washington Consensus' was a term coined by John Williamson, of the Institute for International Economics, when summarizing the new position that the IMF, World Bank and the US Treasury had reached in 1989 on dealing with indebted states. Here, a 10-point recommendation was made for states to restructure their economies in order to manage their debt. These included strict fiscal policy discipline, a reduction of public spending, tax reform, trade liberalization, privatization and regulation. It was expected that such policies would result in a significant increase in foreign direct investment (FDI), which would lead to a dramatic rise in economic growth.

   Using the terms of the Washington Consensus, the World Bank devised structural adjustment packages that were offered to developing states unable to meet the conditions for outstanding loans. There were multiple consequences of this action. First, many developing states were compelled to take on the conditions and by doing so engaged with private companies in order to provide welfare, health and education services, which the state could no longer afford. Second, the onset of privatization allowed companies to place their own conditions on their operations within a country. Third, it provided a 'one size fits all' solution to debt alleviation, regardless of the actual situation (Stiglitz 2002). Finally, it provided a set of economic governmental conventions that were to resurface when states faced fiscal crisis. What was provided conditionally to developing states in the 1990s would be applied similarly to more advanced economies two decades later in response to the global financial crisis.

As the 1990s progressed, the strict conditions proposed initially on such loans made way for more specialized assistance, such as the Heavily Indebted Poor Countries (HIPC) Initiative, which focused more specifically on states that were spending a high percentage of GDP on debt repayment, and the conditions of the consensus were not easing the situation. This changed again by the early years of the twenty-first century, as public opinion and the Millennium Development Goals (MDGs) for human development pointed at the injustices of the Washington Consensus. G8 summits, such as that held in Gleneagles, Scotland, in 2005, pledged a greater commitment towards debt cancellation and put conditions that placed political democratic reform on the same level as economic restructuring. Yet the precedent had been set by the World Bank. While over time the need for partnerships between the public and the private sectors were encouraged, the message in terms of development could not have been clearer. The path to prosperity was through marketization and an engagement with external investors. In this way, it is stressed, globalization can work as a force for development and empowerment (World Bank 2010).

This neoliberal incentive was a clear break from developmental strategies of the past. The establishment of the UN and the process of decolonialization in the years after the Second World War gave a clear mandate as to how newly independent states should progress with development. Influenced by Walt Rostow's model of 'take-off', it stressed that industrialization was key for economic growth. Just as Britain had embarked on its Industrial Revolution in the late seventeenth and early eighteenth centuries, and the rest of Europe and North America followed, then developing countries, once in control of their own affairs could emulate these. In Rostow's 'stages of development', prior to industrial take-off states needed to ensure the preconditions for industrialization are in place. These include greater centralization of the state and the embedding of certain forms of infrastructure (Rostow 1960). The post-war years thus encouraged centralization and state intervention in their respective development. The U-turn by the 1980s centred on the notion that states spent too lavishly in their post-colonial development. Despite being prompted to move towards industrialization through various stages of development, states were penalized when spending on this led to debt problems. The confidence in the modernization theory espoused by Rostow and the UN had certainly waned by the time of the financial turmoil of the 1970s. States were not able to develop in the manner that had been prescribed by those in Europe in the nineteenth century and as a result had ended up further in debt.

The move towards engaging with the global market has been one that has also been used by states in the developing world itself. President Fernando Cardoso of Brazil, a one-time leading advocate of the dependency school critique on modernization, stressed the importance of globalism in terms of development (Cardoso 2001). In his position as president of Brazil he urged states to engage with the market to maximize its potential. Moving against a state-led focus and the rise of isolation, he suggested that developmental states needed to engage specific strategic objectives at both regional and international levels in order to become more empowered within the global economy. This was to further reinforce the hegemonic conviction that economic growth and development were best served by market engagement.

The position taken by Cardoso mirrored development across the developing world, particularly by key state players within it. The long-term relevance of the new manufacturing powerhouses will be discussed in depth in Chapter 6. But the economic mobilization of states such as India and China has been marked by their successful ability to attract FDI and inward private investment. In addition, they have been further aided by the ability to offer a flexible and cheap labour force to multinational firms. While a great deal of attention has been paid to the relevance of power assumed by the so-called BRIC (Brazil, Russia, India and China) powers, the way they have built such a power base has come from market-led initiatives. While rightly discussing the growing significance of such powers, they have nevertheless succeeded in the accumulation of wealth through the successful pursuit of external private investments from successive companies (Shirk 2004). In this sense, the idea of the competition state has been taken to a new level.

The rise of China has also led to many suggesting that the Washington Consensus has been replaced by the Beijing Consensus. The precise meaning of this seems to suggest that China favours a form of development that allows a greater role for the state and favours a gradual engagement with market reform (Williamson

2012). Whether this refers to a type of capitalism that will serve to challenge the neoliberal model (Ramo 2004), or one where the state plays a more controlled role in its engagement with the neoliberal model (Harvey 2005) is a point I shall take up in depth in Chapter 6. What has been apparent is that China's engagement in Africa has seen African states learn from the Chinese experience and adopt similar tactics towards developmental goals. At the same time, China has claimed that investment should be seen along the lines of a 'South–South' relationship and along the premise that both partners can maximize their developmental potential. As a result, the engagement with a state considered as a developing rather than Western has been a favourable one. Market engagement is made without the negative connotations associated with the form of neoliberalism preached by Washington.

The Third Way

The mid-1990s saw a series of social democratic and centre-left political parties across Europe and North America alter their directional outlook. In response to the success of market economics and to the end of the Cold War, they sought to engage with the policies that had proved to be successful with the neoliberal right. Traditional social democratic policies such as high taxation, intervention in the economy and economic redistribution were seen as untenable in light of the transformation of the global economy. As a result, the 'Third Way' emerged as a suitable ideology that would facilitate the main objectives of social democracy through engagement with the market.

The position was best summarized by Anthony Giddens' *Third Way* and subsequent follow-up books (Giddens 1998, 2000). In this, he argues that the centre-left needs to distance itself both from the traditions of old left, which could not realistically provide their intended objectives, and the neoliberal right, which believed in the unfettered market. Instead, he suggested that the market could be steered in a direction that could fulfil the main principles of social democracy. Rather than understanding the market and the private sector as being the antitheses of socialism, Giddens argued that the main tenets of social democracy –full employment, greater inclusivity and welfare provision – can be realized through public/private collaboration (Giddens 1998: 101–18). The main focus of the Third Way was to ensure forms of 'inclusion'. Market economics left unfettered might produce forms of inequality and polarization, but if the state plays a significant role to ensure that private actors facilitate both welfare provision and provide opportunity for those marginalized by the market to gain access to its wealth potential.

The epoch of the Third Way was embraced by leaders such as Bill Clinton in the USA and Gerhard Schröder, Tony Blair and Lionel Jospin in Europe. To a degree this followed on from Jacques Delors' vision at the end of the 1980s of a social Europe. Yet what it did in fact was to embed and legitimize the wider principles of neoliberalism. Because, by accepting the principles of market economics and by compromising on Keynesian forms of intervention and wealth redistribution, the left has strengthened the general working formula of neoliberalism. As Gramsci originally indicated when looking at the formation of the Italian state, it was only when the opposition accepted the overriding conditions that had been bestowed upon them that a hegemonic order was able to be fashioned (Gramsci 1971: 55–102). This was demonstrated well by Stuart Hall, when he argued that the Thatcher revolution in the UK only matured when New Labour came to power a decade later on the premise of accepting its key foundations (Hall 2011). Elsewhere in Europe, neoliberal social forces appeared to gain ascendency in key EU institutions (Bieler and Morton 2001). While the pursuit of a social Europe remained a central objective, the realities of economic globalization have led to a greater engagement with neoliberalism. The Third Way also played a significant role in moving the EU towards an entity that could regulate the market to enable the main social objectives that Delors called for to be achieved though neoliberal principles.

It was not just in the European or North American financial heartland that the Third Way was popular. The Chinese used a variant of it to underpin their state-managed approach to the market. Whether this can be seen as the form that Giddens suggested, or as a different form of capitalism that counters rather than embeds the process of neoliberalism is another question that will be given more attention in Chapter 6. The general principle of using the state to facilitate positive engagement with the market remains similar. The Third Way was backed more explicitly in South and Central America by leaders such as Vicente Fox in Mexico and Michelle Bachelet in Chile. As with his understanding of globalization, Cardoso in Brazil was perhaps more forward in his endorsement of the Third Way. During his term as president, his rejection of traditional ideologies in favour of using the state to facilitate a wider global transformation was central to his arguments (Cardoso 2001).

To an extent, the Third Way allowed the Hayekian ideals on the nature of the state to be realized more than the more concentrated applications of the economic right. As Hayek was keen to stress, the role of the state was to provide a basis for market principles to flourish. While the Third Way might have seen the state use more resources than Hayek would have endorsed, in terms of using public funds to secure public–private partnerships, it ultimately led to the normalization of core neoliberal practices. The many ideas of inclusion have also found support from several entrepreneurs and philanthropists (such as Bill Gates and Alan Sugar), who have backed the Third Way or the new centre-left approach to the market economy. Central to this is the conviction that the innovation and competition provided by the private sector can generate enough wealth to trickle down to levels that would eradicate exclusion and extreme poverty (Gates 2010).

Neoliberalism on the Defensive: Austerity and Crisis

The advances of neoliberalism during the latter part of the twentieth century spread to embrace economic, social and cultural dimensions. The era of market-driven mass consumerism sought to legitimize the common sense of neoliberalism. Politics, nationalism and even religion have been formulated in a manner that complies with the hegemony of free market capitalism (Murray and Worth 2013). As outlined in Chapter 4, hegemony is forged and articulated in a number of different ways and through a number of different media. Yet it also needs to respond to the potential forms of resistance and potential hegemonic crises that may emerge. As a result, the nature of hegemony is not stable; it (to paraphrase Stuart Hall) is constantly on the move, and able to reinvent its character to keep potential opposition forces at bay (Hall 1988).

The rise of protest movements that first started symbolically with the protests at the World Trade Organization's Ministerial Conference in 1999 in Seattle, USA, began to challenge the nature of neoliberal development. Protestors pointed to the vast inequalities that the globalization of neoliberal principles have produced, as well as highlighting how international organizations were seeking to maximize the influence of corporate power at the expense of labour and civil groups. This led to a number of protests during international summits and meetings. The attacks on the World Trade Center in New York in 2001 provided another demonstration of discontent with the contemporary system of global capitalism. The response from the USA was to reassert its authority at the international level.

The years following the 9/11 attacks saw a neoconservative response being enforced by the Bush administration that sought to ensure that the principles of liberal democracy were enforced through the interventionist policies in Afghanistan and Iraq. The main premise here was that the USA needed to be more hands-on in its policing of the international system. The flexing of US power was discussed in depth in Chapter3, but what is apparent is that, through military inven-tion, the USA is looking to protect the legitimacy of neoliberalism. Yet, as I stressed in Chapter 4, hegemony is best facilitated through consent. The use of force or coercion in the enforcement of conditions and values is often a sign of instability and a lack of confidence in the overall system (Gramsci 1971). For those who maintain a belief in unipolarity, and for those who endorsed the 'project for the new American Century', force is a necessary requirement to ensure the continuity of American leadership at the international level. The 'project for the new American Century' was a think tank formed by Robert Kagan and William Kristol that had close links to the Bush administration. It stressed the need for greater US involvement in international affairs and a greater commitment to ensure that rogue states and potential extremists groups that threaten the neoliberal order are kept at bay.

By the end of the Bush administration, this approach did indeed attract some of the problems that Gramsci (and Machiavelli before him) were warning about. The use of force and the inability to terminate wars successfully led to a backlash amid the growth of anti-American feeling. By the time Obama took office, the process of intervention-ism was becoming unpopular, not just within the international community but also within the USA itself. However, the fabric of neoliberalism was about to be threatened by something far more serious in terms of its overall survival. In 2008, in the aftermath of the bursting of the housing bubble, Lehman Brothers Holdings, the fourth-largest investment bank in the USA dropped its stock value rapidly and filed for bankruptcy. This was to precipitate the most significant international financial crisis since the Wall Street crash of

1929. It doing so, it firmly questioned the sustainability of the neoliberal financial system.

Austerity as a Form of Common Sense

In the immediate aftermath of the banking crisis, world leaders and leading economists called for a new financial system based on a new set of regulations (Krugman 2008). This was followed by a number of world leaders, such as Gordon Brown and even George W. Bush suggesting that a new form of Bretton Woods system was needed. The move towards Keynesianism continued as a succession of failing banks were bailed out and given a capital injection from states. Many early, detailed accounts of the global financial crisis predicted that it was unlikely to see neoliberalism survive in its current format (Gamble 2009). Yet, as a post-crisis era began to emerge, it was not a change in the overall character of the hegemonic system that was to take place, but instead a firm defence of its workings. This was to be understood through policies of austerity.

For post-crisis governments, austerity has been the central policy in the attempt to instigate economic recovery. The logic behind austerity mystified many Keynesians, who had insisted that austerity measures would only serve to plunge economies into a further, deeper recession (Krugman 2012; Blyth 2013). Austerity, however, has been presented as a necessary measure that is required for the market to be re-stimulated. The reasons for this are twofold. First, rather than attempting to intervene in the market to stimulate growth, what is required is that the market should be as free and unregulated as possible to enable the private sector to regain its confidence. This would then attract greater investment, thus leading to economic growth. As a result, the state needs to maintain a minimum presence in the economy to maximize competition in the market. Second, austerity measures have been brought in to lower the burden of debt which had increased sharply in a number of countries during the preceding decades and had multiplied in the light of respective government bailouts of national banks.

In terms of the second point, the growing debt burden has been such that international and supranational bodies have pursued and insisted on austerity measures in the light of economic restructuring. This has been especially noticeable in the Eurozone, where the build-up of sovereign debt in certain states has placed great strain on the overall functioning of the euro. As a result, states hit hardest by the financial fallout, such as Portugal, Ireland, Italy, Greece and Spain (commonly referred to as PIIGS) have embarked on stringent austerity measures in order to meet the euro's fiscal restrictions. Governments in the PIIGS countries have considered such measures as being both necessary and inevitable, yet austerity has also built a distinct narrative that moves beyond the notion that no alternative exists.

Austerity has been 'sold' as a logical framework for action in a number of ways. Just as individuals have to break even during times of crisis, so do states. Therefore, debt management and prudence is essential during times of difficulty (Blyth 2013; Worth 2013). Governments have also been quick to blame previous administration for over-spending and for failing to take the necessary measures to deal with the amounting debt. While in many cases external or public debt is not distinguished from government debt (Krugman 2012), the opportunity for points-scoring has not been missed. For the centre-right it has also gone some way towards reconfirming the necessity of market economics over the Keynesian alternative. Aided by international media groups, the necessity for debt reduction has thus been used as almost a natural consequence of a crisis.

In real terms, austerity has appeared as a suitable policy for the defence of neoliberalism. Its main significance has been to facilitate a belief that austerity is a normal and correct process during a time of crisis. Perhaps more important, it has been preferred to a wider and more comprehensive change. Part of the reason for this is that no real recipe for a hegemonic alternative has been strong enough to seriously challenge the main fabric of the current order. The ideas that were being talked about in 2008 and 2009 regarding a new international economic arrangement disappeared as austerity measures became embedded within governmental circles.

This has not been to say that discontent regarding austerity has not emerged. As I shall explain in Chapter 8, a number of contending ideologies that were already prominent before the crisis, gained greater relevance. Movements such as *Occupy* made a great impact on public consciousness, and in certain parts of Europe, the far right, which had steadily grown as a political force since the end of the Cold War, has continued its upward mobility. At the same time, the resurgence of religious-based movements kept up their own critiques of global capitalism (Worth 2013). However, no firm practical alternative has emerged from these critiques. What has emerged instead are a number of well-framed criticisms of the consequences of austerity – such as growing inequality and poverty brought on by the cutting of welfare and raising unemployment. Despite this, the lack of any firm strategic alternative has merely gone to strengthen the validity of austerity.

The policy of austerity has thus contributed to a new key form of neoliberal common sense. The narrative that austerity is a necessary process of political and economic life has added a new layer to the hegemony of neoliberalism. The central idea of neoliberalism – that the market and the private sector provide the basis for wealth creation – is further strengthened, adding a new dimension in the process. Not only does austerity act as a form of survival, but it is also a useful defence mechanism against criticism. Yet this will only work realistically if the self-regulated market does succeed in stimulating the economy towards a new period of growth. The period of austerity has also led to a wider debate about the nature of neoliberalism, and whether the state should be more minimalist in its role within the market economy.

Too Much Regulation?

One of the more surprising reactions to the financial crisis has been from neoconservative movements that have pointed to the interference of regulatory bodies as its main cause. The age-old laissez-faire tradition that was popular with the physiocrats in eighteenth-century France and with the liberals in nineteenth-century Britain rested on the philosophy that financial institutions limited the market from reaching its potential as a wealth creating mechanism in society. Following from this, many contemporary laissez-faire positions believed that it was indeed the actions of key central banks and of international financial institutions that had caused the financial crash. As central banks had intervened in lowering interest rates artificially and allowing the credit bubble to build up, it had denied the market the opportunity to act as the true enforcer of economic outcomes. Without such an intervention, the market can act to find equilibrium in the economy that will cancel out long-term periods of crisis. This position has been taken up by neoconservative movements such as the Tea Party in the USA, and with right-wing political parties such as the United Kingdom Independence Party (UKIP) in Britain and Lega Nord in Italy.

The main complaint that such groups have is that there has been too much taxation and regulation in the economy, which has eroded individual liberties. They also believe that governments have been spending excessively on a wide collection of unnecessarily areas, and this has resulted in the debt build-up. Taking an intellectual cue from Ludwig von Mises and Murray Rothbard, they believe that the state should ultimately cut right back in its fiscal responsibilities, and that central regulatory bodies should either be restricted in their authority or should cease to exist. This new wave of libertarianism has perhaps been best associated with US politicians such as Ron Paul and Michele Bachmann, who made their position on the role of the state explicit during the Republican nomination campaigns for the 2012 US presidential election.

Paul, in particular has often been considered as the godfather of the Tea Party movement. A veteran of political campaigning, and author of books such as *The Revolution* (2008) and *End the Fed* (2009), Paul has thrived in the post-crisis environment. He has suggested that both central banks and institutions such as the WTO should be disbanded as they hinder the global free market from reaching its real potential (Paul 2008: 88–97). This follows the arguments made by von Mises, where he claimed that intervention and regulation in the economy leads to a spiralling process where more and more regulation is required in order to supervise such a process (von Mises 1949). Ironically, this observation is similar to Polanyi's claim that free markets lead to a double movement that looks to regulate its workings, and then becomes unsustainable over time (Polanyi [1944]/2001). For those that believe in a truly unfettered market, no such movement or process of regulation needs to happen, provided that states have the courage to let it develop.

This position was identified during the Mont Pelerin era as one that was termed anarcho-capitalism because of its deep scepticism of the state, and has seen a popular revival in light of the emergence of the movements, such as the Tea Party, that have accompanied it. The low-tax agenda has found great popularity within large sections of society, and the pursuit of less regulation and the growth of welfare chauvinism has appealed to those who supported Reagan and Thatcher in the late 1970s. For them, the financial crisis has been the result of the softening of these principles, heightened by an increase in state debt and undisciplined state spending. They share Hayek's suggestion, put forward in *Prices and Production* (1931), that the artificial lowering of interest rates leads to necessary instability, but Ron Paul's supporters prefer Rothbard's dilution of the state to Hayek's more hands-on approach to the state as market facilitator (Gamble 1996).

The contribution from the right to the crisis has breathed new life into the defence of neoliberal hegemony. From starting at a point where regulation was essential to avoid long-term instability, a new position has gained momentum that has questioned the claim that the financial crisis was the result of the unregulated system. On the contrary, it has been argued that the market has not been allowed to reach its potential as the central mechanism for growth because of the constant regulation and interference from different governmental and bureaucratic bodies. By highlighting mounting debt and opposing bailouts for commercial banks, this position has received growing popular support and created a debate on how the international system should be radically changed so that the real benefits of a market society can be realized.

Conclusion: The Longevity of Neoliberal Hegemony?

This chapter has illustrated how neoliberalism grew from an ideology debated within exclusive academic circles to become a widespread global hegemonic project. Through initial experiences in Chile, it became synonymous with the Thatcher government in the UK, the Reagan government in the USA, and via the auspices of monetarism, the West German government under Helmut Kohl. The embrace of free market principles, combined with the support for private enterprise, saw the ideology flourish during the 1980s. Yet it was the following decade that saw neoliberalism gain global ascendency in the light of the end of the Cold War and the decline of state socialism.

Formed around the notion that private enterprise provides the main impetus for economic growth, the development of a truly global economy began to emerge, where states altered their economic outlook and focused on attracting inward investment in order to compete with the demands of the global market (Palan and Abbott 1996). The rise of consumerism has also played a vital role in the articulation of hegemony, and allowed potentially hostile factors such as nationalism and religion to find a place within the wider dimensions of neoliberalism. The embrace of the market by the left has also taken away a political platform for contestation. As a result, the main avenues of contest have generally come from civil society, quick to illustrate the wider social problems, such as increasing inequality and social fragmentation, that neoliberalism has created in abundance.

The financial crisis was expected to signal the slowing down or reform of the neoliberal agenda, but instead austerity measures have been widely used by countries as a means of cutting back on the debt that has accumulated because of the widespread bank bailouts of 2007–9. These austerity measures have had the intended effect of freeing up the market in order to stimulate international trade towards a renewal of growth. At the time of writing, it remains to be seen whether this process can indeed spark off another cycle of growth or whether this proves to be inadequate as a solution. It also remains to be seen how long neoliberalism can remain on the defensive without a concrete alternative gaining momentum.

What should this tell us about the overall fabric of hegemony? There is no doubt that neoliberalism has provided a basis for the globalization of a hegemonic order. It is also apparent from this chapter that neoliberalism is not merely a US- or state-led project, but something that has emerged over time through different channels, and articulated in contrasting ways. One might suggest that hegemony should be viewed through the lens of an overriding ideology, rather than through the lens of a state. However, as was suggested in the earlier chapters, it is imperative that we look at the manner in which states have sought to lead the wider state system when discussing the workings of hegemony. While the USA has not been responsible for the development and articulation of neoliberalism, it nevertheless remained as the only existing superpower after the Cold War, and was allowed to flourish as a result. As Francis Fukuyama (1992) was quick to point out in the immediate aftermath of the Cold War, it was the form of liberalism and liberal democracy waged by the USA that triumphed and allowed the freer version of liberal economics to trump both state socialism and the Keynesian-inspired form of social democracy.

The USA also played a significant role in the forming of the Washington Consensus. Even if one accepts the argument that it was economists, policy-makers and pressure groups that drew on a wide body of national and international opinion (Williamson 2012), it was the USA, having majority voting rights in the World Bank, that secured the authority for the structural adjustments programmes. The USA therefore allowed neoliberalism to flourish through its international supremacy. To rethink hegemony we therefore need to understand it as a process where a leading state (or states) allows a coherent world order to develop, and then we examine the complex ideological components that allow it to function. If neoliberalism is to be transformed or challenged in some way, the genesis for change might come from an emerging state or region capable of challenging the role of the USA as the 'policeman' of international affairs. The potential for this will be outlined in Chapter 6.

6
The Rise of China and BRICS

As discussed in Chapter 5, the main result of the Washington Consensus was to forge a form of market-based logic within the developing world. Whether this emerged primarily as a US-led incentive, or whether it merely demonstrated the ideological strength of neoliberal principles, is harder to ascertain. However, as the 1990s progressed it became noticeable that the influence of neoliberalism had grown to a level where it appeared to be truly global. As such, the much heralded idea that a 'variety' of capitalisms exist within international politics had been questioned as a result of this dominance. This is an acknowledgement that different types of capitalism exist within different national traditions. The 'Anglo-Saxon' tradition, favoured by the anglophone countries (the UK, the USA, Australia, New Zealand, Ireland and so on) provide the general characteristics of neoliberalism – minimal state interference in the economy, low taxation and little regulation. This contrasts with the continental form of 'Rhine capitalism' that was for a long period a feature of German capitalism. Here, a more regulated form of capitalism has traditionally been practised, relying on tighter regulation and greater corporate control of economic output, which is at odds with the neoliberal tradition (Hall and Soskice 2001). Added to that has been the Scandinavian or Nordic model of capitalism, where low corporate tax and flexibility have been coupled with high welfare protection and high individual income tax (Palan and Abbott 1996).

In reality, by the end of the twentieth century within the global economy, these contrasting forms of capitalism were being compromised increasingly by the growth and spread of the neoliberal model twentieth (Peck 2007; Jessop 2011). In the aftermath of the East Asian crisis of the late 1990s, structural adjustment loans from the World Bank/IMF resulted in similar restructurings to the economies that for years had come to embody state-led forms of neo-mercantilism. As a result, market reforms were ushered in as fiscal spending was reduced to meet the conditions of the loans. This development demonstrated how the neoliberal model had made inroads into competing economic traditions. By enforcing certain compromises during a period of crisis, the general principles of neoliberalism succeeded in making inroads into any previously preferred form of capitalist model.

Despite this, the increase in inequality and the failure of neoliberalism to deal with issues such as poverty and socio-economic stability has seen a rethink by some regarding its suitability as a sustainable economic model. Others have argued that neoliberalism has not reached or maintained the dominance that some have assumed. Much of this has added to the wider observations that the age of American dominance on the international stage is being seriously challenged. This is a position we discussed in depth in Chapter 3, but in that case largely in relation to the USA. Here, it is not just the USA that is being contested, but the economic model it has promoted. Given the way that we have discussed the complex relationship between 'neoliberal' and 'ideological' hegemony on the one hand and state leadership on the other in the preceding chapters, we should avoid reductionist assertions. It is highly debatable that the failure or the stumbling of the neoliberal model mirrors the similar decline of the USA. Equally debatable is the notion that the Washington Consensus itself was (or is) coherent as a directive. Indeed, this questions the extent to which we can link US power to neoliberal hegemony. As I identified in Chapter 5, neoliberalism has been a project that has gone in many directions and assumed many guises. Any attempt to understand it by locating it within a singular departure point proves to be quite problematic, unless one understands it as a wider, class-based phenomenon.

Nevertheless, the rise of newly emerging economies, and of China in particular, has led many to suggest that the global hegemony of neoliberalism is being challenged by fresh versions of capitalism favoured by these new states. This chapter will look at whether China and the newly emerged BRICS (Brazil, Russia, India, China and South Africa) can fashion a South–South developmental mandate that can radically challenge the neoliberalism that has been prominent since the end of the Cold War. Subsequently, in light of the financial crisis, can new economic models emerge, driven by BRICS, that could challenge the main practices of austerity and fiscal prudence that have been used predominately as a method of managing the crisis? Similarly, could a geopolitical situation emerge where separate regions pursue different policies that resemble a multipolar world? These questions will be considered and discussed in this chapter and the next.

The Rise of China

In terms of economic growth, the rise of China has been the most noticeable development since the end of the Cold War. Having seen high rises in the 1980s, the Chinese economy was to continue at a double-figure rate of percentage growth per GDP throughout much of the 1990s. Despite a brief cooling of growth as a result of the Asian crisis in the late 1990s, the economy was to sustain even higher growth rates during the first decade of the twenty-first century, which tailored off slightly as the world went into economic decline, but, comparatively, still maintained a very high level (World Bank 2013). More prominently, this surge has seen China move from being the eighth-largest economy at the end of the Cold War to become comfortably the second-largest. In addition, while nominally Chinese GDP remains at just slightly over a half of the level of the USA, if calculated though purchasing power parity (PPP), then China is closer in terms of its economic might (World Bank 2013).

China's very real economic gains since the mid-1990s have been coupled with huge increases in investment and trade. In terms of foreign direct investment (FDI), China surpassed the USA in becoming the leading recipient in 2012 (and the second after the UK in 2013), while its entry into the World Trade Organization has seen the amount of trade and capital flowing in and out of the country increase to levels undreamed of a decade before. China has also become the largest single holder of foreign reserves, surpassing Japan in 2006. By 2013, this stock had grown to the extent that China had nearly three times more stock than its nearest competitor. This not only reflected the Chinese state's ability to expand its account surpluses and vastly increase its balance of trade in a world marked by stagnation and debt, but it has also allowed China to purchase US 'treasury securities' in the aftermath of the 2008 crisis, becoming the top foreign owner.

With China's rise to become the second-largest economic power prominence in terms of world politics, many commentators have been quick to assess its validity as a rival to the USA. One of the most prominent theorists in international politics, John Mearsheimer, has firmly held the view that China's rise is not just inevitable, but that this rise is likely to lead to a violent struggle. In his *The Tragedy of Great Power Politics*, he suggests that the structural nature of international politics is such that emerging powers are bound to clash with existing ones, unless strategic manoeuvres are put in place (Mearsheimer 2001). To a degree this complements the view of the neoconservative writer, Robert Kaplan. Following Mearsheimer's arguments, he suggests that, as the leading power, the USA should take the lead in ensuring that the threat of China is contained (Kaplan 2005). As China appears to represent a threat to American dominance, a collection of balancing coalitions would be required to keep potential instabilities at bay. Despite this, as we saw in Chapter 3, Kaplan favoured a unipolar system where the USA would need to maintain an offensive line in order to keep its position (Kaplan 2005). This position was, of course, used by the neoconservatives during the Bush administration and during the Iraq War. Conversely, Mearsheimer, who was criticized in certain quarters for being opposed to military action in Iraq, argued that, as powers seek to expand offensively, it is the job of the leading state to make sure that it defends the status quo and does not do anything that might unbalance the system. He believed that, by embarking on wars and campaigns that were unnecessary at a wider structural level, the USA was weakening its own long-term position and encouraging others – in this case China – to lay down the foundations for a later challenge (Mearsheimer 2004).

We also saw in Chapter 3 that there are a number of different ways to understand how dominant states seek to maintain their influence. From positioning themselves strategically so that a contending state is limited in its potential growth, to actively seeking to limit forcefully any potential danger, a number of suggestions have been put forward by those who favour the maintenance of the current status quo. The distinction between those who maintain a belief in a unipolar world, and those who fear that the emergence of states such as China and India will lead to an unstable multipolar world, is also evident (Mearsheimer 1990; Krauthammer 2004). However, as alluded to in Chapter 5, if the neoliberal form of capitalism remains in the ascendency within the global economy, then a crisis of hegemony might not result from the rise of a contender state such as China. Such a crisis will only occur if China endorses a model of production that seeks to contest the hegemonic fabric of the neoliberal model.

It is precisely through an evaluation of China's model of capitalism that such an assessment is currently being made. Many students of China have claimed that the Chinese form of capitalism differs significantly from the US-inspired free market capitalism on which neoliberalism rested (Arrighi 2007). Many have also argued that the Chinese model is strong enough to sustain a viable challenge to the supremacy of the neoliberal model (Lampton 2008; Beeson 2010; Bisley 2011). China's economic development has often been described as one that is state-managed. Rather than relying on the free market for its internal dynamic, the Chinese economy is closely managed by the state. In line with Deng Xiaoping's goal to embrace a socialist form of market economy, China revised its previous stringent form of planned socialism that was associated with the great leap forward of Chairman Mao. The term used during the 1980s within the Chinese Communist Party was that of creating a 'socialism with Chinese characteristics'. This was to form the basis of China's economic recovery and, unlike the USSR's perestroika, survived the fall of the Soviet Union. The development of capitalism has thus been managed and directed strategically by the state, and every development of marketization has been planned by the Communist Party and its advisers. While investment has been welcomed, it has also arrived via protracted forms of state negotiation and management. In addition, the precursor to China's capitalist development was one that was mercantilist, rather than liberal, in its nature (Strange 2011). Strategically, for example, it drew much from the emphasis on the pursuit of a positive balance of trade, and the comparative national advantage that China has obtained has been a central component of the country's emergence. It has been this national economic might that has been used to continue to spread its influence both regionally and globally.

Paradoxically, the Chinese model has moved from one that introduced a capitalist dimension to a form of socialism, to one that is becoming increasingly recognized as having a social dimension to its capitalism (Jacques 2009). This, despite the official line of the Communist Party that it retains the wider premise of socialism. This social dimension can be seen with the so-called 'Beijing Consensus'. Characterized by Joshua Ramo, the Beijing Consensus appears to be an alternative for development to the neoliberal Washington

Consensus. For Ramo, the model emphasizes equity alongside growth, and national self-determination against economic openness (Ramo 2004). John Williamson, himself, the author of the term 'Washington Consensus' suggests that the Beijing Consensus has real alternatives in its central understanding of growth. He argues that it endorses incremental reform, as opposed to 'big bang' growth, is geared around state-led strategies of innovation, and is largely export-led in its wider objectives. Hence, it maintains the traditional mercantilist trait of placing a positive balance of trade as its overriding aim, but is also authoritarian or autocratic in its execution (Williamson 2012). This potentially sees the growth of a new familiar rivalry. In echoing the Cold War, the free-yet-unequal Western form of production might be seen as forging a new competition against a more equitable, yet more authoritarian, Eastern form.

The model that China seems to endorse also appears attractive to the developing world. China's courtship of Africa has received great attention in recent years, and it has been perhaps the most significant development in trade relations in the twenty-first century. In statistical terms, estimates show that China's trade with Africa prior to Deng's reforms of the 1980s was around US$1 billion. By the start of the twenty-first century this had risen to around US$7–10 billion. The greatest increase occurred in the first decade of the twenty-first century, however, as trade had increased drastically to around US$170 billion by 2012 (IMF 2013). The increase of trade with the African continent has been coupled with a gradual reduction in imports and exports between Africa and the EU/USA. This trade incentive was one that was strongly encouraged by Du Jintao, during his period as premier of China. It could be suggested that part of this was a necessity, as China, despite its size, lacks an energy resource base, and Africa appears to be a useful supplier of oil (Jacques 2009). Yet it has also been understood as a wider expansionist project and one that has looked to transport the Beijing model internationally. The Chinese have been quick to claim that collaboration with Africa forms the basis of a 'South–South cooperation', where China takes the lead in order to empower African states to get what they can out of the international economy. Certainly, China has won praise from several African leaders for the Chinese commitment to infrastructural investment (African Union 2012), a further indication that the Beijing model of development seems far more appealing to developing economies than the ideological constraints of the Washington

Consensus. If this trend continues, it might indeed be reasonable to suggest that a Chinese presence in the developing world would compete with the neoliberal form of development as prescribed by the Washington Consensus.

Yet there is also plenty of evidence to suggest that China is merely a cog in the wider practical machinery of the global economy. Rather than providing an alternative model to contest the legitimacy of the free market model that became dominant after the end of the Cold War, China has instead acted very much from within its influence. Others have argued that China does not offer a firm alternative to neoliberalism as such, as its own economic development relies on providing cheap labour for the multinational firms that drive the global free market economy (Dirlik 2007). Indeed, rather than providing a more socially inclusive form of capitalism, the Chinese state has aimed to provide cheap skilled labour for multinational companies, while suppressing the growth of labour unionization. By retaining state control over labour purchasing power China has made it easier and cheaper for firms to do business with them. In addition, it is the reliability on foreign direct investment (FDI) and on employment by multinational companies that has led to China's rise. This reliance on FDI and on the manufacturing sector to provide products marketed primarily in the developed world shows that the Chinese have very much appeared as serving and appropriating the character of the global system, rather than confronting it.

Some have gone further, and have argued that China has actively pursued a neoliberal agenda, and looked for a model that fits and is highly compatible with the wider hegemonic project implicit within the contemporary global economy. David Harvey, for example, makes it clear that China has developed a form of 'neoliberalism' that is not just highly compatible with the wider global project, but also actively enforces and strengthens its overall hegemony (Harvey 2005). The role of the state serves as a way of facilitating China's own entry into the global market. While the state intervenes in a manner that might appear to contradict the overall principle of the free market, it does so to facilitate the wider practices of the global economy. This is a position that has been adopted by other observers. While they would not suggest that China has accepted or embarked on the neoliberal model put into practice by the west, it has endeavoured to apply forms of the neoliberal doctrine to enable it to succeed as a global economic entity. In doing so, China has provided something of an enigma, by developing in a manner that both appeals to the vanguard of Chinese socialism and contains the strategic objectives that have appeared in its form of state-managed capitalism, but has also remained entwined and influenced by the overall principles of the wider neoliberal project (Wu 2010; Lim 2013).

The debates on the nature of the rise of China and its relationship to the longevity of neoliberalism are relevant to some of the questions discussed in Chapter 5. One of the major problems with debating neoliberalism is that it appears as a contested and multidimensional term. If, as suggested in the previous chapter, neoliberalism is understood as the belief that the private sector is the main generator of economic growth, and that the role of the state is to provide a basis where the private sector can flourish, then we could suggest that China is contributing to and complying with its overall framework of action. Yet, as many Asian specialists are correct to remind us, the rise of China should not be seen merely within the general functioning of the global economy. The pursuit of sovereign wealth funds by the Chinese state, and direct investment into the infrastructure of developing countries would suggest that China is not merely taking a passive role within global economic affairs but is seeking to make a significant contribution. In terms of leadership, China has also taken on a leadership role that has challenged traditional dominant players in multilateral trade forums. For example, at the WTO, China has been seen as the dominant player in the G20 trading bloc. The G20 includes the major representative states of the developing world and has pursued an aim of challenging the dominance of the established countries of North America and Europe in building trading regimes. The standoffs that have occurred over tariff reductions during the Doha round of trade negotiations have shown that China can provide a useful and powerful ally when tackling the double standards of the advanced nations. Again, the irony here is that, by trying to put pressure on powerful states to reduce their own tariffs so that developing countries can gain entry to their markets, China is actually encouraging a free market system based on a more generic set of neoliberal rules.

BRICS

The role of China has also fed significantly into the wider role of BRICS. The term emerged as an acronym representing the four emerging powers that seemed to gain prominence in the aftermath of the global financial crisis. The term first appeared in a piece by Goldman Sachs' Jim O'Neill in 2001, in a paper entitled 'The World Needs Better Economic BRICs'. This looked at the potential Brazil, Russia, India and China had as economic players on the world stage and suggested that the G7/G8 would have to include China sooner rather than later, and with Russia's earlier inclusion in the G8, both India and Brazil would logically follow. By 2009, the BRIC countries collectively had formed their own formal institution and held their first summit in Yekaterinburg in the Russian Urals in June of that year. Since then, the group has had an annual meeting, officially becoming BRICS (as opposed to BRIC) in 2011 with the inclusion of South Africa. BRICS now represent the most influential emerging economy within a specific region, suggesting that each state speaks to some extent on behalf of its particular region. Yet the rise of BRICS as economic entities in their own right became apparent in the first decade of the twenty-first century. India, for example, entered the top ten economic entities measured by GNP during the decade, but if one were to take into account PPP, its rank jumps to fourth in the world (World Bank 2012). Similarly, Brazil had risen to levels in 2013 where it had overtaken the UK on both forms of analysis (*Economist* 2013). Significant rises in South Africa's economic growth and the continued recovery of the Russian economy have added greater clout to the forum of BRICS.

As a collection, the five have assumed the mantle of the leaders of the 'South' and have also looked at ways of expanding the forum so that other potential regional leaders are added to the mix. Alongside China, the individual BRICS countries have emerged as potential sites where an alternative, and more equitable, form of capitalism could be built. These states have had a variety of recent histories in terms of their respective forms of growth.

Brazil

Brazil's move to become a 'top six' economy was the result of decades of unrest that arose from periods of military dictatorships, economic turmoil and failed attempts at neo-mercantilism conducted through a variety of import-substitution programmes. The move towards liberalization was aided by the former dependency school sociologist Fernando Henrique Cardoso. Cardoso became president of Brazil in 1995 and continued the privatization programme that was begun a decade earlier by the conservative president, Fernando Collor de Mello. But, following the social democratic re-orientation process that was being popularized by Clinton and Blair in the USA/UK, Cardoso argued that such liberalization programmes could be employed in a manner that would reduce inequality in Brazil (Cardoso 2001). The increase of FDI amid the process of privatization could be levered towards dealing with the problems of social exclusion to which an unfettered free market inevitably leads. Yet Cardoso's own regime was marked by a coalition that put free marketers at odds with those who favoured a more developmental approach to the economy. Neither of these reflected the 'neoliberalism with a human face' he was attempting to achieve. As his time in office lengthened he also became increasingly unpopular within Brazilian civil society as indigenous groups began to emerge to challenge the neoliberal programmes he was pursuing. In addition, Cardoso's 'Third Way' approach had not succeeded in tackling the problems of inequality and, as a testament to this, a world social forum was established by the oppositional 'Workers' Party' (Partido dos Trabalhadores – PT), which would sweep to power in 2002 through the presidency of its leader, Luís Inácio da Silva, popularly known as 'Lula'.

Lula's period as president has often been understood as a post-neoliberal one, where social equality and local democracy were considered as necessary components for national development. In line with the left turn in Latin America, Lula looked to embark on a 'post-neoliberal' form of governance. The term 'post'-neoliberalism is one we shall deal with fully in Chapter 7, when discussing regionalism, but it is one that has had tentative links with the state-capitalist model in China. Post-neoliberalism has been associated with Latin America to explain an economic model that has moved beyond a solely market approach to the economy towards one that looks to retain elements of previous export-led strategies, with the aim of using the increased revenue for social welfare and on decreasing relative poverty (Grugel and Riggirozzi 2012). However, while there has been a great deal of enthusiasm around the emergence of such an approach, many feel that the party has largely retained many of the ideas that Cardoso put in place. Even as Lula was being sworn in as president some felt that his policies were following the similar 'Third Way' agenda, but, without having to work with a coalition that included many from the free market right, it appeared to be far more committed towards its social objectives (Petras 2003). The success of the Workers' Party ensured the smooth transition of the position of president to Lula's colleague, Dilma Rousseff, in 2011. However, the demonstrations that dominated Brazilian society in 2013 and 2014 have led to more question marks over the validity of post-neoliberalism as a meaningful alternative model for BRICS to pursue (Yates and Bakker 2013).

Russia

Just as Brazil (and India) underwent a period of financial restraint under the Washington Consensus conditions, Russia too embarked on a strategy of fiscal restraint. The marked difference was that this was under the auspices of economic shock therapy, which aimed to see the Russian economy transform from a planned to a market economy over a short period of time. The notorious plan backfired spectacularly as inflation spiralled out of control because of price liberation that resulted in a series of U-turns by the government over how the transition should be managed. The outcome of this was that the economy became dominated by an elite group of individuals who had gained prominence in the Soviet system as a result of the hierarchal system of bureaucratic control that existed throughout the regime, known as the *nomenklatura* system. At the end of the Soviet Union, those with influence in the system used it to gain considerable personal advantage during the transition. As a result of this, contemporary Russia became a country where its vast wealth was situated in the hands of a few powerful individuals as the country developed what became known as 'crony capitalism' (Kagarlitsky 2002). Its development was also hampered by a number of economic crises, which would unsettle any attempt at maintaining a stable political system. As a state, the Russian Federation was to slide down the international ranking tables of wealth and productivity as the oligarchic system that emerged became uncompetitive and unable to attract outside investment.

The emergence of Vladimir Putin as leader at the start of the twenty-first century saw the state take on a firmer line in developing the economy. The centralization of the state, the restrictions on funding for political parties, the seizing of assets from certain oligarchs and the restrictions on certain liberties have all seen the state take on a more centralized and authoritarian role in political and economic

Role of UnitedRussia

life. As with China, the main purpose of involving the state has not been to introduce protectionist measures, but rather to take on a greater role to ensure that FDI and investment enters the country (Worth 2009). The paradox with Russia is that while it intended to adopt an idealistic approach to the free market to allow for a neoliberal experiment, the economy that was to emerge was uncompetitive and unproductive. Yet when the state took on a much more active role in economic affairs, it became more appealing to investors. Here, the state sought to direct change by intervening in the economy to allow the market to work effectively. This could be said to be very much within the ordoliberal tradition discussed in Chapter 5. For a market economy to operate properly it sometimes requires the intervention of the state.

However, any suggestion that Putin's main incentive was to intervene in a chaotic and failing economic system in order to allow it to function within a global market should be considered with caution. While this has certainly been a feature of Putin's Russia, the overtly authoritarian system he has rested on is not one generally associated with an attempt to appease global forces. The re-emergence of Russia as an economic power under Putin has coincided with its re-emergence as a geopolitical force. Under Putin, Russia has seen relationships with Europe harden, and a renewed rivalry arise with the USA alongside the maintenance of its strategic superiority in Central Asia. Flashpoints such as Georgia, and more recently Ukraine, have seen Russia looking to protect its geographical sphere of influence in any manner it sees fit. As a result, it appears to be the beginning of a potential source for an alternative economic strategy to neoliberalism. Certainly, Russia might adopt the use of state aggression if a clear alternative does emerge. Historically, Russia has been marked by its contestation of Western-backed projects that internationalize (Neumann 1996) and is certainly reasserting itself as a geopolitical force. The likelihood of this emerging towards challenging the hegemony of the neoliberal global economy is less apparent.

India

Like China, India has seen its economy rise significantly as a result of the specific development of one source of labour. In India, the information technology (IT) industry and the outsourcing of business processes have been targeted and have flourished, accounting for nearly 8 per cent of its total GDP and 25 per cent of its total exports in 2012 (NASSCOM 2013). More prominent has been the fact that around half of all outsourcing companies in the world are based in India. The targeting of the knowledge economy as a potential growth spot has seen India gain a considerable niche at the international level along with its emerging prominence as a military power (Rothermund 2009). Coupled with a rising population of over 1.2 billion, India has cemented its position as the powerhouse of South Asia and sits as the dominant member of the South Asian Association for Regional Cooperation (SAARC). However, when looking at pursuing a partnership with China and facilitating a model of capitalism that might compete with those favoured by more established economic powers, we see a number of problems emerging.

First, the viability of India and China to form an active political partnership is problematic in itself. The Sino–Indian War of 1962 is still fresh in the minds of Indian political society, and ongoing border disputes between the two countries have strained relations ever since. Second, the recent history of Indian economic liberalization differs from that of China. Rather than use the state as a facilitator for development, the Indian model has followed a far more concentrated neoliberal form (Ahmed 2009). Despite being hesitant to remove certain regulations within the domestic retail industry, economic liberalization has very much followed the Anglo–Saxon line. The explosion of FDI advances into the country was not strategically controlled by state or governmental bodies, but arose as a result of the financial crisis of the early 1990s. As a result, India followed a process of liberalization that was very much in line with the objectives of the Washington Consensus. Finally, as with China, India's economic advance has occurred by using (as opposed to contesting) the neoliberal global economy. It has relied on foreign companies to build an effective labour force and, also like China, has looked to limit unionization in order to keep wages competitive and attractive to client firm. Having found a growing niche to press home its competitive advantage, it seems unlikely that India would opt for a system that might compromise its economic advances. That said, it might look to use the BRICS forums to strengthen ties in groupings such as the G20 trading group or the G77. This would further the potential power shift from the North to the South, which might also see a shift in the wider form and content of the production of international capitalism.

South Africa

South Africa's joining of the BRIC group has been cited by some as being incidental rather than meaningful. *The Economist* magazine has suggested that South Africa's inclusion was merely to ensure that an African state was needed to provide the legitimacy of the group, and even suggested that South Africa benefited over other potential African inclusions such as Nigeria because its name began with 'S' – meaning the acronym would not have to be changed by its inclusion (*The Economist* 2013). A less cynical view would point to South Africa's vast comparative advantage in mineral reserves and its position as Africa's prominent financial centre. It also shares with most of BRICS a recent history of transition. It has experienced the market prescription of neoliberalism through the Washington Consensus and an opening up of trade highlighted by the reduction of tariffs that marked the end of the apartheid system.

South Africa's form of development has thus been characterized by a familiar process that has seen an initial embracing of the free market that accompanied the end of the apartheid years followed by a period when the state looked to focus on certain areas of the national economy that might heighten its position within the global economy. As a result, the state focused on the area of skills and technology to establish itself as the African continent's leader in the knowledge economy (Scerri 2013). The African National Congress's (ANC's) commitment towards trade union inclusion has also been a hallmark of South Africa's emerging economy, yet its form of corporatism has been developed alongside an economy that is seen as becoming increasingly deregulated and open as it has progressed (Nattras 2011). South Africa has also had concerns with unemployment, which has remained consistent high, and inequality, which has increased steadily since the end apartheid. In this sense it appears as very much the junior partner in BRICS as these factors have been obstacles for any substantial growth such as that experienced by other emerging economies.

Some have concluded from this that South Africa's inclusion as one of BRICS has largely been a Chinese initiative. China has been central to South Africa's recent economic development because of the export to China of minerals such iron ore, gold, copper and aluminium that have become vital to the Chinese economy. As such, the inclusion of South Africa, China's leading bilateral partner in Africa, will allow for greater access to other parts of the African continent (Park and Alden 2013). At the same time, China can strengthen its existing ties with South Africa through the formal institutional set-up of BRICS. It would certainly appear from this that South Africa might appear as something like China's 'junior partner' amid the power brokers in BRICS, yet its strategic and geographical position provides a potential site as a more prominent partner to any wider alternative economic project.

Other Potential Members

The emergence of acronyms such as TIMBI (Turkey, India, Mexico, Brazil and Indonesia) and CIVETS (Colombia, Indonesia, Vietnam, Egypt, Turkey and South Africa) have been applied as an alternative to understanding emerging economies. The first of these has been suggested in a response to the power of China, with the belief that both China and Russia will ultimately falter as emerging economies (Goldstone 2011), while the latter were understood (before the admission of South Africa) as the next potential candidates to the BRICS forum. O'Neill himself has gone further and suggested a potential 11 that include the once-pioneering export-led state of South Korea, Iran, the Philippines, Nigeria, Vietnam, Pakistan and Bangladesh (O'Neill *et al*. 2005). Some of these are included more as a result of their size, population and potential rather than their contemporary position as emerging economies. It is difficult to know whether these might emerge to bolster a viable and coherent alternative South–South strategy to contest neoliberal hegemony, or whether they will serve merely to reiterate their respective positions within the wider global economy. While the list includes some (such as Iran and Vietnam) that have had a history of resistance to Western forms of capitalism, they also seem to reflect economies that have adopted outward-looking developmental strategies. This would again suggest that emerging states look to find a niche and 'internationalize' their economies in order to progress. If any alternative is going to emerge from the G77 states it appears that it would be by engaging and transforming the character of the global economy rather than revisiting any national strategies based on neo-mercantilism.

Another question posed by potential BRICS is that many of the states discussed are either ones that are overshadowed by a larger BRIC (such as Pakistan and Bangladesh with India, or Vietnam with China) or are actively pursuing entry into a leading regional organization (as the case with Turkey). As a result, it remains difficult to imagine that BRICS will dramatically increase in terms of their numbers, and it seems more plausible that they will continue to represent a forum where dominant states within specific regions meet.

Emerging Powers or the Semi-Periphery?

Another way in which the emerging BRICS can be understood is though the concept of the semi-periphery. In general, the semi-periphery refers to states that have an equal level of basic and advanced forms of production (Wallerstein 1985) and have also largely been reliant on manufacturing. Traditionally, the term semi-periphery was associated with relatively underdeveloped areas of Eastern and Southern Europe, with East Asia, Latin America and later with state socialist countries. Primarily, they were states that were independent entities by the end of the nineteenth century, but were not at the forefront of capitalist development. As a result, they often experienced forms of authoritarianism well past the end of the Second World War.

More prominently, some have argued that semi-peripheral states are the instigators of resistance in an international system (Chase-Dunn and Hall 1997). Such an observation could be seen with the role of Russia at the time of the Russian Revolution, when, as Lenin himself indicated, it had not been involved in the process of imperialism either as an imperial power or as an exploited region (Lenin 1939). The subsequent revolution was to have a profound effect on the world order as it altered the shape and character of international capitalism significantly. In the contemporary post-communist, post-Cold War era, it could be argued that the semi-periphery has continued to contain potential seeds of resistance. For example, not only does China appear to contain a potential threat to the contemporary US-led neoliberal form of capitalism, but also other semi-peripheral areas such as the Middle East have been the source of religious conflict, and Latin America has seen an attempt to renew a form of socialist opposition. These are areas I shall discuss in greater depth in Chapters 7 and 8. The point here is to examine whether China, India and other successful emerging economies should be considered more as a contemporary form of semi-periphery within the wider international economy.

The presence of China and India as manufacturing and technological powerhouses within the global economy provides us with one such example of this. Both facilitate a role where they are dependent on suppliers and companies from the advanced regions of the world, yet have exploited this relationship to great economic success. They appear as states that have adopted a position that produces for a consumer market largely in Europe and North America, and by doing this successfully they have increased their productivity to unexpected levels but still remain dependent on the outsourcing of companies. This form of dependency is not limited to the so-called emerging economies, however. Increasingly, leading companies that originated orientated from G77 states have themselves been courted for investment by governments of the more advanced economic world (Nederveen-Pieterse 2000). Certain states in the EU (Ireland, the Baltic States and so on) have long relied on investment from multinational corporations for their development. Yet India and China have moved to provide cheaper labour costs and have mobilized part-time workers, flexible workers and female workers (known as pink-collar workers), who are all paid at a cheaper rate as a means of lowering labour standards. As a result, both have gained productivity via means that regulations in the developed world would consider exploitative.

Some recent studies have shown, therefore, that BRICS have a number of characteristics typical of previous definitions of the semi-periphery, but also have certain new traits showing a switch from the adoption of a national strategy to an international or a global one (Worth and Moore 2009). For example, authoritarianism has remained a significant condition within BRICS. From China's one-party system to the form of 'managed democracy' that has emerged in Putin's Russia, elements of authoritarianism have remained in certain guises. The role of the state in society has thus remained as a key factor behind the success of BRICS (Scerri 2013). As we have seen, it has provided the basis for economic development, as the state has sought ways in which it can offer a competitive utility within the global economy. Therefore it could be said that the role of the state *vis-à-vis* the economy has changed significantly in the semi-periphery of the twenty-first century. The role of the state is not to generate forms of state-led import substitution to counteract an international system that works against its interests, as previous wisdom dictated (Frank 1966). Instead, it has increasingly taken on the form of 'competition states', where states look to centralize the importance of competitiveness and seek to internationalize their economies in order to increase their productivity (Cerny 1997). As semi-peripheral states, BRICS and CIVETS have used natural resources, manufacturing, technology and cheap labour as assets for economic growth, have encouraged foreign investment and huge interest from multinational firms, and have improved their economies as a result. From understanding these emerging economies as semi-peripheral entities, it can be argued that they have remained as providers rather than leaders within the global economy. In this sense they appear to be very much dependent on providing a service that is largely employed in the consumer markets of the developed world.

There are, however, a number of additional points suggesting that such conclusions might be too dismissive of the emergence of BRICS. The new middle classes in India, Russia and China, and some of those in energy rich states, have gained considerable influence in terms of their input to the global economy. It should be a reminder, however, that the newfound wealth of such classes has strengthened the wider class relations inherent within contemporary capitalism. As we know from the developed world, the notoriety gained by certain businessmen in purchasing sports teams and well-known fashionable companies have not sought to challenge the workings of the global capitalist system – far from it. They have looked to strengthen and contribute towards its overriding workings. It should also be remembered that change and resistance is often instigated in the semi-peripheral areas. When trying to decide where a challenge to neoliberal hegemony might appear, it seems highly plausible to suggest that it might come from these emerging economies (Chase-Dunn 2013).

To summarize, then, how might this discussion of the semi-periphery and the rise of BRICS lead us to rethink the wider question of hegemony within world politics? What we can see here is that the rise of China does not necessarily mean that the contemporary condition of hegemony is in the process of collapse, decline or transformation. Instead, its rise provides us with an interesting dilemma for further analysis. China's rise might challenge the wider, US-inspired neoliberal hegemonic model by adopting a different model of capitalism. Yet the dynamism of modern capitalism is such that China's surge in economic development might reinforce existing norms of the capitalist system. The much-discussed emergence of BRICS provides us with more questions about how this will affect the nature of hegemony. Many traditional accounts in IR will point to the institutional emergence of BRICS as being an indication that US power will be challenged in the twenty-first century and onwards. However, as O'Neill mentioned, when defining BRICS, their emergence was needed to contribute to the increased productivity of the international economy, rather than lead to any potential conflict (O'Neill 2001). Looking at Chapters 4 and 5, this brings us back to the importance of Robinson's suggestion of a transnational hegemony based on earlier understandings of the formation of a transnational class (van der Pijl 1998; Robinson 2005). The obvious implication here is that the contemporary form of hegemony – that is defined through a US-led form of neoliberal capitalism and organized through a transnational class formation will only strengthen with the rise of BRICS (Saull 2012; Stephens 2014).

Ultimately, the significance of BRICS often differ when assessed through the lens of high and low politics, and whether they have the capacity and the means to consent towards or to contest the prevailing hegemonic order. As a consequence, this chapter might conclude that China and BRICS in general have been overplayed and underplayed, respectively, in terms of their significance for the longevity of US-inspired neoliberal hegemony. The economic development of China has been highly significant in terms of the change in influence at the global level. The construction of BRICS as regional powers within what used to be called the developing world has also been highly significant. Yet, because BRICS have looked at internationalizing their economies and because they looked to advance their economies by offering specific services that enabled investment, it is also unlikely to see at present how they would challenge the appearance of the world order. Equally, as some economists have suggested recently, BRICS remain marked by excessive inequality and a lack of innova-tion at the global level, so it is hard to see how they will become a significant force in terms of leadership of the world economy (Beausang 2012).

What might move 'high' politics back on to the agenda in terms of potential hegemonic conflict could be the increase of geopolitical tension that has long been predicted by declinists of all political persuasions. The American 'imperial overstretch' discussed in Chapter 3, which was seen in the aftermath of the wars in Iraq and Afghanistan, has certainly left a mark of unpopularity on the American regime. This might certainly lead to implications if the BRICS look to contest American foreign interests. Recent conflict with the USA/EU and

Russia over Ukraine has added to the potential for this to escalate, particularly if Russia requests the support of partners within BRICS. The geopolitical aspect takes on greater significance when looking at the emergence of regionalism in global politics. As I shall show in Chapter 7, as the world has increasingly been ordered geographically by regions, it has been regional projects in certain semi-peripheral areas that have provided some of the more successful resistance to the American-inspired spread of neoliberalism.

7
Regionalism

The idea that a hegemonic order can be challenged by promoting regional groupings within global politics is not a new one. The liberal era of the nineteenth century was to an extent challenged by the emergence of European rivalries that sought to use the politics of imperialism to extend territorial power (Keohane 1984; Cox 1987). The geopolitical world that emerged was one that created a number of regions run and directed by their European 'masters' at the centre. The result was the emergence of conflict between these European spheres of influence that culminated in the two world wars in the first half of the twentieth century. The idea of regionalism as a continued potential for conflict did not disappear with the end of the Second World War. Just years after the end of the war, George Orwell, writing from his home on the Scottish island of Jura, satirized in his book *Nineteen Eighty-Four* a world split into three regional blocs. The characteristics of the blocs were marked by continued conflict and constant fear of attack.

Forty years later, and the end of the Cold War saw a form of optimism play off against a form of pessimism in a manner that had similarities with international society during Orwell's time of writing 1984 in the years following the end of the Second World War. While great optimism was placed by some on the victory of capitalism and liberalism over socialism and authoritarianism, others saw the end of the Cold War as an event that would provide new problems (Little 1995). In terms of the latter, as outlined in Chapter 3, many structural realists were quick to point out that the more stable bipolar world of the Cold War would be replaced by a more unstable multipolar world in the future (Mearsheimer 1990). Others were indicating that the shape of such a world might be defined through regional powers and their satellites (Waltz 1993). Out of these, it was Samuel Huntington's *Clash of Civilizations* that had the greatest impact. He argued that a set of competing civilizations would emerge in the post-Cold War environment that would be tied loosely to different regions of the world. Unifying through culture, religion and wider expressions of civilization, they would form the parameters of world politics in the future (Huntington 1996). Huntington's arguments did not really gain any considerable attention outside of academe until after the events of 9/11. In light of this, the optimism of the 'new world order' that seemed to characterize the 1990s had been cut short by the dangerous realities that accompanied the attacks on the Twin Towers. Suddenly, the dangers outlined by Huntington began to look very real. Indeed, as the rise of Islam has provided regional unity in the Middle East, and the rise of China and India has led to a growing civilizational presence in East and South Asia, then Huntington's vision has gained mass appeal, particularly in neoconservative circles during the George W. Bush administrations. The dystopian nightmare that Orwell perceived was suddenly re-imagined. Rather than the political ideologies of Ingsoc, neo-Bolshevism and Obliteration of the Self, which were the central organizing principles of the regions in *1984*, post-Cold War regionalism would be defined through historical and cultural traditions rather than through political ideology.

Like Orwell before him, Huntington's main arguments were to suggest that the state would not play as big a role as it had previously in world politics. The shared cultural ties would be enough to bind regions together and would serve as competing entities on the global stage. The main point we can take from Huntington's study is that it is assumed that the cultural and political form of hegemony based on the liberal democracies of North America and Europe would ultimately be rejected. This assumes that any move towards regional or cultural groupings will lead to the end of the type of neoliberal hegemony I have identified throughout this book. However, the growth of regional blocs in global politics has not been something that is necessarily defined by conflict or by the rejection of a specific form of hegemonic order. On the contrary, many of the debates in the recent literature surrounding the emergence of regionalism has suggested that regional arrangement have often been employed, both to regulate the processes of the global economy and to co-ordinate strategic global objectives (Hurrell 2007). Similarly, regional organizations have been set up to intervene in conflicts and instabilities within their geographical areas, and to gain support for this from other regional and international bodies (Aning and Salihu 2012). If the world is moving towards one defined increasingly by regional plurality, the implications of this therefore need to be looked at more closely.

Old and New Regionalism

One of the main discussions in the study of regionalism has been the distinctions between the 'old' form of regionalism and the 'new' form. Old regionalism refers to the bodies of (largely military) organizations that were founded during the Cold War and were to define the period. Organizations such as NATO and the Organization of American States (OAS), as well as the original institutions of the European Community (EC) were examples of regional organizations that were within the influence of the West. Conversely, organizations such as Comecon and the Warsaw Pact were built on Soviet socialist principles. Other examples of old regionalism include the Organization of African Unity (OAU) and the Arab League, which both looked to establish a pan-national movement with the intention of mobilizing independently from the East/West axis.

New regionalism, on the other hand, refers to the wave of regionalism that has appeared since the 1980s, as a result of greater forms of trade liberalization between states and the move by states to break down economic barriers with their neighbours to encourage greater productivity. Coinciding with the birth of the neoliberal doctrine, new regionalism was to gain greater significance by the end of the Cold War as states looked to forge partnerships in an attempt to regulate the wider processes of globalization that were arising through the rapidly changing global economy. The obvious example of new regionalism can be seen with the integration of Europe from being a common market of Western European states to becoming a wider Union encompassing economic, political and cultural unity, and emerging as a power in its own right on the global stage (Telo 2007). Other examples include the Association of Southeast Asian Nations (ASEAN) in South East Asia; the North American Free Trade Agreement (NAFTA) in North America; and Mercosur in South America. The revamping of the OAU to become the African Union (AU) provides us with another case of the shift away from a body bent on the acquisition of power to one geared towards economic cooperation.

Another development of new regionalism is the crossover of bodies into different spheres of influence. By this we mean that states have chosen to join a number of organizations, irrespective of whether they belong to one specific regional body or another. With this in mind, it is problematic to suggest that geographical regions might logically conflict. As regional bodies have emerged, they have not created fortresses as such, but instead have merged, which allows states to join many different entities (Perkmann and Ngai-Ling 2002). For example, while APEC (Asia-Pacific Economic Co-operation) might have been the brainchild of the Australian Prime Minister, Bob Hawkes, it has created an economic community that includes China, Japan, Russia and the ASEAN states on one side of the Pacific and the USA and selective states in the Americas on the other, despite their membership of other free trade bodies. This has led many to suggest that what is emerging is a form of 'open regionalism', where states can join many bodies to suit their own interests (Bergsten 1997). From the point of view of world order, open regionalism facilitates the practices of neoliberalism very well. As the construction of such bodies has aimed to create more trade, increased liberalization and greater harmonization on regulation on investment, then it could be argued that they have added to the structural conditions of the prevailing neoliberal order (Gamble and Payne 1996). This does have a great deal of validity. One popular way of using a neo-Gramscian approach to international politics has been in understanding regional institutions as bodies that serve to facilitate forms of neoliberal hegemony. This has largely been used within the EU to deal with questions of the Union's development and enlargement (Bieler and Morton 2001; Bohle 2006). However, it should also be stressed that open regionalism represents only one stage in the development of regional bodies. Organizations such as the EU, ASEAN, Mercosur, SAARC, and to some extent NAFTA, are based on more solid foundations that can look to form alternative strategies to neoliberalism. As well as these, China has emerged as a key regional leader in Asia, which has led to the potential of a larger form of regional unity in Asia that might in time clash with developed entities such as the EU. To scrutinize this further, it is necessary to look at the current developments of regional integration to assess their form, content and see the direction in which they are heading.

Europe

Process

The project of European integration has had a long and well documented history, from its early days as a US-backed coal and steel
community through to its consolidation as a political entity in the
post-Cold War era. In terms of its emergence as a regional superpower
in world politics, its newfound economic might, aided by the rise of
the euro and its bloc vote in the WTO, Europe has seen its prominence
as a unified actor grow on the global stage. That said, the political and
economic integration of the EU is one that remains highly complex
and unequal. It also remains a body that attracts great divisions in
terms of its larger role. The various theories that have been put
forward to describe the evolution of the EU have been complicated by
constant moves and changes to the structure and scope of the organization. As a result, the way the EU has been understood has never
produced a definitive answer. We have seen how the EU has emerged
from a federal organization to become one seeking to stress that it
existed primarily as a state-centre intergovernmental organization by
the end of the 1960s. It has also been understood as a neo-functional-
ist organization that developed through necessity (Rosamond 2000).
In recent years we have seen the emergence of a twin-speed Europe,
where certain states opt in and out of certain protocols within the EU.
The obvious example of this is with regard to the euro, where states
are divided into Eurozone states, states that have entered an exchange
rate system, and those who have opted out of the currency altogether.
While only the UK and Denmark formally arranged opt-out clauses
(Denmark staying within the ERM II), the sovereign debt crisis and
the fallout from the resulting bailout has led to a cooling of interest
from states outside the Eurozone with regard to joining the currency.

The EU's development as a single entity on the global stage has not
been consistent. While its unity on economic affairs appears to be
unique and is often put on a pedestal as an example for other regional
blocs to follow (Fawn 2009), in other areas the EU has not succeeded
in cementing a unified voice. There are some areas within foreign
affairs that have found certain amount of unity, but these might be
described as being within a context of 'low politics'. (such as in developmental issues and in human rights). The 'high' political areas of
foreign policy have failed to find agreement. As one might suspect
when the situation is examined closely, states such as France and the

UK, who maintain a significant presence at the international level, have ignored calls by other large states within the EU to move towards a single entity (Young 2012). The reality of two key states being unwilling to compromise their positions as permanent members of the UN Security Council for a wider regional one have led to another obstacle to wider European unity. The new position of High Representative for Foreign Affairs, created as a result of the Lisbon Treaty, did provide a figurehead for the wider EU umbrella and this has allowed the EU to adopt a common position on relations with certain states and regions, which has strengthened its trade. The idea of a single position on foreign relations is a long way from fruition, however.

Content

When understanding the significance and content of the EU as a global player we hear familiar arguments. As I noted above, one understanding of the EU is as a neoliberal entity that merely seeks to consolidate the wider structures of the global order. Here, the EU appears as a body that looks to form a constitution basing itself around the principles of neoliberalism (Gill 1998). The EU has been developed increasingly into an organization that has looked to tighten fiscal expenditure at the national level, to privatize public-owned property and bring it under wider regional market competition, and has sought to pursue flexible labour conditions as opposed to favouring wider European forms of unionization (van Apeldoorn *et al.* 2009).

Despite this, Euro-sceptics from the right have long argued that it has provided precisely the reverse. For them, the EU has merely created a set of regulations that have interfered with the market system underpinning economic production (Minford *et al.* 2005). As an addition to eroding national sovereignty and identity, conservative positions have also argued that the EU has diminished individual economic liberty through its restrictions, conditions and laws on industry and business (Taggart and Szczerbiak 2008). Consequently, the Union is dismissed as an interventionist institution that is ultimately socialist in nature.

In reality, the EU as it stands is highly ambiguous in terms of its content. It provides a strong structural foundation where social forces can struggle and attempt to build on their respective visions of regional governance. This would suggest that the EU is neither a social interventionist nor a neoliberal entity, but is the product of a protracted political development where one set of forces gains ascendency over the other. This, of course, brings us back to the classic Gramscian understanding of society discussed in Chapter 4, where contrasting social forces compete until one gains hegemony. However, such an ascendency can be challenged consistently and transformed over time. Therefore, while the neoliberal ideology appears to be central to EU governance at present, it remains highly contested (Rosamond 2012). Certainly, since Jacques Delors outlined his vision for a social Europe, there has been a clear commitment towards opposing any overhaul of social protection against market reform.

So where does that leave the EU at present? The crisis gave rise to a number of questions regarding how the EU would react to the failings of the financial system. The numerous bailouts and cash injections provided by the European Central Bank (ECB) suggested that the EU might be looking to seek a Keynesian alternative to the excessive deregulation of the recent past. Yet, instead, the EU has maintained its recent neoliberal principles and has been one of the main actors facilitating the politics of austerity (Blyth 2013). As a result, the EU is more orientated at present towards maintaining the neoliberal status quo within wider international society. However, the position of the EU remains unclear. It is a body that offers a potentially different form of leadership at the international level from that of the USA. European regionalism has always been marked by a form of capitalism that has tried to maintain its continental style of a mixed economy that was prevalent in the economic development of Germany (see Chapter 6). This position still competes with a more variegated form of neoliberalism with which the EU has become associated since its development and expansion (Bohle 2006).

East Asia

The central issue of Asian regionalism has been dominated by the rise of China. The question here is whether the region as a whole is being led by China and, more important, whether the region is happy to accept China's role as such. The other significant factor in the region is in its historical legacy and the influence in the Cold War period of a large American presence. As such, there are two distinct lines of argument concerning the nature of regionalism. First, that the region looks to China to lead ideas on development. Second, and conversely, that regional organizations are constructed so that they can protect themselves from Chinese influence and dominance. Both these have further connotations relating to wider issues on the nature of hegemony at the global level.

During the Cold War, the huge military and economic presence in the region was comparable to that of Western Europe in the immediate aftermath of the Second World War. With the presence of the Soviet Union and China, and the events in Vietnam, the East Asian community viewed the US very much as a protecting influence and as a 'stabilizer of the last resort' in the region (Clark 2011: 177). With the Cold War over, certain heavily pro-US narratives claim that a renewed Cold War policy is needed to fight off the twin threat of Communist China and its allies, and the growing resurgence of radical Islam (Feigenbaum and Manning 2009). Many of those who follow the structural, strategic and state-centric understandings of international politics have been quick to point out that China has gained significant influence in the region as a natural consequence that sees the transformation of a bipolar and then a unipolar world towards a multipolar one (Layne 2009). Following from this, Ikenberry has suggested that China's presence can be one that compliments the contemporary liberal order (Ikenberry 2008). China has the tools and regional know-how to provide stability to the region in partnership with the USA in the same manner as Europe has done through various EU–USA–NATO partnerships.

There is still the question of whether the region itself is keen to embrace the Chinese sphere of influence, or whether it is perceived to be more of a threat. Certainly, the increase of trade in the region has centred on China, with the region becoming more and more reliant on China for trade. Countries such as Australia, one of the few advanced states in the region, have also expressed the need for the central importance of China within the Asia-Pacific community, pointing to its strategic importance as a trading partner. The Beijing Consensus has attracted popularity in the region, especially in the light of the Washington-inspired neoliberal reforms that occurred in the aftermath of the Asian financial crisis in the 1990s, and which proved to be unpopular. Despite this, the fear of China, and particular of Chinese dominance, still resonates with some. For example, ASEAN can be understood at one level as an institution aimed at limiting the extent of both US and Chinese power within the region. As a regional body, ASEAN has been successful in pursuing a collective position in dealing with its trading partners. As a result, China and Japan (the latter a former big presence and still a major economic presence in the region) can be dealt with individually. Hence the ASEAN+1, ASEAN+2 and ASEAN+3 forums that take place with China, Japan and South Korea allow the organization to keep any potential threats at bay.

Power relations aside, ASEAN remains the only substantial regional bloc within the area with any significant institutional ties. Despite this, it has been criticized for not adopting a commitment to political and economic unity like that in the EU. ASEAN has been distinguished by its commitment towards sustaining the sovereignty and self-expression of its members. While some have criticized ASEAN for its weak institutional framework and its shortcomings in failing to deliver a more profound collective unity (Leviter 2010), its principle concern was to allow its members the right to autonomy in the light of external larger influential powers (Yahuda 2006). Other than ASEAN, there have been no further regional organizations in the area. While APEC provides a large framework for open trade, the sheer size and scope of the body makes it far too loose to sustain a substantial organization of any political significance.

In terms of hegemony, East Asia is an interesting and significant region to examine. While the more state-centric accounts of hegemony might see it as a battleground for states to assert their influence, others looking for a more nuanced understanding should see it as a semi-peripheral region where hegemonic conditions can be built and contested (Beeson 2009). The period after the Second World War saw the USA provide influence against a backdrop of conflict in Korea, Vietnam and Cambodia. The different types of state socialism espoused by China and Russia, which became notorious with the Sino-Soviet split, saw less communist resistance than might have been expected. In recent years, the move from the export-led forms of mercantilism that provided the successful 'tiger economies', to more globalized, knowledge-based economies has been significant to the extension of the neoliberal epoch (Moore 2010). Yet the presence of China and the Chinese version of capitalism has gained much interest in recent years, especially as China's rise continues. However, as I outlined in Chapter 6, the Chinese alternative for development might provide a different role for the state in terms of directing its economy in a manner that is more effective than merely leaving it to the market, but nevertheless does not offer a drastic ideological alternative for world order. In addition, to return to Ikenberry, the presence of both the USA and China in the region does not necessarily lead to a conflict of interests but can result in the mutual acceptance of their respective roles within the contemporary (neo)liberal system (Ikenberry and Moon 2008).

The lack of an EU-style structure or vision is also significant in terms of foreseeing any wider unity within the region. While ASEAN is often attacked unfairly for its lack of strategic endeavour in terms of its unity, it has not sought to provide a foundation for greater regional integration. Without an organizational body that can unite the various parts of the region, it remains doubtful whether it can produce a coherent set of regional bodies that seek to embrace their regional partnership(s). That is not to say that such organization might not emerge, especially as China continues to gain significance and Japan maintains its economic position within the elite, but that at present there is no institutional base for such a process to develop.

Latin America

Nowhere has the very fabric of neoliberalism been challenged more than in Central and South America and nowhere has the call for a regional response been more noticeable than from these areas. It is here that neoliberalism has been openly discussed, debated and criticized, and alternatives have been suggested. It is also in this region that a far greater distinction exists between the right and the left in terms of their respective understanding of neoliberalism. Dating from the Cold War and the establishment of the OAS, which looked to enshrine the whole American continent as a sphere of US influence, a divide grew up between the political right, who favoured US aid and the development of capitalism, and the left, who saw US influence as a form of imperialism. The revolution in Cuba and the various military coups reinforced these divisions, with one-party governance being rife throughout the region, which often resulted in the suppression of the opposition. This polarization was to set the conditions of the post-Cold War era, when the right and left renewed their hostilities.

Perhaps nothing was more poignant in the development of this than with the Pinochet regime in Chile. As outlined in Chapter 5, not only did this oust Salvador Allende, who was seen as the darling of the left, but it also propelled Chile towards becoming a laboratory for neoliberal development (Peck 2010; Worth 2013). By the end of the Cold War, and with the end of state socialism, the economic (if not the political) arguments of the Pinochet regime appeared to be won as the 1990s saw a neoliberal revolution sweep through South America. Much of this emerged from the debt crisis, where some of the first structural adjustment policies provided the impetus for the later Washington Consensus. More significantly, it allowed US firms to gain access to the Latin American markets through the selling-off of state assets (Cypher 1989). Neoliberal development was to continue after the end of the Cold War, with some key figures arguing that no alternative existed to its reality (Cardoso 2001), and others insisting on the need for an open market when trying to build democratic societies after the years of military dictatorship and authoritarianism within the region (Weyland 2004).

The turn against neoliberalism was seen initially with the Zapatista uprising against Mexico's entry to NAFTA in 1994 (for a discussion in greater depth, see Chapter 8). This set up public debate on the essence of neoliberalism and what it meant to the region. It was the electoral process, however, that fuelled the idea that an alternative bloc could be set up to counter it. The elections of Hugo Chavez in Venezuela, Evo Morales in Bolivia and Rafael Correa in Ecuador were pivotal in bringing about this regional transformation. The success of Brazil's Workers' Party (Partido dos Trabalhadores (PT)) both in electoral terms and in the establishment of the World Social Forum also provided a stimulus for the success of the left in many parts of the continent (Peru, Uruguay and Chile, for example). The mobilization against neoliberalism can be seen in a number of different ways. First, there is certainly a populist element in this renewal of the left (Seligson 2006). The rhetoric of Chavez and Morales certainly relied on popular issues that often laid blame squarely on the shoulders of 'American imperialists', and the right/conservative opposition are often depicted as the unpatriotic 'agents' of the USA. This has provided a popular front to tackle the hegemony of neoliberalism and follows Gramsci's argument that a nationally popular mobilization of social forces is required for the pursuit of political success (Gramsci 1971).

There have also been different types of new left within the region. There are differences between the more internationally focused form of cosmopolitanism, which seemed to be the position favoured by Lula and the Workers' Party, and the more radical Bolivian position, favoured by Morales and Chavez (Castaneda 2006). Here, there is an argument that, in states where democratic institutionalism is more established, the left are more favourable to pluralist coalition building. However, in places such as Bolivia and Venezuela, where politics has been marked by authoritarian populism, left/right disputes and the lack of institutional democratization, a more radical position appears (Roberts 2007). At this more radical level, the re-nationalization projects, welfare programmes and land reforms that have been ushered in by certain regimes have indicated a strong collective response to neoliberalism. This has led to the creation of organizations such as the Bolivarian Alliance for the Peoples of Our Americas (ALBA). Launched in 2004 as a dual initiative by Cuba and Venezuela as a move to contest any US-driven free market agreement in the Americas (such as the FTAA/ALCA – Free Trade Area of the Americas), ALBA expanded to include Correa's Ecuador, Enrique Ortego's Nicaragua and Manuel Zelaya's Honduras, before they withdrew after Zelaya was ousted from power in 2009. It has also increased its membership to include a number of Caribbean states and has attracted further interest from states outside of the region. Despite this, such radicalism has been rejected by the more moderate position of the left in places such Brazil and Uruguay, who have both decided against joining ALBA. Nevertheless they still endorse a regional commitment towards what they see as a 'post' neoliberal position (Yates and Bakker 2013).

While South America has been defined as a region that is embracing an era of post-neoliberalism, it begs the question what exactly is it that has made it so 'post' neoliberal. For example, much of the practical co-ordination in organizations such as Mercosur has followed conventional practices as a regional bloc in the global economy and has not looked to challenge the wider system, with the exception of arguing for the better social management of market economies (Panizza 2005). In addition, it is hard to ascertain the precise extent of the radical position the late Hugo Chavez was trying to achieve alongside Fidel Castro, Morales and others. On one level it can be seen as a radical transnational attempt at building a socialist alternative, while on the other it can be interpreted as an attempt to foster a Bolivarian form of populist authoritarianism at the regional level. This would imply a more traditional fortress form of protectionism than anything revolutionary. Yet there are other issues that should also be looked at when considering a wider regional response to neoliberalism in Latin America.

First, despite having a great cultural and historical unity, Latin America as a region has a poor record of performance in terms of political and economic unity (Phillips 2005). Both Mercosur and the Andean Community of Nations (CAN) are intergovernmental bodies and lack the unity for wider integration. The big hope for greater unity is through the Union of South American Nations (UNASUR). Set up in 2008, this encompasses all of South America, (with the exception of French Guyana, which remains a colony of France) and pledges to join both Mercosur and CAN towards a wider supranational union. This organization intends to integrate the region gradually, with the intention that UNASUR would become a complete union, based on a similar model to that of the EU by 2019 at the earliest (ALADI 2013). This still leaves the OAS and the FTAA, which, while now shelved, is still supported by opponents of the new left. This brings us to the final point. Despite a certain amount of democratic pluralism being reached in most Latin American parliaments, there remains a sharp division between the right and the left. Certain states, such as Colombia and more recently Paraguay after the impeachment of former left-wing President Ferdinand Lugo, have rejected the move to the left, while states such as Chile have adopted a centrist stance as the government has passed through a more traditional centre-left/centre-right axis. The question thus remains as to whether the left turn across the region appears to be merely a temporary process, or whether all political persuasions are moving to accept the mantle of post-neoliberalism.

Other Regional Formations

Central and Southern Asia

Other members of BRICS have situated themselves in regions where they appear not just as the most influential state in the area but are also so powerful that they dwarf other, smaller states in their regions. Russia and India are two examples of this, but they have different relationships with their neighbours. In the case of Russia, the sheer power and influence they have possessed over central Asia and what has become dubbed the 'post-Soviet space' makes them pivotal to any collective decisions taken. The establishment of the Conference of Independent States (CIS) as the Soviet Union collapsed provided a shield for Russian influence to develop. As many observers have commented, the main developments in terms of regional influence in recent years have been seen with the shifting of Russia's influence eastwards since the end of the Cold War. In the immediate aftermath of the fall of the Berlin and the Eastern bloc, there was great enthusiasm that a wider unity could be forged between the EU and the Russian influenced areas of Eastern and Central Asia (Neumann 1996). Yet the reality has been that the frontier between Russia and Europe has merely moved east (Robinson 2012). As Eastern European and Baltic states have been integrated into the liberal democratic structure of the EU, the CIS states have tightened ties with Russia and, mirroring Mother Russia, have emerged to embody authoritarian forms of managed democracy.

As a result, there has been a distinct border between European regionalism and Russia's regional sphere of influence. The unrest that has gathered around the borders – as in Georgia and Ukraine – is often characterized by conflicts that have emerged over whether states should look to Brussels or to Moscow. As a regional body, the post-Soviet space has generally served to reinforce Russia's sphere of influence and cushioned it from potential isolation. To this extent, it has been successful. With the exception of states such as Georgia, the Ukraine and independence movements that have emerged from within the Russian Federation itself, Russia has generally been successful in building its 'near abroad' around its own strategic interests. Indeed, increasingly, the main source of instability for the region lies not with the stand-off with Europe or with other regions, but with the emergence within the civil society of radical and political Islam (Rashid 2002; Louw 2007).

India has a similar dominance of the South Asian region in terms of its economic output. The difference compared with Russia, however, is that South Asia has been marked by the conflict between India and Pakistan since their independence from the British empire in 1947. The civil war that brought the partition of the sub-continent provided the historical basis for a confrontation that has proved difficult to manage. Wars in 1965 and 1971 which led to the establishment of Bangladesh saw open hostility between the two countries continuing after independence. More recently, the ongoing territorial disputes over Kashmir and nuclear testing in the late 1990s, which resulted in sanctions from the international community, increased the animosity between the two states. Despite the improved relationship between the two since the start of the twenty-first century and the establishment of the South Asian Association for Regional Cooperation (SAARC), there remain significant barriers for wider integration. For example, while one of the cornerstones of SAARCs has been in establishing a free trade zone to enable a dramatic reduction of duties and tariffs within the region, the trading routes between India and Pakistan have been formally curtailed, meaning that trade between the two is routed via Dubai.

SAARC has more potential to form a basis for a vibrant regional organization than the symbolic CIS, but it remains largely problematic because of the combative history between India and Pakistan. In terms of whether SAARC can form a unique position as, to borrow from Huntington (1996), a 'civilization', or as a competing form of production, it has a long way to go. At least, the Russian-dominated area of post-Soviet space seems to represent a model of state-managed capitalism that appears at odds with North America and Europe. With the India–Pakistan conflict dominating the South Indian sub-continent, it seems very difficult, despite the intuitional promise of SAARC, that the region would offer the same.

Africa

If the OAU had grandiose plans for the construction of a pan-African union, its successor, the AU, has been more modest in its aims. Primarily, the AU acts as an umbrella organization, with sub-regional bodies charged with dealing with crisis situations, such as war and ethnic conflict, within their respective areas (Okumu 2009). The reality of this is that groupings such as the Southern African Development Community (SADC) in the south and the Economic Community of West African States (ECOWAS) in the West have benefited from the relative powerful intervention of South Africa and Nigeria. The ascension of South Africa to the BRICS has provided another significant development for AU leadership. This, as suggested Chapter 6, has brought a significant trading opportunity with China. The AU's potential in aligning with China should not be underestimated and could be used as a strategic attempt to forge a South–South alliance in order to create a market that is separate from that of the West. At this stage, however, the AU has no grand plans to forge an alternative power bloc, as they might have in the past. The partnership with China is a complex one and forms the basis of many a moral maze (Chan 2013). Yet it largely appears to fulfil the developmental goals of the continent as a whole, particularly (as mentioned in Chapter 6) if the Chinese offer a partnership free of the market conditionality of the Washington Consensus.

Africa is thus a region in evolution. As an institutional body around the AU, it has been successful in securing membership of all states (with the exception of Morocco) on the continent. As a region, it does not have any strategic interest in looking to create a bloc aimed at contesting the current world order, yet, with the emergence of states such as South Africa, Nigeria and the more developed Northern Arabic states, and their resources, it appears likely to have some impact on any future development. The African region remains one that needs to be won over in any potential wider struggle for hegemony.

Regionalism versus Variegated Neoliberalism?

The formation of regionalism could lead to the suggestion that a new geopolitical climate is growing in the global economy. One, it can be further argued, that may be understood in a multipolar form. This might open up space for wider challenges to the US-inspired form of neoliberal hegemony that, as we have outlined, has been the focal point of this book. However, any change to the ideological underpinning of the global system would depend more on whether the emerging economies and regions are successful in setting up their own markets, and not if they continue to rely on investment and markets largely for consumption in the developed world (Desai 2013). The larger question for us is whether regionalism can lead to a significant change in the appearance of hegemony in world politics. As we have discussed in the past few chapters, the change to the economic capacity of the state does not necessarily lead to a challenge to hegemony, especially if a consensus has been formed around a specific form of production. As we saw in Chapter 5, the strength of neoliberal hegemony is that it is multifaceted in its nature. One argument would be to suggest that the financial crisis has left a mark on the fabric of the economic global landscape so that a hegemonic crisis is inevitable (Overbeek and van Apeldoorn 2012). Despite an attempt to introduce austerity measures in an attempt to re-establish free market principles, neoliberalism will ultimately be challenged through a set of regulatory bodies acting at national and regional levels (Germain 2010). Yet what we have seen in reality is that regionalism has generally assumed different positions in the global economy to enable it to compete within existing markets. As with the emerging economies of BRICS, regionalism has been established in a manner that might imply a wider hegemonic change, but in practice seems to play very much within the parameters of the contemporary international system.

One alternative understanding of the post-crisis period has come from the perspective of political geography. The idea of variegated neoliberalism is one that tries to make sense of the different spatial levels that exist within the international capitalist system. Essentially, it suggests that neoliberalism has been developed through a number of waves and applied unevenly (Brenner *et al.* 2010). The geographical dimension of space is one that sees the understanding of free market hegemony not being reinforced at either the international or the national level, but at different spatial levels of society. This accounts for the intensity of market society within urban areas and urban financial centres, and explains how neoliberal practices are embedded at different urban/rural levels across societies (Gough 2014). This in turn can be understood more widely at the international level, where institutions have sought to forge different ways of articulating neoliberal principles. This ties in with what was suggested in Chapter 5, that neoliberalism is articulated at different levels and by different means. Recent accounts, for example, have been quick to show that there have been distinct governmental differences in the way that neoliberalism has been carried out. This has been particularly noticeable since the recent financial crisis, where some institutional bodies have been more interventionist in protecting the market system, while others have looked to a more ideological laissez-faire position (Macartney 2010; Jessop 2012).

This can be extended to regional governance. Here, institutions have looked to embed neoliberal principles at different levels. Regions also reflect the uneven development of such principles and, perhaps more prominently, the different varieties of neoliberalism. For example, the Chinese-inspired form of state-managed capitalism might appear to be offering an alternative to neoliberal hegemony, but could also be understood as a variety of neoliberalism – one that takes some of the main principles of neoliberalism, but allows a certain amount of guidance and management in order to function (Birch and

Mykhnenko 2010). As mentioned above, the same might be said of the EU. As many have mentioned, and as I argued above, the EU should not be considered as an organic neoliberal organization, in the same manner that the US-inspired NAFTA or FTAA are. Yet, as we have seen, the EU has developed into an organization that has promoted neoliberal principles, and has done so in a way that facilitates other models of production (Macartney 2010; Rosamond 2012). This could even be extended to South America, which, while it has forged a very real alternative to US-inspired neoliberalism, especially in places such as Bolivia and Venezuela, has also looked to integrate itself within the global market. Indeed, as noted in Chapter 5, increasingly, Lula, the champion of the left, was seen as a 'Third Way' practitioner in the same manner as Cardoso (Petras 2003). This was perhaps best expressed when he was honoured at the World Economic Forum (WEF) for his commitment to enterprise, the great irony being that the World Social Forum (WSF), founded by his PT Party in Porto Allegre, was presented as an alternative to the WEF.

That said, the emergence of both BRICS and regional organizations have served to disrupt the fabric of US power. What the state-centric and traditional accounts we saw in Chapter 3 give us is an indication of a change in overall state influence in the global political system. The relative decline of the USA in terms of its economic influence over developmental policy and its geographical spheres of influence does not necessarily mean that a change in hegemony will occur, if we understand hegemony principally as an ideological form. However, we also need to note that a change or decline in US power is bound to have an effect on the nature of neoliberalism. As the end of the Cold War and the victory of liberal capitalism built on the neoliberal ideologies backed by the USA in the 1980s and 1990s and allowed for its class-based international spread, it seems logical to suggest that more hybrid forms popular in other regions that are based on alternative forms of production will gain greater prominence. Chapter 8 will look at the wider question of counter-hegemony to expand this further. For while alternatives might emerge from changes to the geopolitical nature of global politics in terms of economic power, greater attention needs to be paid to how alternative counter-hegemonic discourses have emerged across global society to challenge neoliberalism. The strength of such discourses will provide us with a better example of potential challenges to neoliberal hegemony.

8
The Idea of Counter-Hegemony

The notion of counter-hegemony is one that has been used increasingly to understand a process that confronts the central principles of a hegemonic order. As a term, it is interesting concept and seems to provide a number of different potential outcomes. As a concept, it has been associated principally with Gramsci, though it is not one that Gramsci himself used. His concern was with building a hegemonic project that could challenge the capitalist structures of his day. As I outlined in Chapter 4, this was largely built on a Leninist strategy. As Lenin argued for a socialist movement that could fashion a working-class consciousness, then so did Gramsci (Joseph 2002). As we saw in Chapter 4, however, Gramsci's understanding of a hegemonic strategy was far deeper than Lenin's, as it tackled the facets and complexities of civil society and popular belief. Gramsci argued that it needed to challenge existing norms and practices that are central to the existing order.

Those who have worked on modern interpretations of Gramsci's hegemony have suggested different ways of understanding counter-hegemony through a wider historical lens. Stephen Gill (2000), for example, argued that if Machiavelli's *The Prince* was a metaphor for the modern state, attempting to establish a form of legitimacy against the Papacy, and Gramsci's modern 'Prince' was to establish a socialist party constructed to counter the forces of fascism and capitalism, then a contemporary Prince would represent something else. Gill's suggestion is that a 'postmodern' Prince has emerged in the era of globalization. This is understood as a collection of transnational social forces geared towards progressively transforming the hegemony of neoliberalism (Gill 2000). The growth of global civil society has provided an avenue for the transformation of a broad alliance. The essence of global civil society can be seen with international pressure and non-governmental organizations (NGOs), with the formation of the anti-globalization movement or the global justice movement, and later with the Occupy movement and the birth of the World Social Forum (WSF) (Kaldor 2003). Therefore, a united front can be understood as a form of postmodern Prince geared towards establishing a new counter-hegemonic project.

Others have followed the idea of a post-hegemonic order (Cox 1996). This is a popular term, both for those who imagine a world free from dominant powers and those who believe that counter-hegemonic struggles do not have to result in a new form of hegemony, but instead can result in a multitude of different positions all looking to contest dominant norms. In an increasing world of globalization, where identities are formed both below and above the state, a single global hegemonic project is untenable (Yúdice 1995). Consequently counter-hegemony can be employed as a series of interconnecting projects that look to democratize neoliberalism from different angles, resulting in a world where different identities can be forged at a variety of levels, without there being necessarily a dominant set of practices.

One of the main problems with counter-hegemony, however, is the fact that respective counter-hegemonic strategies lack a coherent alternative to challenge the fabric of neoliberalism. Indeed, for a long time the main criticism of the anti-globalization movements and the various social forums was that they lacked a comprehensive alternative vision of what a post-neoliberal world might look like. This has been one of the hallmarks of the post-Cold War era. With the decline of state socialism and the post-war Keynesian interventionist state, there has been a lack of a comprehensive opposition to market-based policy. As noted in Chapter 5, when social democratic political parties embraced new strategies such as the 'Third Way', any alternative within mainstream party political intuitions became increasingly untenable. While both social democratic parties and communist parties had firm alternatives to market capitalism in the past, there has been no anti-capitalist or anti-neoliberal manifesto as such that is geared towards centrally challenging the status quo. Within global politics, it also appears difficult to find wider networks and linkages for such an alternative to emerge. However, as we shall see, the idea of a 'progressive' 'international' front to capitalism is not a new one, and has, of course, a significant history through the socialist movement and the first, second and third internationals they produced. In understanding counter-hegemony we need to look at other alternative counter-hegemonic projects that can both disrupt and be potentially more successful than a wider internationalist solution. In particular, the move to de-globalize world politics through the re-emergence of nationalism has also occurred. This would provide greater battle lines for the kinds of conflicts that Huntington (1996) envisaged.

Understanding Counter-Hegemony

In Chapter 4 I referred to the work of the late, great academic and founding father of cultural studies, Stuart Hall. Writing in opposition to the growth of Thatcherism, he argued that the only way the neoliberal advance of Thatcherism could be challenged was through an equally popular alternative. Hall had argued that Thatcherism had succeeded in Britain as it had great popular appeal. The ideas of greater personal responsibility, home ownership, less taxation and greater freedom from the state were concepts that seemed revolutionary to the stale stagnant political ideals of the day. These ideas, coupled with the strengthening of the British identity through the attack on Europe, victory in the Falkland's War, and through the clamping down on law, order and welfare for 'criminals' and the 'lazy' in society created a form of authoritarian liberal democracy that would provide a hegemonic mind-set (Hall 1988).

Commenting in the 1980s, and within an entirely British context, Hall was quick to point out that Thatcherism has yet to succeed in its objective of achieving ideological hegemony, as wider society as a whole had not consented to it. In fact, it was quite the contrary. As we explored in Chapter 5, Thatcher's form of divide-and rule took far more from the style of Pinochet in Chile than it did from any attempt to create a universal set of values. The early observations by Hall were interesting in a number of ways. First, he was correct in saying that in order to confront an emerging hegemonic ideology, an alternative was needed that is just as strong and built on popular lines. The assumption is that, if opposition forces accept the general mantle of an ideological project, then it gathers momentum and an alternative becomes more difficult to construct. What Hall could not have realized was that the fall of the Berlin Wall would signal the end of Cold War and would result in the neoliberal doctrine – still highly contested in both the UK and the USA – gaining an international footing. Ultimately, as we saw, social democratic parties went into retreat in the 1990s and accepted the general principles espoused within neoliberalism. It was at this time that hegemony had won. Hall argued that projects such as the New Labour project within the UK were adding to the legitimacy of neoliberalism (Hall 1998).

The second observation Hall made is more pertinent to us when looking at counter-hegemony. To forge a challenge to an existing order it must do a number of things. Not only does a counter-hegemonic challenge have a central ideological focus, but it also needs to find a popular front across civil society. Again, when observing Thatcherism, there were a number of key actors across civil society who would lend their support during the 1980s. The most obvious of these were the tabloid press, who served to unleash a form of populism for the Thatcher government and against the opposition that had not been seen before. The small business community and civil bodies that favoured home ownership also yielded popular support. This was, perhaps, maximized more importantly by the mobilization of a nationalism that was historically endemic within Britain, but had not been stimulated by political forces for some time. This form of national populism was also employed as a form of welfare chauvinism to support cuts in welfare.

By looking at how a hegemonic strategy initially emerged, we have some idea of what is needed for the current order to be challenged. The case that Stuart Hall made is obviously specific to Britain and Thatcherism, naturally, and as we have seen, other states, regions and parts of the world have had different experiences in their respective transformations. However, if we are to understand what (and how successful) a potential counter-hegemonic movement might be, we can assess it by looking at whether it has (a) a clear ideological alternative to the current status quo; (b) support from civil society that can be mobilized at different levels; and (c) a popular appeal which can challenge the overriding common sense of a specific order (see Chapter 4). Before we look at whether potential counter-hegemonic strategies fulfil these criteria, we should observe more closely what Gramsci looked at when understanding resistance to a specific system. Here, he distinguished between what he called the wars of position and the wars of movement.

Wars of Movement versus Wars of Position

In Chapter 4, I outlined the two different strategies used by Gramsci in the fashioning of hegemony. The two terms have increasingly been understood by those who have looked at resistance in the contemporary era (Chin and Mittelman 2000). The war of movement could be understood, certainly in the era of Gramsci, as a form of revolution or insurrection against the state. He also extended it to areas such as mass strikes and protests that affect the functioning of the state (Gramsci 1971: 230–1). In contemporary terms this could be extended to the actions of the anti-globalization or global justice movements, as these have aimed to confront the shortcomings of neoliberal globalization through mass demonstration. In recent years, the Occupy movement could be understood as another form of war of movement (Worth 2013). The Occupy movement was geared towards confronting global capitalism with simple messages such as the 'We are the 99%', illustrating the concentration of wealth in the world. By occupying public space in front of symbolic financial institutions, the movement has confronted the inequalities of the neoliberal system by meeting them head on (Mason 2012). In addition, as the Occupy movement spread across more than 80 countries, it can be considered a truly global phenomenon, with the shared purpose of confronting the global process of neoliberalism. As a result, a war of movement does not have to be understood as one where violence or an insurrection occurs, but where political confrontation occurs in some form or other.

The war of position is the longer process, and, for Gramsci, it was here that his theory of hegemony rested. It is the process during which ideas are discussed, contested, challenged, replaced and defended. As examples, Gramsci cited forms of boycott, and non-violent demonstrations or confrontations that occur at all levels of civil society (Gramsci 1971: 229–30), but primarily, though, the war of position is where the key assumptions of a hegemonic order are challenged, most prominently in areas such as the media, popular culture and religion. In Italy during Gramsci's time, the support for the Catholic Church was obviously a major actor in the war of position as it had huge significance in terms of its role as a disseminator of information, knowledge and morality across civil society (Gramsci 1995: 1–87).

In the contemporary era, the key tenets of neoliberal assumptions need to be challenged in a war of position. In different ways, therefore, consumerism, the idea that the market and the private sectors are the generators of production, free trade, US-led initiatives, individualism, greater integration and interdependence are all assumptions that need to be contested and challenged. At the same time, new principles need to be put forward that are firm and strong enough to transform existing ones. Therefore, at the level of civil society such challenges need to appear within dominant forms of the mass media and information technology that have emerged as key components of global society. Similarly, the key facilitators of civil society in different parts of the world – whether they are cultural, political, social or religious, need to be put into service in a manner that similarly contests these norms.

Perhaps more important, it is within the sphere of party politics that the key principles of neoliberalism really need to be countered. As Stuart Hall commented, the lack of imagination from the political left in terms of innovation has been a characteristic of recent decades (Hall 2012). As a political force, certainly in some parts of the world, the left has failed to forge an opposition with enough guile to challenge the main tenets of the existing global economy. Socialism since the nineteenth century and social liberalism in the Keynesian sense all produced, in their different guises, a system pertinent to the state system at the time. They all looked to intervene in the economy via the state at the national level, and all looked to stimulate the economy though varying degrees of intervention and ownership. With the move towards regional and global integration, the left has shelved its national-based strategy, but has failed to replace it with an alternative. The exception, as we saw in Chapter 7, has been in Latin America, where the left has gone some distance towards constructing a regional alternative, but lack the institutional capacity to put it in place.

With these in mind, when looking at potential counter-hegemonic alternatives we should be mindful of both the shortcomings that exist within their ideological foundations and in the diversities in different parts of the world. At the same time we can at least look at the some of the counter-hegemony discourses that have emerged to contest neoliberalism. The interesting contradiction here is that while neoliberal globalization has been comprehensive enough to keep certain alternatives at bay, its de-stabilizing nature has left it open to contestation. Or, to borrow from Barry Gills, it both reduces and stimulates the forces of resistance (Gills 2000).

Types of Counter-Hegemonic Discourse

Increasingly, a typology of discourses is being used to show the difference between the types of counter-hegemonic resistance that have grown up to neoliberalism. For example, Alex Callinicos has offered different types of what he calls anti-capitalist movements, as opposed to anti-neoliberal. He identifies bourgeois anti-capitalism, localist anti-capitalism, reformist anti-capitalism, autonomous anti-capitalism, socialist anti-capitalism and reactionary anti-capitalism as six strands of resistance that have emerged to contest contemporary capitalism (Callinicos 2003). Some of these are called 'anti-capitalism' rather debatably. For example, bourgeois anti-capitalism largely refers to forms of corporate responsibility and to improving the corporate welfare of workers against the unprotected free market – a position that certainly would not be described as anti-capitalist by those who subscribe to it (Callinicos 2003: 71–3). Similarly, reformist anti-capitalism looks to strengthen and sustain capitalism rather than destroy it. Very much influenced by the Keynesian tradition of reforming rather than transforming capitalism, or, to borrow from Keynes himself, of saving capitalism from itself ([1926]/2004), reformists have suggested a number of changes to global governance and towards regulating the global economy. What he does show is that there is a long tradition of reactionary anti-capitalism. These are again not really anti-capitalist per se, but form a critique of globalism around national populism, with the primary attack being over the loss of national identity and tradition in the contemporary era.

Others have brought in further distinctions. Manfred Steger, for example, distinguishes between the international-egalitarian left, which is embodied in the rise of global protest movements such as the global justice/anti-globalization movement and Occupy, from the more national or regional campaigns that were endemic with Hugo Chavez (Steger 2005). In my book, *Resistance in the Age of Austerity*, I argued that resistance could generally be split into 'progressive', 'left' and 'internationalist' (at least in spirit), 'national populist' and 'religious' or 'fundamentalist' (Worth 2013: 42–6). My argument here was that while there are some distinct differences between those within the first category, essentially they are geared towards replacing neoliberalism with a form of social transformation. In this respect they are united, despite having contrasting strategies of how this might come about. Similarly, 'religious' accounts obviously differ depending on their respective religious belief, but they nevertheless understand the global system as being one that can be understood through religious interpretation. I shall take this further and look at how each of these has unfolded, and how they stand up as potential hegemonic challengers.

Progressive Internationalism

In this category, we can place not only the various strands of global demonstrations, but all forms of global civil society and NGOs as well as those that have argued for a reformed economic governance. They also include left-wing political parties who have looked to reject neoliberalism by suggesting alternative socialist policies and the various social forums: the World Social Forum that was set up to counter the World Economic Forum, and the various regional social forums such as the European, American and Asian Social Forums. The first signs of opposition from this position was seen with the Zapatista uprising in 1994, on the day that the NAFTA treaty came into force. The Zapatistas were a group of indigenous Mexicans from the Chiapas region of Mexico, who rebelled against the NAFTA treaty after it compromised the indigenous right to land that was constitutionally won by Emiliano Zapata in the revolution of 1910. In rebelling against the 'neoliberalism of NAFTA', the Zapatistas brought in a local/global dichotomy that aimed to show how local and everyday politics are eroded by free market policies (Zapatistas 1998).

The Zapatista uprising might have been seen symbolically as the spark for progressive movements against neoliberalism, but it can also be said that it set the precedent for ambiguity in terms of strategy. Because, as has been discussed in depth by many, the main objective of the Zapatistas was not to take power as such, but merely to reinforce and protect the local objectives from neoliberal development (Holloway 2002). The lack of a wider political project was one that was to become a feature of progressive critiques to some extent which took their cue from the Zapatistas. From the various civil movements, social forums and various direct action groups very little has emerged in terms of firm mandates. Certainly, in the aftermath of the financial crisis a number of practical solutions were emerging that were gaining significant support and looked to erode the fabric of the neoliberal system. Ideas for a new Bretton Woods style of governance were put forward, with suggestions coming from China that a global reserve currency be created that would stabilize the financial system (Xiaochuan 2009). This revisited J. M. Keynes' plan for his fictional 'Bancor' currency – a neutral global currency that he suggested should be used as a reserve currency to which others could be tied and stabilized. This would also neutralize any supremacy that one currency might have over another. As it was, it was the US dollar that did precisely that and ended any attempt to reduce one-state dominance over the post-war system.

The Bancor solution had been placed alongside other international campaigns such as the financial transaction Tobin tax that would raise a levy on international monetary transactions, a bank tax and a significant form of financial regulatory governance so that future credit spirals are curtailed. Elements of this have been taken up by some bodies. For example, watered-down regulatory processes have been agreed on by the EU with the aim of having it phased in by 2016. This will attempt to provide some protection against the worst excesses of the free market. However, it has not been agreed to as an attempt to challenge the neoliberal system radically, but rather to alter and reform it. In addition, if the proposals for the EU's financial transaction tax goes through it will only be partial as only 11 states signed up to it, with the more Anglo-Saxon states (including the UK and the Netherlands), most of the Eastern European states and the Nordic states opting out. The wholesale changes to the international system therefore have never appeared, and no serious attempt to make radical alterations to the financial system have emerged.

Outside Latin America, political parties of the left have also failed to back an alternative hegemonic project. For example, those left-wing parties in Europe who have rejected the centre-left consensus have often failed to explain clearly what an alternative world order would look like. Some favoured a return to national-first forms of social democracy, while those who have favoured a more global or regional form of unity have failed to convince in terms of their clarity (Dunphy 2004).

Part of the lack of clarity can also be seen with the debate over whether a hegemonic alternative is needed at all. As indicated above, debate exists over whether an actual hegemonic project at a wider level is needed, or whether different forms of resistance are better understood through disparate challenges at the local level. Following on from the Zapatistas, resistance is best carried out not through clear strategic ideas, but rather through different devolved struggles that look to counter all forms of hegemony and domination (Scott 1990). Some arguments here very much follow the line suggested by Rosa Luxemburg when she argued that spontaneity from below was equally as important as strategy from above in building a socialist alternative (Bailey 2014; Worth 2012). Others see this as a more postmodern approach to hegemony that has some similarities with that of Laclau (see Chapter 4) but tends to go further as it suggests that a post-hegemonic order, free from a form of universal ideology, is possible. However, as we have seen with the various types of progressive resistance, the lack of such a mandate for change has led to its weakness. In addition, it has allowed some of its criticisms to be picked up by actors who have used them merely to maintain the status quo. Hence the measures to regulate banks and financial institutions that were intended as wider campaigns to transform the neoliberal system have been used as an attempt to stabilize it.

National Populism

The rise of popular nationalism as a form of counter-hegemony is one that has been around for a number of years (Rupert 2000; Worth 2002, 2013; Callinicos 2003; Steger 2005). As an alternative discourse it looks to demonize neoliberal globalism by criticizing social developments such as multiculturalism, immigration, the wider forms of globalization, and regionalism. It argues that they have served to threaten the unique character of the nation state and erode historical national traditions and sovereignty (Worth 2013: 44–5). The increasing support of the far-right political organizations in Europe have highlighted this position, with parties winning support across the continent and in states such as Austria, where they have been highly prominent and served in government. Outside Europe, national populism emerged in the post-Cold War era in both the USA and the former Soviet Union as the era of globalism came to represent a new danger.

The sources of popular national criticisms of the contemporary world order differ in the extremity of their views, but in general they look to blame or scapegoat certain groups who they believe are responsible for the loss of national identity. From 'new world order' conspiracy theorists, who believe that a transnational elite is bent on globalizing the whole world and eroding national cultures and values (Rupert 2000), to those who point to the fallacies of multiculturalism and to immigration, national populism focuses on how the sovereign state is being threatened. As a consequence, regional organization, such as the EU and NAFTA, are a focal point of ridicule. In the light of the aftermath of 9/11, Islamophobia has intensified in Europe and North America, with many suggesting that the fear of Islam has replaced anti-Semitism as a source of racial attacks (Mayer 2007).

In terms of a counter-hegemonic project, the general vision of national populism is to re-create the national in lieu of globalization. Yet there are some distinct differences between such positions. Increasingly, many national populist positions appear to support free market principles, while some actively seem to endorse them (Betz 1994). For example, while political parties such as Greece's Golden Dawn and Marine Le Pen's Front National in France openly approve of a return to national protectionism, and politicians such as Pat Buchanan in the USA condemned the principles of free trade in favour of tariff restoration, many anti-immigration, anti-multiculturalists favour general neoliberal principles. In addition, groups such as the Swiss Popular Party and the United Kingdom Independence Party (UKIP) go further. For them, the idea of a retreat from state spending appears attractive and adds another populist slogan that can aid their campaigns – that of welfare chauvinism (Mudde 2007). This refers to the belief the state spends too much on welfare subsidization, which certain sections of society 'manipulate'. This also extends to immigration and refugee relief, providing another area for such groups to exploit. In Europe, Euroscepticism can also be located within the neoliberal mantle here, as one of the criticisms of the EU from a concentrated market position was that it was an unnecessary regulatory obstacle to the free market. We also saw in Chapter 5 how populism was a central component of the development of neoliberalism in the 1970s and 1980s. As a result, it can be understood how a similar populism used by the new far right could be contained within the very fabric of neoliberalism.

Those who favour a de-globalized world and a world where nation states and national cultures retain their autonomy, remain something of a contradiction. At one level they appear to embody a coherent alternative to neoliberal globalization. A reactionary set of responses to the global free market that propels the return of the nation state is certainly one that many have predicted. As we saw in Chapters 2 and 3, structural realists have long suggested that a multipolar world would in time emerge from the post-Cold War period because of an inevitable clash of nations (Waltz 1993). The forces of nationalism would certainly complement such a move. They also represent the other side of the coin, the Janus-like face of resistance from those who have visions of a more tolerable, more equitable world (Worth 2002). Yet many of the main ideas that were imposed by neo-nationalist forces have been found to be compatible with neoliberal forces. In some quarters, such as adopting an opposition to regional bodies, the promotion of a more concentrated form of neoliberalism has been argued. The ambiguity over the economy has seen a weakening of clarity of a national populist alternative.

Religious Fundamentalist

If the national populist discourse has largely emerged from the developed world and from advanced economies, than religious fundamentalist forms of counter-hegemony have emerged from the developing world. For them, the globalization of society has not resulted in the imminent destruction of their respective identities but has offered an opportunity that could be understood through scripture. Religion played a pivotal role in Gramsci's own understanding of hegemony as we know it, and other accounts have been quick to show how religion has manifested itself to strengthen the neoliberal discourse (Marsden 2008; Murray 2012). As a counter-hegemonic strategy, religion has also become central to forms of opposition. Long before the events of 9/11, Manuel Castells mentioned how the Japanese cult, Aum Shinrikyo, which gained notoriety in the mid-1990s for gas attacks on the Tokyo underground, looked to forge a critique of contemporary society based on spiritual interpretation and belief (Castells 1997). Many extreme forms of fundamentalism have emerged from more recognized religions. Fundamentalism has appeared in both Christianity and Hinduism in a manner that provides a basis for ideological contestation (Worth 2013: 105–11), yet it is with Islamic forms of fundamentalism and with political Islam that such opposition is mainly associated.

The different strands of Islamic fundamentalism have understood neoliberal globalization as something that is 'unholy' and 'ungodly', and modern consumerism as a form of US imperialism. In addition, the cause of Islam can be aided at both the level of the state (through the Islamic State) and through a transnational process. In the case of the former, counter-hegemony is constructed by contesting the idea of reason, which is central to liberal society, and replacing it with the idea of 'revelation' (Evans 2011). Sharia law serves to question such hegemony even further, by contesting the very fabric of private property, and declaring that the state itself is not answerable to representative democracy as such but to God and the scriptures. Islamic republics or kingdoms can form the basis of a counter-hegemonic challenge, especially if the clerical orders that interpret the form of the state according to God's will argue for a more rigorous challenge to contemporary capitalism. This does not mean that Islamic states are likely to act in this manner. Such is the open-ended nature of religious interpretation that it is just as easy for this to be compatible with neoliberalism. Indeed, it should be remembered that the large majority of Islamic republics embed themselves around the general principles of the world order. This can be seen with the much-heralded alliances the USA has enjoyed (and in many cases continue to enjoy) with oil-rich Islamic republics and kingdoms.

What, then, of transnational forms of radical Islam? Rather than attack forms of globalism, transnational radical Islam has exploited globalization for its own ends and interpreted it as a significant moment for potential advance. Transnational Islam is a stateless phenomenon and is opposed to the fabric of territoriality in world politics. The idea of a global society has been a stimulation to its cause, particularly the technological developments that globalization has produced. The reliance on forms of communication and technology to organize its advancement has been another feature. One of the more popular accounts of the rise of radical Islamic globalism has been from Benjamin Barber, in his book *Jihad vs McWorld*. Written in the mid-1990s (with subsequent editions after 9/11), Barber argued that a clash of globalization was emerging where the world of liberal consumerism would conflict with forms of radical Islam. Here, Jihad, the contested pledge of duty and sacrifice, which those who follow the Islamic faith commit themselves towards, is understood to be an act against the fabric of Western-inspired capitalism (Barber 1996). Counter-hegemony is also fought along two fronts. As radical clerics look to build a war of position through religious teaching, jihadists have gone on the offensive with violent attacks.

While we can see a counter-hegemonic project that both looks to counter neoliberalism from the war of position and movement, we still need to be very cautious in reading too much into such forms of contestation. The only way that religious fundamentalist counter-hegemony can be successful is if it reaches its intended outcomes from its respective religious interpretation. So, for radical Islam, success depends on the globalization of Jihad and the eradication of contemporary society; for Christianity, the coming again of the Son of God and so on. As a result, there is no single end-game for such positions. What they perhaps do instead is to bring us back to the idea of the clash of civilizations that was discussed in Chapter 7.

Fragmentation and *Trasformismo*

As we have seen, there are a number of potential counter-hegemonic projects that have emerged to contest neoliberalism. Yet we can also see that each type of opposition has been fraught with shortcomings that have left them open to criticism and fragmentation. Many of the counter-hegemonic discourses suffer from some of the key weaknesses we outlined at the beginning of the chapter. To a degree, all three positions outlined above lack coherence when it comes to providing a distinct alternative to existing principles. In the case of the first group, the 'progressive internationalist' group, the sheer size and diversity preclude any hope of uniformity. Also, the differences and the unequal development of neoliberalism across the world mean that this form of uniformity should not be expected at a systematic level. Yet the concern remains that there seems to be no direction to any form of alternative. The different socialist internationals of the nineteenth and twentieth centuries that contributed to the decline of Victorian liberalism had specific strategies that were related at first to the building of socialism in their respective countries. Where the forms of nationalism and internationalism did conflict – as in the well-known debates between Lenin and Luxemburg – they did so, not because of a difference over their understanding of the development of socialism, but rather on how it would be organized and achieved (Luxemburg 1976). In the contemporary era there seems to be no clarity over what should replace neoliberalism. While much criticism has emerged over the problems and failures of neoliberalism, the only objective that is unequivocal is, to quote a well-known banner used in an anti-globalization protest in London, to 'Replace capitalism with something nicer'.

The other two approaches I have mentioned here also have problems. In the case of the first, the contradictions of national populist discourses are rife. Especially in terms of the economy, where certain forms of national populism actually look to support neoliberalism and in some cases openly back more concentrated forms of it. Yet it remains difficult to see in practice how a system can work where such a concentrated form of free market capitalism is appropriated, while insisting upon an anti-immigration policy that would lead to a restriction of the mobility of the labour market. However, the populist right relies on a form of anti-intellectualism in its interpretation of social and political life, and the result relies on a series of reactionary and emotional generalisms when examining the wrongs of the world (Hainsworth 2000). As a result, such approaches are understandably fraught with contradictions and lack any consistency to amount a significant challenge to the status quo, unless (as in the case of the 1930s) a highly suitable environment exists to enable this to happen. As Robert Cox shows in his *Power, Production and World Order*, the emergence of fascism arose from an environment where the free market had collapsed and where nationalism was in advance (Cox 1987). As a counter-hegemonic force it appears to be less successful.

Finally, as already indicated, religious criticisms can be effective in distinct discourses and are certainly able to upset the fabric of world politics, as was seen with the events and aftermath of the 9/11 attacks. As a wider counter-hegemonic form, however, they appear unrealistic. Even if we take out the reliance on scriptural interpretations of current and future development of global society, the idea of one religion gaining global supremacy over others is in reality unfeasible, and in essence is what such challenges rely on. In addition, nowhere can fragmentation be seen more than within these groups. While both right and left oppositions are renowned for their splits in terms of organization, religious ones go even deeper. The often violent clashes that can occur between different denominations have been documented historically and are a painful feature of this fragmentation.

The subsequent direction of world politics in the aftermath of the crisis has not followed any of the potential reforms that were originally considered in 2008. Instead, much of the reform that has been discussed since then has been aimed at re-energizing the power of the market. The preoccupation with sovereign debt, fiscal conservatism and regenerating the neoliberal system have replaced any substantial need for change. In terms of social forces, a further development has occurred: in the USA a body of populism has emerged that openly endorses a greater marketization of society. With the rise of the Tea Party, a movement has materialized that has effectively turned all forms of counter-hegemony on its head by arguing for greater amounts of de-regulation. In the spirit of von Mises and later of

Murray Rothbard and his brand of state minimalism, the Tea Party has emerged as a grassroots organization geared towards criticizing state bailouts and federal spending. Encouraged by popular fiscal libertarians such as Ron Paul, it has pushed for campaigns such as 'End the Fed'. Having believed that the economic crisis developed primarily from the artificial lowering of interest rates by the Federal Bank, this looks to its abolition, to allow the market to find its natural equilibrium, free from bureaucratic control of any kind (Paul 2008).

The grassroots support for market-generated responses might be limited to Republican factions within the USA, but the defence of neoliberalism that has emerged since is one that has tried to claim that austerity, debt reduction and the re-stimulation of the economy are the only realistic options in the light of the crisis (see Chapter 5). At the same time, many of the concerns that have been highlighted by some of the criticisms of neoliberalism discussed above have been kept at bay and pacified through one means or another. We can see this with the EU's support for financial regulation and for a financial transaction tax. The intention here is not to look for radical changes to the functioning of the global economy but to even out some of its insecurities. The pathway where dominant classes look to co-opt certain criticisms in order to maintain the general status quo is one that Gramsci recognized well in his studies of Italian history. In his writings he referred to a process of *trasformismo*. In the years after the unification of Italy, Gramsci commented how the left-leaning Prime Minister, Agostino Depretis, forged an alliance with the conservatives in order to maintain a broad, stable coalition. This move meant more than just a coalition building exercise for Gramsci. It was a class manoeuvre where the dominant political classes maintain a form of continuity by co-opting previous areas of dissent (Gramsci 1971: 53–60). This move is vital in terms of preserving hegemony. Counterhegemonic discourses are controlled by the successful mobilization of co-option, whereby dominant forces at the centre give certain allowances and certain concessions but maintain the hegemonic character of the order in place.

Trasformismo is more effective when disagreements come from the opposition. Certainly, the divisions as well as the contradictions of counter-hegemonic positions have enabled neoliberalism to construct a viable defence. We have also seen that some of the opposition to neoliberalism has been reorientated so that it appears to back, or at least work within, its economic scope. The ambiguity of national populism has left it liable to co-option, in some cases – such as in inviting far-right parties to form governments – perhaps dangerously so. However, the reactionary elements that embody the far right can easily be incorporated within the wider neoliberal project and indeed were, in their initial inception, through the leadership of such figures as Pinochet, Thatcher and Reagan (Harmes 2012; Worth 2014). *Trasformismo* has also been a feature where religious forms of counter-hegemony have been in play. As I mentioned above, Islamic kingdoms and republics have both been able to engage with the global market system. This is not seen only with oil-rich, US-friendly states such as Saudi Arabia, but also with states such as Malaysia, which looked to employ neoliberal reform while maintaining Islamic principles (Hilley 2001).

Trasformismo *in Action: The Tea Party and Fellow Travellers*

In understanding the emergence of groups such as the Tea Party, we can see exactly how the process of *trasformismo* has worked, so that the neoliberal agenda not only survived the financial crisis but also re-established its underlying credentials so that its main forms of common sense are maintained. For while there have been a number of accounts illustrating their surprise at the longevity of neoliberalism (Crouch 2011; Mirowski 2013), the way that its main principles survived its legitimacy have not been explained to the same level. What the Tea Party and similar populist movements such as some Eurosceptic parties have done is to appear as protest groups, but strongly endorse such key principles. In doing so they have looked at other factors for the breakdown of society that has resulted from the financial crisis. While the intellectual arguments that underline such responses might borrow from Rothbard and von Mises, the popular success of the campaigns has employed some of the populism that was evident within the campaigns of Reagan and Thatcher in the 1980s: the neo-conservative elements that were implicit within these campaigns, such as welfare chauvinism, anti-immigration, and distrust for governmental organizations of any kind which they regarded as 'socialist' (Worth 2013: 10–14).

How have such groups gained such popularity from a crisis that seemingly had its roots in the very core of neoliberal practice? In the USA, the Tea Party has drawn its popular support from the ideals of small governance and in the conviction that state intervention of any kind erodes individual liberty. To some degree, the Patriot movements that emerged in the aftermath of the end of the Cold War, and have been discussed by authors such as Manuel Castells and Mark Rupert, provided the initial basis for the Tea Party (Castells 1997; Rupert 2000). However, as I indicated earlier, these largely appeared as forms of opposition to globalization. The Tea Party has managed to take some of the concerns that the Patriot movement was expressing and use them for their own purpose. For example, the paranoia regarding international organizations that the Patriot movement focused on with campaigns such as 'get the US out of the UN' has been subsumed into campaigns against central banking regulation and federal state spending. As such, the reactionary contestation of the post-Cold War era that embodied the Patriot movement has been replaced by forms of protest that do not look to contest the essence of neoliberalism, but endorse them rather strongly. By mobilizing a movement that targets the federal banking system, 'big government; spending' and excess taxation as the main sources of discontent, wider resistance has been co-opted from providing a counter-hegemonic opposition to neoliberalism to one that wishes to see its theoretical principles be more forcefully applied (Worth 2014).

If the Tea Party has succeeded in co-opting potential nationalist resistance into its brand of free market populism, then similar forms are also occurring in Europe. As mentioned above, the far right in Europe has gradually emerged from the margins and joined the mainstream as a form of protest but it has often been ambiguous in its economic orientation, especially in terms of its opposition to neoliberalism. Since the financial crisis, Eurosceptic groups have become more prominent which have followed the spirit of the Tea Party movement with attacks on the EU. A number of popular parties in Scandinavia and Eastern Europe have strengthened their Eurosceptic credentials, while the emergence of the United Kingdom Independence Party (UKIP) has seen perhaps the closest formation to the Tea Party. UKIP has emerged as a serious political player in Britain. Favouring a programme that includes withdrawal from the EU, welfare spending cuts and a greater deregulation of the economy, UKIP have attracted support by supporting these alongside a rejection of social liberalism, multiculturalism and immigration. As with the Tea Party, they have managed to co-opt nationalist feeling that might be used against neoliberalism in order to sustain a programme endorsing greater forms of economic liberalization.

We have thus seen how the process of *trasformismo* can work on both sides of the Atlantic. When the financial crisis hit, there was certainly the expectation that a hegemonic crisis would emerge in the economic heartlands of Europe and North America. Through the process of *trasformismo* we can understand not only how a hegemonic order can survive but also how it can transform itself to re-establish its founding principles. In this case, it also explains the irony of the emergence of groups such as the Tea Party as benign protest movements.

The Significance of Counter-Hegemony

The idea of counter-hegemony remains a notion that is largely suggestive in terms of its wider significance. There are a number of different interpretations of what might or might not constitute a counter-hegemonic project, and what serves as a strong form of contestation that might lead to a transformation in society. The sheer nature and diversity of the construction of hegemony makes it very difficult to ascertain the significance of its contestation. If a more nuanced concept of hegemony is understood, then, as suggested in Chapter 4, we should consider the social construction of hegemony as one that consistently shifts in order to survive. The various forms of economic, political and cultural agencies that are used for its construction are constantly being updated and altered in order to maintain the status quo. It is through these agencies that we can look for signs of resistance, and where the battle for consent is played out.

However, counter-hegemony has taken on an even more fragmented dimension with the various studies that have occupied many postmodern understandings of resistance. The idea of building a post-hegemonic system is one that moves beyond both Laclau's and Mouffe's arguments of multiple identities towards one that has more in common with Foucault. Here, the argument would suggest that, as every social interaction depends on its cultural relativity, a broad hegemonic project would always result in marginalization of some kind. This is demonstrated well in the genre of post-development studies. Here, development is understood as a project constructed through Western eyes to project economic advancement. The result is that all forms of development are defined and measured through this Western-inspired construction and enshrined through institutions such as the UN. As a result, all forms of cultural and social diversities are marginalized because of the wider international hegemonic understanding of development (Radnema and Bawtree 1997).

This same logic is applied to the notion of hegemony. Any attempt to organize an alternative hegemonic project would fall into a similar trap. Here, we see a move away from a Gramscian position to a sort of post-Gramscian one, and this post-hegemonic world being one where power is increasingly devolved and relative to its local surroundings. Some significant interpretations of anti-globalization movements have suggested that the reason there appears to be no strategic order is that it is not needed. Instead, they resemble a 'multitude', appearing too complex to commit to and fit into a central counter-hegemonic strategy (Hardt and Negri 2004). As the state system has become challenged by the forces of globalization, and by global civil society, then so has the traditional understanding of hegemony. This view suggests that the notion of power across all forms of politics – local, national and, more prominently for us, the global, need a rethink.

Yet the concept of hegemony, as we know, remains central and, as I have shown, both a contested and a developing and evolving concept in the study of world politics. While the study of IR might have been guilty of reducing the nature of the concept to the level of the state, it might also argue that it serves to remind us that the state still remains the central, most pivotal director and transporter of hegemony. It is here, where the subject of IR can remind other disciplines in the social sciences that the state and the state system, singularly and in all of its regional and intergovernmental re-creations, has retained its prominence, and its significance does not just fade away in light of transnational movements, as most textbooks on world politics will reaffirm (Beeson and Bisley 2013). The idea of post-hegemony is also one that has been understood differently in IR. The possibility of post-hegemony has been questioned by many when looking at the current evolution of the international system, and post-hegemony would differ from the idea of a non-hegemonic world (or a world where one state does not appear to be dominant). Rather than understand the world through a multipolar lens, or one where regional powers assert authority over their own spheres of influence, a post-hegemonic world would be one where power is dispersed relatively equally and international norms are embedded through strong forms of institutionalism (Cox 1987; Halliday 2009; Vezirgiannidou 2013). For neo-Gramscians this would also go further, as it would serve to neutralize the forms of productive hege-mony that are central to world order (Cox 1996: 126). This would require some form of progressive attempt to neutralize neoliberalism, through the sum of social forces outlined in the first counter-hegemonic discourse discussed above, with state endorsement that would lead to institutional reform.

It is here that we can find the usefulness of exploring these different counter-hegemonic strategies within the study of global politics. Each discourse might not provide any clues as to the potential transforma-tion of the global system, especially as we might argue that they have not sustained any strong unified alternative, but they do give us some ideas on where these discourses might lead. If, for example, resistance grows across global civil society towards the workings of neoliberal-ism and finds significant support with states or regions within the international system, then contestation will increase. Again, such support might be facilitated through another form of *trasformismo*. To an extent, both the EU's stand on regulation since the crisis and the Beijing Consensus favoured by China can be seen as examples of such a process. One could even add the post-neoliberalism within parts (not including the more radical left bloc of the Bolivarian Alliance of the Americas – ALBA) of Latin America could be seen though a similar lens. However, it is also through this medium that hegemonic change might occur.

Similarly, for those who see that either a multipolar world might attract instability or a clash of civilizations is on the horizon, the other counter-hegemonic discourses discussed here could provide a foundation. Continued disagreements among religious or nationalist forces might lead to a wider fragmentation within global politics, which similarly could find greater state or regional support. This fragmentation could also have grave implications over time for neoliberalism and its US-inspired leadership. To date we have seen states that have formed radical breaks from the global system (such as Afghanistan under the Taliban, and North Korea) have suffered deep consequences from their exclusion. As a result, it seems unlikely that a successful counter-hegemonic strategy will arrive from anywhere other than with the firm support of either a powerful state and/or region. What we have seen, however, is that such social forces exist and provide a basis for similar developments to occur in the future.

Conclusion

The concept of counter-hegemony is one that has been used in many different ways and is also a process that can be understood from a number of positions. Generally speaking, counter-hegemony is seen as a process related to ideological contestation at the level of civil society. Counter-hegemonic movements are those that seek to challenge the form and content of the existing order, and to replace it with an alternative model. It is also seen as one that owes central gratitude to Gramsci, despite Gramsci himself not using the term, preferring instead the idea of competing hegemonic projects. From counter-hegemony we can conceive of a possibility of a post-hegemonic world. This is the idea that a world can exist where there is a recognition that power appears at all levels of society. It also suggests that neoliberalism can never be successful in its hegemonic ambitions, as power is relative and dependent on the manner in which social relations are constructed. As a result, multiple forms of resistance to neoliberalism can be understood, providing opportunities to forge a multitude of new social alternatives.

We have also seen that this has a number of problems in terms of the more central question of the real purpose of hegemony. It remains rather presumptuous to assume that a 'post-hegemonic' society can be achieved without a hegemonic ideology. The purpose of Gramsci's understanding of hegemony was that it would inspire a unifying strategy capable of challenging the bourgeois narratives in ascendency at the time. Unless such a coherent strategy exists, central hegemonic principles are reorientated through a process of co-option that Gramsci referred to as *trasformismo*. As we have shown here, neoliberalism has re-asserted itself through policies of austerity and the insistence that the market remains the best mechanism for economic growth. We have also seen how the weaknesses of counter-hegemonic challenges have allowed this to occur. This might suggest that no matter how far power can be devolved, and how far post-hegemonic worlds can be imagined, the central workings of neoliberalism remain. For that reason, many accounts have been highly sceptical of the idea of 'post-hegemony' (Johnson 2007).

The larger question of how far the concept is relevant when we add the dynamics of the state system was also discussed in this chapter. The state remains the key actor in shaping the wider form of hegemony that we see in existence at the international (or the global) level.

Yet, without understanding the many dimensions of struggles that exist at the civil level in forging an ideological character complementing the structure and production of global politics, we leave ourselves open to accusations of state-centricism. Through studying the dynamics of counter-hegemony we can see how stable the current world order is, and whether any potential power shifts in real terms (that is, in terms of the statistical power of states) are imminent. It also poses questions such as whether an era of regional formations is indeed a possibility, and whether a new age of global politics might emerge that radically transforms the international state system. Counter-hegemonic forces provide us with what the world might look like, but the various processes of *trasformismo* can also show us ways in which an order can be altered in character, while its central principles remain in place.

Conclusion: Rethinking Hegemony in Global Politics

What can we conclude from this study of hegemony, and how can we look to provide a more nuanced definition to avoid the confusion of the dual meaning it sometimes attracts? As outlined at the beginning of the book, two different understandings of hegemony have often been used in the area of international politics: one that understands hegemony as a mechanism where one state controls others in the international system; and the other being the process that occurs when one class in society asserts its dominance over others by establishing certain ideological principles through which order can be maintained. As we have seen, the historical distinctions between these two are not as different in their understandings of hegemony as one might have thought.

We have also seen that the two different meanings of hegemony are not entirely divided between the studies of international politics and the rest. The assumptions here stem from a belief that the historical roots of hegemony in international politics differ fundamentally from those in other area of the social sciences. However, those that share a structural understanding of the way the international system works also have a similar way of understanding the role of hegemony. For example, world-systems theorists look primarily for the decline of the leading state and the rise of a competitor state to ascertain the potential change to a system. As we have seen, many look to understand the USA as a hegemon that provides leadership for a system of capitalism that provides a form of imperialism for core financial centres over peripheral states (Arrighi and Silver 1999; Wallerstein 1979, 2004). Similarly, hegemonic stability theorists look for the emergence of a dominant state in the state system to assess whether the world can be described as hegemonic (Robinson 2005). Both positions look to

170

analysis to decide whether the current system is sustainable, whether the USA is still in a position to maintain its role, or whether we are witnessing the beginnings of a change in guard in terms of the hegemon or in a wider transformation of the system itself.

The alternative position in IR has been to engage with the 'other' understanding of the term that has been used with the revival of Gramsci's work in the social sciences and in the development of Western Marxism. As we saw in Chapter 4, the neo-Gramscian understanding of hegemony within IR/IPE is one that has been applied in different ways and that has led to further confusion when approaching the concept.

This book has attempted to investigate the evolution of the term hegemony and tried to make sense of the confused and almost contested way that it is understood. It has also looked at ways in which hegemony can be approached, to try to develop a wider interpretation that bridges the various subject divisions and provides a greater clarity for the term in IR. To reiterate what was said earlier, the concept is one that is used liberally, but often without clarity. This is obviously a problem for those who are approaching the subject as students and find that the term is used under the assumption that the reader is aware of its definition. As a result, students are bombarded with a variety of different applications and understandings of the term, but without the clarity of the term being put across. This is made worse when the term is treated differently in other traditions. One of the main objectives of this book has therefore been to bring these definitions together and provide more clarity to the term. Its main goal, however, has been to rethink the term and provide a more nuanced understanding of it that is developed from its many guises. In doing so, we can make several observations that have come from this book and a number of conclusions that might allow us not just to rethink but also to reformulate the concept of hegemony in world politics.

The state-centric model of hegemony that has been applied within traditional forms of hegemonic stability theory (HST) is underdeveloped as a theory of hegemony. It originally stood by the suggestion in the 1980s that the USA was in decline and considered whether a new hegemon (Japan) would emerge. Robert Keohane poured scorn on HST by pointing to an institutional framework of integration that would not rely upon a dominant state (Keohane 1984), yet this in itself acknowledged the role that leading states would have to play and as a result could in itself be categorized as hegemonic (Strange 1987). The end of the Cold War and the re-creation – as it was – of HST in the form of unipolarity was to create a new narrative and almost obliterate the follies that preceded it. The idea that Japan would take over where the USA left off is now considered unimaginable. However, the logic now prevails that China is now the threat to the leadership of the USA. The statist argument that one leading state inevitably challenges another, and then assumes the role of 'the hegemon' for a period of time, lacks a deeper understanding of the fabric of power. Even Thucydides, the godfather of HST, stressed the importance of consent. Indeed, as we saw in Chapter 1, the more one looks into his historical accounts of the wars in ancient Greece, the more similarities can be found between his account of the building of hegemony and the ideas of Gramsci than with the HST theories in contemporary studies in international politics. His observations that the use of consent and of appeasing governing states and their citizens provide the foundations for hegemony is something that was repeated by Machiavelli through his fictional Prince many centuries later. It was this, as we know, that formed the basis for Gramsci's own ideas for a communist party, which he called 'the Modern Prince' to avoid prison censorship.

This is not to say that HST has not provided us with useful places to go, or with reminders when we look to understand hegemony. From the shortcomings with the early predictions, prominent scholars such as Joseph Nye and John Ikenberry have developed theories of state power so they attach far more to the ideas of consent through their work on soft power and liberal democracy repressively (Nye 2004; Ikenberry 2006). Here, far more is focused on how hegemony is not just built but also how it is maintained and developed. It also provides us with ways of understanding the workings of global civil society, and how these can be subsumed into the extension of US-led hegemony. Building on this, we have also seen how accounts of international society look to develop the concept. Ian Clark's study (2011) provides a holistic account of how we can understand several different ways that hegemony can be built. The different types of state-led hegemony he mentions allow us to think of a deeper, more complex understanding of international society through the interactions of the state system. Here we see how leading states interact with other prominent states at different levels of the international system. Therefore the international system contains different types of hegemonic order – both singular and coalitional – operating at both regional and the international levels. For example, while the USA might appear to the leading state within the international system, it requires an interaction within other states to carry out distinct operations in international society. These complex relationships form the basis of what we can understand as hegemony at the international level (Clark 2011).

These accounts show that, if we develop the concept of hegemony beyond HST – or to use Clark's term – beyond 'singular hegemony', it becomes much more than merely the sum and the outcome of the actions of one dominant state (Ikenberry 2001; Clark 2011). These do provide us with greater detail on which we can build and add the class-based dynamics implicit within Gramscian definitions. State-centric accounts such as these are important as they show the increasing complexities that exist within formal policy-making and reaffirm the state as the main actor in the process of consolidating a hegemonic order. They are vital when considering the ideological undertones that bind an order together, and they allow us to understand power in real terms and how it is developed.

The argument that a Gramscian or neo-Gramscian hegemony cannot be understood at the international or the global level is debatable. However, for us to understand the complexities of the international system, a model of hegemony needs to be built that looks at the multitude of agencies involved in forging a hegemonic order between social classes. These need to be understood at the local, national and global levels. The Amsterdam School, which introduced the idea of transnational classes, and Robert Cox's inspired Italian School that tends to favour the primacy of state power in its understanding of world order, have done much to introduce ways of applying Gramsci to world politics (Gill 1993; Overbeek 2000). But if we extend this so that we pay attention to elements of agency that Gramsci argued were vital for the fashioning of hegemony – popular culture, religion, national mythology – then we can look for a more comprehensive understanding of how it might play out. We see this even more when we look at the contemporary neoliberal world order. The varied manner in which neoliberalism has developed provides us with an opportunity to understand how we might assess the levels of hegemonic strength. As Chapter 5 showed us, neoliberal hegemony is articulated differently depending on both geography and the way societies are organized. So, as we have seen, in the Anglo-American centres where neoliberalism is at its strongest ideologically, its main principles can be centralized at the level of civil society. In other areas, particularly those that are culturally hostile to Western-inspired projects, neoliberalism has been legitimized through different cultural forms. As a result, nationalism, religion and different forms of popular and consumerist culture have been forged across civil society in a manner that complements neoliberal forms of production.

The sheer depth of Gramsci's understanding of hegemony can be applied to a global political system that has been inspired by the USA and by class interests at a transnational level. The ways in which hegemony has been constructed and articulated differ not just across borders but also across societies more generally. Therefore a theory of hegemony at the global level needs to look first at how world order is constructed both through ideology *and* through state-led initiatives; and then, second, look at the various ways it is articulated and reproduced across international society. This provides wide opportunities for students of global politics to look for innovative empirical studies in order to expand on the variety of socio-cultural ways in which hegemony develops across the different layers of civil society. In order to do this, a greater link with other areas of the social sciences should be encouraged: the fields of geography, urban studies, cultural studies, media studies, religious studies and literary studies have all made contributions to the ways hegemony is constructed. In return, international politics can provide a global framework for these studies. These linkages should be encouraged, if for nothing more than to create a wider understanding of the term and to avoid the confusion that currently exists when the term is used in IR.

The term 'neoliberalism' is another that has been used widely and in a number of confusing ways. The actual meaning of the term has often been vague and been used inconsistently. Furthermore, if we talk about neoliberal hegemony we have to pinpoint precisely what it is, especially if we are suggesting that it can be articulated in a number of different ways. This would also allow us to understand whether other new or competing models of political economy actually confront neoliberalism, or whether they merely allow it to be managed in different ways. I have suggested in this book that neoliberalism rests on a number of central principles, and it is these that form the basis of its hegemony. First, the belief that the market and the private sector form the basis for economic growth. This is a key departure from the post-war years, when state-owned enterprises of varying degrees formed an important component of the economy. In the communist world, this went further as state planning became the main fulcrum for growth. By the end of the Cold War, however, this changed drastically and rapidly. Aided by the Washington Consensus and the various transition programmes that had been set up in post-communist states, it became increasingly apparent that there was a shift of focus to the private sector and/or the market. The events that have followed – the East Asian crisis, the credit crunch, the sovereign debt crisis, and the embracing of austerity – have all strengthened this assumption. To some degree, the essence of neoliberalism can be seen with Karl Polanyi's depictions of economic man and of a market-based society. Here, the market takes on the central role in society, with other forms of practice being built and co-ordinated around it. Society is then consumed by a market mentality, whereby all economic activity becomes dependent on the workings and function-ing of the market (Polanyi [1944] 2001; 1968).

This market mentality forms the central principle of neoliberal hegemony. As we have seen from studies in the 1990s, states had suddenly looked to rearrange their economies, not necessarily by the amount of output they could generate, but by how competitive they could be in attracting investment and bolstering economic growth (Cerny 1997). The state might have looked to spend to allow this to occur, but the primary objective has been to become competitive. From this, the second hegemonic principle of neoliberalism can be seen through the internationalization of the state; namely, that states must look to compete internationally to attract investment and contracts with private companies. Again, this is a distinct move away from state concerns in previous eras. Rather than being a wealth generator and a provider of employment within its sovereign sphere, the state has looked to the global economy in order to develop. The growth of the global economy has facilitated this change, and the more the state restructures its strategic economic objectives towards this competitiveness, the more the global economy grows in its influence. This is especially important when dealing with the growth of BRICS. As we have seen, a great deal of attention had been paid to the new political economic models, or at least to the new variety of capitalism that China in particular has promoted. But this has also relied on the structure of the global markets in order to advance. The offer of cheap labour, a skilled, flexible workforce and additional attractions for transnational companies has seen China rise as a manufacturing hub, and India as a technological home for outsourcing. This has served to reinforce both of these central forms of neoliberal hegemony.

Therefore, neoliberalism, if we are to understand it as a wider form of hegemony at the global level, is based on a mind-set that rests on certain economic assumptions. It is these basic principles that have allowed it to flourish globally, but the ways in which these assumptions are realized and managed differ. For example, debates have emerged that show how different variations (compared with varieties) of capitalism emerge within and beyond different regions of the world (for a recent collection of useful debates on this, see Bruff and Ebenau 2014), and we can see how different forms of cultural and political practices are followed. This diversity does not mean that they necessarily operate through different or competing ideologies, as those who remain sceptical to the idea of a wider global hegemony might suggest. Instead, they are both used in a manner that complements the wider hegemonic principles that bind the global economy and the world order together. This provides the general essence of contemporary forms of hegemony at the international level.

The various forms of regional blocs that have emerged to prominence since the end of the Cold War are neither facilitators of neoliberalism nor bodies of resistance. Instead, they are institutions that can be used for a multitude of purposes and have the potential to embed, manage, curtail or resist hegemonic practices. What we have seen are forms of regional integration that appear as open bodies in terms of their potential. As a result, the assumptions made about a future clash of civilizations can be seen as a future possibility. At the same time, the idea that new regionalism appears as a form of constitutionalism (as put forward by Stephen Gill, 1998), which serves to legitimate the practices of the global market, can also be true. Certainly, many of the developments made by regional bodies in recent years would reflect this. While the EU had set out its commitment towards establishing a social Europe, the actions taken throughout the 1990s represented a distinct turn towards enshrining free market principles and, through the euro, strict monetarist fiscal restraints (van Apeldoorn *et al.* 2008). The NAFTA treaty was never intended to be anything other than a free trade agreement and one that would aim to de-politicize economic policy between the three North American states. However, events occurring in Central and South America have sought to challenge free market rhetoric and halt the growth of the neoliberal principles that had escalated with the debt crisis and the establishment of the Washington Consensus, and had spread across the region throughout the 1990s. There also appear to be mixed interpretations of regionalism in East

Asia and its wider intent, both in terms of its relationship to China and to the wider workings of the global order.

Regionalism has emerged as a new phenomenon in world politics in effectively dealing with or governing world order. Yet, as with the fabric of the tradition state system, it is within these institutions where the struggles for hegemony take place. Therefore it would be wrong to label them merely as structural blocs looking to facilitate neoliberal hegemony. Similarly, it would be equally wrong to suggest that, as these regional organizations have emerged, we are halfway towards a dystopia like that depicted in Orwell's *Nineteen Eighty-Four*, in which they would naturally compete among themselves. As we have seen, regional organizations differ greatly in terms of their integration and how unified they are as bodies (Farrell *et al.* 2005). The EU, on the one hand, has sought to integrate both politically and economically, while others such as the AU and ASEAN have committed themselves to using their collectivism to safeguard the sovereignty of member states against external factors. Organizations such as APEC provide an altogether different set-up, as it appears to be more of an umbrella for free trade than a substantial body as such. It can be said that, in terms of its functional capability, regionalism can be seen as a mechanism to strengthen a hegemonic order. Certainly, the establishment of bodies such as NAFTA and APEC are a testament to this. Yet there remains much conflict in the EU over the future of global capitalism, and there is certainly potential for the current course of fiscal prudency in support of a wider neoliberal programme to be challenged from the left by a renewed socialist opposition of some kind (Worth 2007). Finally, as we saw when discussing Latin America, regionalism can be constructed along lines that can contest and use their institutional foundations as a direct challenge to the wider workings of the global order. Regionalism might have arisen from the reality of globalization, as the traditional nation state became increasingly unable to deal with the rigour of a technologically transformed global environment. Yet regionalism as a process is an open one and can be determined through political struggle. As such, these regional bodies can complement and strengthen a hegemonic order through policy-making that endorses its central principles. Conversely, it can try to resist, contest and ultimately transform the hegemonic character of the international system.

The idea of counter-hegemony is one that has also been used extensively in recent studies on resistance. For us here, counter-hegemony is important because it provides an indication of how a specific order might be challenged allowing us to understand the character of counter-hegemonic discourses and the potential alternative worlds and ideologies that look to challenge it. From an analytical point of view, two questions stand out for consideration. First, whether a counter-hegemonic challenge is potentially strong enough to threaten the stability of the contemporary order, and second, if a competing ideological challenge is to emerge, which states might support it. In looking at the contemporary neoliberal order, a number of answers can be given to – or at least comments made about – these questions. There remain significant shortcomings in the counter-hegemonic strategies that have been developed to date towards neoliberal economic globalization. While, the three counter-hegemonic strategies outlined here – broadly, 'left', 'right' and 'religious' – are not without their typological problems (as acknowledged in my more detailed book on resistance – Worth 2013), they do illustrate significant weaknesses with regard to challenging the contemporary neoliberal order. This has been particularly noticeable in light of the financial crisis, where the neoliberal order should have come under a great deal of opposition from competing alternatives, but instead succeeded in regrouping with its key principles largely unblemished.

In many cases, counter-hegemony within global politics is understood by judging whether a contender state can challenge the hegemonic legitimacy of the leading state. While the term counter-hegemonic is not one that is used to explain this challenge – HST instead prefers to look at international structures that appear hegemonic and those that do not, while world-systems theory defines 'counter-hegemony' in terms of 'anti-systemic movements' (Arrighi 2004). As we have discussed here, the neo-Gramscian use of counter-hegemony provides a wider understanding of the likelihood for change. Yet, it is also within these contender states that might be located a specific counter-hegemonic movement which has the ability to become prominent within such a state and as a result challenge the wider global order. One only needs to go back to 1917 to see the effect of a counter-hegemonic movement once it has embedded itself within one such rising state. The birth of the Soviet Union and the state-socialist economic model led to a change in the wider global system and the fragmented world that followed the First World War. Economically, the failure of the liberal economy would strengthen the different forces of socialism, which would lead to the different forms of mixed economy post-1945.

As we suggested in Chapter 8, the current neoliberal order has benefited from the shortcomings in counter-hegemonic opposition. The lack of cohesion in constructing viable alternatives to neoliberalism has allowed the present order to defend itself against its weaknesses. We have also suggested that China might emerge as the type of contender state that could facilitate some kind of counter-hegemonic project. China's distrust of the unfettered neoliberalism of the Washington Consensus and its alternative offerings that have been termed the Beijing Consensus, has led many to suggest that China is leading a frontal attack on the US-led form of neoliberalism (Beeson 2009; Strange 2011). Conversely, we can also observe that China's influence has yet to lead to a form of political economy countering the contemporary model in a manner that attacks the fabric of the global order. By adopting economic strategies that seek to attract investment from prominent actors within the global economy, China can be seen as a state that actively complies with the current order. Despite this, China has positioned itself as a key player in its own right, not just in terms of its economic influence but also its military and political prowess. This has been seen with the growing regional significance that China has wielded not just in Asia, but also more significantly in the developed world and especially in Africa. As a result, the debate over the significance of China in terms of hegemony will continue to grow, with great attention being placed on whether China might provide the catalyst for counter-hegemonic forces to develop.

The above observations provide us with a broader understanding of the term hegemony and suggest questions that can be debated in greater depth. However, at this point, I should return to a key issue discussed in the first chapters of the book. While I have tried to provide a wider understanding of hegemony in this book, the breadth of the concept as an explanatory tool will still depend on its purpose. For example, if hegemony remains a concept that is tied to narrow forms of economic and political measurement, it will still attract great criticism. However, it should be noted that many of these studies have been revised so they now engage with many of the criticisms that were levelled against them in terms of their over-reliance on positivist methodology. Robert Gilpin and John Ikenberry, respectively, have been explicit in their more recent work in looking to develop a wider understanding of the complexities that exist within global power in order to compile such a concept (Gilpin 2001; Ikenberry 2006).

This indeed flies in the face of recent accounts suggesting that a divide exists in certain studies within the social sciences regarding the way that international economic power is understood. Benjamin Cohen, for example, has illustrated in his work how a transatlantic divide has defined the way in which the study of IPE is approached: the Americans are more scientific in their approach to understanding the nature and construction of the international political economy, while the British are more multidisciplinary (Cohen 2008). However, it might be more useful to return to the scepticism of the notion of objectivity that was argued by Robert Cox, when he suggested that 'theory was always for the purpose of someone or something' (Cox 1981). This would certainly hold true when we see how Robert Keohane, who has always been located very much within the American (and as a result, the objective) school, argued for an end to the egotism of states and for greater co-operation in world economic affairs (Keohane 1984). Ikenberry too has never hidden the fact that he supports a form of liberal interventional and has been vocal in his belief in the greater American investment into international institutions (Ikenberry 2001). Moving to the right, both Huntington (1996) and Barber (1996) can be seen as looking to equalize the potential threat of religious and cultural opposition to the American-inspired form of liberal democracy.

In contrast, a Gramscian-inspired understanding of hegemony has always arisen from a commitment towards critiquing the world in which it exists and looking to transform it. In terms of applying this to contemporary forms of neoliberalism, any account is similarly committed towards demonstrating why and how the contemporary order is failing humanity. As a result, the normative approach is not one that is dismissed in favour of any claim to objectivity by those who borrow from Gramsci, but in fact is very much central to its purpose. Following the wider tradition of critique within social theory, hegemony facilitates both a commitment to critique and a similar commitment towards emancipation and transformation. In this way, it follows Marx's immortal statement that the point is not merely to interpret the world but to change it (Marx 1977). Ultimately, then, we can rethink the meaning and complexity of the concept of hegemony within global politics many times, but its application may still depend on the political persuasion of the individual in question who is applying it.

Rethinking Hegemony: Moving Forward

This provides us with the final question. How can we rethink hegemony in *international/global* politics in a manner that retains its Gramscian focus from a normative position but also takes into account the many and diverse studies we have discussed in this book? How also can this lead us to come to conclusions about the state and nature of the current hegemonic order and, following the normative commitment towards transformation, how might the system ultimately be transformed? Chapter 8 certainly provided answers to some of this, but some of the points raised there might provide us with greater clarity into how questions of hegemony and counter-hegemony might be tackled.

For all the debates about what form hegemony might take, the question that still remains central is whether the current order is under threat or in a downward spiral. Certainly, many HST declinists and world-systems theorists have concluded that the era of US hegemony is reaching the end of its tenure (Arrighi 2007; Mearsheimer 2009) and, as outlined above, many within IPE have suggested that China's form of the Beijing Consensus will provide the basis for a hegemonic challenge. As we have also seen, counter-hegemony projects that have looked to form a social base for wider transformation have had problems in establishing themselves as sustainable oppositional forces to neoliberalism. So what possible developments might there be to the current world order in the near future? Following from the belief that the financial crisis, along with expansive US foreign policy, has left the idea of American leadership in peril, we might be entering a period of uncertainty, from which a new order will slowly emerge (Silver 2014).

Conversely, we have also suggested that if we take the ideas and practices of neoliberal hegemony to be the driving force behind hegemony, it can be questioned whether a specific leading state is required at all. Rather, a set of leading states that practise different forms of neoliberalism can facilitate the continuation of the current order adequately. Following from this, Richard Saull has offered an account of hegemony that both maintains the Gramscian tradition of historical bloc construction, and retains the idea of a leading state as an enforcer (Saull 2012: 329). Yet Saull also stresses that the ideational levels of hegemony often undermine the material conditions of capitalism that shape the general global order. Like others, he argues that China should not be seen as a state on the verge of challenging the USA in terms of hegemonic leadership, as its growth has arisen as a result of its successful integration into the neoliberal system, but he underlines the importance of the USA in maintaining the current order (Saull 2012: 331–4). While the neoliberal historical bloc has been character-ized by a set of key principles, the USA has still retained its unique role as the leading instigator of the system.

This might go some way to answering the dilemma of what a model of hegemony might look like if we wished to create a wider, more nuanced model. Yet, it does not allow us to realize exactly what that might be. As we have suggested here, hegemony might have been used as a means of understanding state leadership in a manner that ignored the complexities of the term as a social process, but this does not necessarily mean that the role of a leading state should be ignored. What we have often seen instead is that the concept at an international level is often puzzling and unclear. Saull's arguments draw on a response to the declinist argument on American power that has resur-faced once again since the financial crisis. As he suggests, the unwit-ting result of this is that the contemporary hegemonic model is one that requires the USA in order to facilitate the wider practices of neoliberalism. This still leaves us with other questions on the nature of leading states; namely, whether the wider processes of neoliberal-ism might still work with another leading state at its helm, or whether a leading state would give a fresh and alternative platform for a new hegemonic order.

At present, however, if we want to see a model of hegemony that would encourage a set of research agendas, a set of proposals might tentatively be suggested that could enable us to broaden its scope as an explanatory model within IR and lessen the ambiguity that has some-times accompanied it as a term:

1. Following on from the accounts offered by Saull and others who reject the declinist idea of the USA, more work needs to be done on examining where the rise of China and BRICS fit in relationship to the wider order. In particular, how state power is realized within the fash-ioning of hegemony. This might involve closer studies contained within international organizations such as the WTO, where certain free market principles are formally embedded (Paterson 2009). If we are to use state interaction as the departure point for hegemonic fash-ioning, then the structural leadership that the USA (first) and then

other 'core' states build need to be looked at more closely. While Gramscians might like to look back at the work of Cox (1996) and Murphy (1994) regarding how this might play out, it might be best if they look at Clark's material on collective hegemony. Detailed historical studies of how the neoliberal order was fashioned have also been a feature of both neo-Gramscian and HST readings of hegemony, but recent accounts need to develop this to show how American leadership maintains its structural influence, particularly in response to declinists.

2. As we have seen throughout this book, state interaction can only go so far in explaining elite formation. The many empirical contributions from Kees van der Pijl and the Amsterdam School have already provided a rich foundation for understanding how transnational classes have been forged across states (van der Pijl 1998; van Apeldoorn et al. 2008), but their work remains a study of the construction of elites. As with point 1, both state leadership and the construction of class elite provides an understanding of the management of a free market capitalism, but understanding how hegemony is fashioned is a different matter. Building on US state leadership and Robinson's model of the transnational capitalist class we need to show how international/ global hegemony is fashioned between social classes. This can be seen as the main focus which has been lacking in accounts in IR. Here, we need to understand the different processes the transnational capitalist class uses to co-opt different social classes into accepting and contributing to the hegemonic order.

Such a task needs to sort out the various ways that hegemony is shaped in this process. As explained in Chapter 4, Gramsci's own way of doing this was to identify a number of different areas where this is achieved, most notably through traditional and popular forms of religion, and popular literature, culture and folklore as well as from the political process (Gramsci 1971: 419–25; 1985: 188–91; 1996: 172–4). The task for contemporary accounts was to distinguish how certain forms of agency would fall into these different categories. This is where the work of the cultural theorists that were prominent in British academia that emerged as part of the New Left from the 1960s is important. The work of Stuart Hall and Raymond Williams might have been written with predominantly British examples in mind, but their descriptions of how hegemony is fashioned provide us with a very useful theoretical departure point to follow. Again, the importance of scale becomes a vital factor here as the forms of agency are articulated across different spatial levels. Therefore studies must show how the core values of a hegemonic order are formed across these different local, national and global levels. Through this, a greater depth of study of every spatial level of hegemony can be applied, and will show a greater diversity in the way that global political society is constructed, shaped and contested.

3. Following on from and developing point 2, regional differences and variations of neoliberal hegemony should also be accounted for. Here, the material on variegated neoliberalism is most useful (Brenner *et al.* 2010). This allows us to understand how neoliberalism takes different forms at regional and state levels in a manner that addresses the concerns put forward by those who reject a hegemonic model in favour of understanding the international system as the sum of a variety of capitalism (Bruff 2011). In this respect it needs to show how the different strategies undertaken by states and regional blocs which might assume a specific model of capitalism remain geared towards an internationalism that is focused primarily on maintaining the practices of the wider neoliberal order.

As with point 2, however, these studies should not be geared only towards looking at how models of neoliberalism – ordoliberal, Anglo-Saxon or more state-managed, for example – are forged within certain states or regions, but how they are embedded socially and culturally. Of particular interest is how local customs and cultures articulate themselves so that they are compatible with the wider process of neoliberal hegemony carried out at the global level. As we have shown in this book, a number of studies have emerged that have provided us with departure points for this, but there is a vast potential for studies that focus on how local, national and regional cultures and customs are articulated in a manner that is compatible with the norms and workings of neoliberal production.

4. Finally, more emphasis needs to be placed on the notion of 'counter' hegemony or hegemonic contestation. Again, this is not to say that there has not been an abundance of rich work on resistance and wider civil contestation to global capitalism or on the possible geopolitical shift from an American-inspired form of leadership to something that might be heavily influenced by China or might fragment into a series of competing regionalisms. What need to be

developed further are the explanations of why an alternative form of hegemony has not succeeded in gaining sufficient momentum to challenge the fabric of the global capitalist order in which we currently find ourselves. Even if we were to concede that China has placed a serious set of alternatives that can be seen as a challenge to free market capitalism, the mobilization of a movement and set of principles that look to challenge firmly the very nature of global capitalism is a different preposition. What this would effectively be asking is what would a potential hegemonic alternative look like, and how would it contest the fabric of the existing order? Such a question is one that Gramsci himself asked, through the medium of twentieth-century socialism, and one that Stuart Hall posed in the light of its collapse in Britain under the advances of Thatcherism. Yet, as we have seen, the era of globalization has produced the potential for a new 'post-modern Prince' (Gill 2000), but until we can understand what form this might take and how it can contest the existing fabric of hegemony successfully, we can only review why this has not yet been achieved (Worth 2013).

Bibliography

Abu-Lughod, J. (1989) *Before European Hegemony: The World System AD 1250–1350* (Oxford: Oxford University Press).

African Union (AU) (2012) 'China–Africa Cooperation Forum'. Available at: http://www.au.int/en/partnerships/africa_china.

Ahmed, W. (2009) 'From Mixed Economy to Neoliberalism: Caste and Class in India's Economic Transition', *Human Geography*, 2(3): 37–51.

ALADI (The Latin American Integration Association) (2013) *Latin America Economic and Cooperation Handbook, Vol. I: Strategic Information, Organizations and Programs* (Washington, DC: International Business Publications).

Ames, G. (2008) *The Globe Encompassed: The Age of European Discovery 1500–1700* (London: Pearson).

Amin, S. (2004) 'Globalism or Apartheid on a Global Scale', in I. Wallerstein (ed.), *The Modern World-System in the Longue Durée* (Boulder, CO: Paradigm).

Aning, K. and Salihu, N. (2012) 'Regional Approaches to State-Building: The Case of the African Union and ECOWAS', in M. Berdal and D. Malone (eds), *Power after Peace: The Political Economy of Post-conflict State Building* (London: Routledge).

Apeldoorn, B.van, L. Drahokoupil and Horn, L. (eds) (2008) *Contradictions and Limits of Neoliberal European Governance: From Lisbon to Lisbon* (Basingstoke: Palgrave Macmillan).

Arrighi, G. (1993) 'The Three Hegemonies of Historical Materialism', in S. Gill (ed.), *Gramsci, Historical Materialism and International Relations* (Cambridge: Cambridge University Press).

Arrighi, G. (2004) 'Hegemony and Antisystemic Movements', in I. Wallerstein (ed.) *The Modern World System in the Longue Durée* (Boulder, CO: Paradigm).

Arrighi, G. (2007) *Adam Smith in Beijing: Lineages of the Twenty-First Century* (London: Verso).

Arrighi, G. and Silver, B. (1999) *Chaos and Governance in the Modern World System* (Minneapolis, MN: Minnesota University Press).

Ashworth, L. (2014) *A History of International Thought* (London: Routledge).

Bailey, D. (2014) 'Resistance is Futile? The Impact of Disruptive Protest in the "Silver Age of Permanent Austerity"', *Socio-Economic Review*. Available at: http://doi: 10.1093/ser/mwu027.

Barber, B. (1996) *Jihad vs McWorld* (New York: Ballantine Books).

Baumol, W. and Strom, R. (2010) '"Useful Knowledge" of Entrepreneurship: Some Implications of the History', in D.S. Landes, J. Mokyr and W. Baumol (eds.) *The Invention of Enterprise: Entrepreneurship from Ancient Mesopotamia to Modern Times*. (Princeton, NJ: Princeton University Press).

Beaudreau, B. (2005) *Making Sense of Smoot-Hawley: Technology and Tariffs* (Bloomington, IN: iUniverse).

Beausang, F. (2012) *Globalisation and the BRICs: Why the BRICs will not Rule the World for Long* (Basingstoke: Palgrave Macmillan).

Beer, S. (1967) *Modern British Politics* (New York: W.W. Norton).

Beeson, M. (2009) 'Hegemonic Transition in East Asia? The Dynamics of Chinese and American power', *Review of International Studies*, 35(1): 95–112.

Beeson, M. (2010) 'There Are Alternatives: The Washington Consensus vs State Capitalism', in M. Beeson and N. Bisley (eds), *Issues in 21st Century World Politics* (Basingstoke: Palgrave Macmillan).

Beeson, M. and Bisley, N. (2013) 'Issues in 21st Century World Politics: An Introduction' in M. Beeson and N. Bisley (eds), *Issues in 21st Century World Politics* (second edition) (Basingstoke: Palgrave Macmillan).

Bentley, M. (1984) *Politics Without Democracy 1815–1914* (London: Fontana).

Bergsten, F. (1997) 'Open Regionalism', *The World Economy*, 20(5): 545–65.

Betz, H.-G. (1994) *Radical Right-Wing Populism in Western Europe* (New York: St Martin's Press).

Bieler, A. and Morton, A. (eds) (2001) *Social Forces in the Making of the New Europe* (Basingstoke: Palgrave).

Bieler, A. and Morton, A. (2004) 'Neo-Gramscian Perspectives in International Relations', *Capital & Class*, 82: 85–115.

Birch, K. and Mykhnenko, V. (eds) (2010) *The Rise and Fall of Neoliberalism: The Collapse of an Economic Order?* (London: Zed Books).

Bisley, N. (2011) 'Biding and Hiding No Longer: A More Assertive China Rattles the Region', *Global Asia*, 6(4): 62–73.

Blyth, M. (2013) *Austerity: The History of a Dangerous Idea* (Oxford: Oxford University Press).

Bohle, D. (2006) 'Neoliberal Hegemony, Transnational Capital and the Terms of the EU's Eastward Expansion', *Capital & Class*, 30(1): 57–86.

Boxer, C. (1965) *The Dutch Seaborne Empire 1600–1800* (London: Knopf).

Braudel, F. (1979) *Civilisation and Capitalism, 15th–17th Century: Vol. I: The Structure of Everyday Life* (Oakland, CA: University of California Press.

Braudel, F. (1983) *Civilization and Capitalism, 15th–18th Century: Vol. II: The Wheels of Commerce* (Oakland, CA: University of California Press).

Brenner, N. (2004) 'Urban Governance and the Production of New State Spaces in Western Europe, 1960–2000', *Review of International Political Economy*, 11(3): 447–88.

Brenner, N., Peck, J. and Theodore, N. (2010) 'Variegated Neoliberalisation: Geographies, Modalities, Pathways', *Global Networks*, 10(2): 182–222.

Bruff, I. (2011) 'What About the Elephant in the Room? Varieties of Capitalism, Varieties in Capitalism', *New Political Economy*, 16(4): 481–500.

Bruff, I. and Ebenau, M. (2014) 'Critical Political Economy and the Critique of Comparative Capitalisms Scholarship on Capitalist Diversity', *Capital & Class*, 38(1): 3–15.

Buci-Glucksmann, C. (1980) *Gramsci and the State* (London: Lawrence & Wishart).

Bukharin, N. (1925) *Historical Materialism* (New York: International Publishers).

Bull, H. (1977) *The Anarchial Society: A Study of Order in World Politics* (New York: Columbia University Press).

Callinicos, A. (2003) *An Anti-Capitalist Manifesto* (Cambridge: Polity Press).

Callinicos. A. (2009) *Imperialism and Global Political Economy* (Cambridge: Polity Press).

Cardoso, H. (2001) *Charting a New Course: The Politics of Globalisation and Social Transformation* (Lanham, MD: Rowman & Littlefield).

Castaneda, J. (2006) 'Latin America's Left Turn', *Foreign Affairs*, 85(3): 28–43.

Castells, M. (1996) *The Rise of the Network Society* (Oxford: Basil Blackwell).

Castells, M. (1997) *The Power of Identity* (Oxford: Basil Blackwell).

Cerny, P. (1997) 'Paradoxes of the Competition State: The Dynamics of Political Globalization', *Government and Opposition*, 32: 251–74.

Chan, S. (ed.) (2013) *The Morality of China in Africa: The Middle Kingdom and the Dark Continent* (London: Zed Books).

Chase-Dunn, C. (2013) 'Contemporary Semi-Peripheral Development: The Regimes and the Movements', IROWS Working Papers, 78.

Chase-Dunn, C. and Hall, D. (1997) *Rise and Demise: Comparing World Systems* (Boulder, CO: Westview Press).

Chin, C. and Mittelman, J. (2000) 'Conceptualising Resistance to Globalization', in B. Gills (ed.), *Globalization and the Politics of Resistance* (Basingstoke: Palgrave Macmillan), 29–47.

Cipolla, C. (ed.) (1970) *Fontana Economic History of Europe* (London: Fontana).

Clark, I. (2011) *Hegemony and International Society* (Oxford: Oxford University Press).

Cohen, B. (2008) *International Political Economy: An Intellectual History* (Princeton, NJ: Princeton University Press).

Coulon, J. (2003) 'How Unipolarity Died in Baghdad', *European Foreign Affairs Review*, 8: 537–41.

Cox, R. (1981) 'Social Forces, States and World Order: Beyond International Relations Theory', *Millennium*, 10(2): 126–55.

Cox, R. (1983) 'Gramsci, Hegemony and International Relations: An Essay in Method', *Millennium*, 12 (2): 162–75.

Cox, R. (1987) *Power, Production and World Order: Social Forces in the Making of History* (New York: Columbia University Press).

Cox, R. (1996) *Approaches to World Order* (Cambridge: Cambridge University Press).

Cox, M. (2004) 'Imperialism and the Bush Doctrine', *Review of International Studies*, 30(4): 585–609.

Crouch, C. (2011) *The Strange Non-Death of Neoliberalism* (Cambridge: Polity Press).

Cypher, J. (1989) 'The Debt Crisis as Opportunity: Strategies to Revive US Hegemony', *Latin America Perspectives*, 16(1): 52–78.

Darwin, J. (2009) *The Empire Project: The Rise and Fall of the British World-System, 1830–1979* (Cambridge: Cambridge University Press).

Der Derian, J. (1987) *On Diplomacy: A Genealogy of Western Estrangement* (Oxford: Blackwells).

Desai, R. (2013) *Geopolitical Economy: After US Hegemony, Globalisation and Empire* (London: Pluto Press).

Dirlik, A. (2007) *Global Modernity: Modernity in the Age of Capitalism* (Boulder, CO: Paradigm Press).

Dunphy, R. (2004) *Contesting Capitalism? Left Parties and European Integration* (Manchester: Manchester University Press).

Economist, The (2013) 'Brazil Overtakes the UK as World 6th Economy', *The Economist*, 5 May.

Ellwood, D. (1992) *Rebuilding Europe: Western Europe, America and Post-War Reconstruction* (London: Longman).

Escobar, A. (1995) *Encountering Development: The Making and Unmaking of the Third World* (Princeton, NJ: Princeton University Press).

Evans, T. (2011) 'The Limits of Tolerance: Islam as Counter-Hegemony', *Review of International Studies*, 37 (4): 1751–73.

Farrell, M., Hettne, B. and van Langenhove, L. (eds) (2005) *Global Politics of Regionalism: Theory and Practice* (London: Pluto Press).

Fawn, R. (2009) 'Regions and Their Study: Where from, What for and Where to?', *Review of International Studies*, 35(1): 5–34.

Feigenbaum, E and Manning, R. (2009) *The United States in the New Asia* (New York: Council on Foreign Relations).

Femia, J. (1981) *Gramsci's Political Thought* (Oxford: Clarendon).

Ferguson, N. (2003) 'Hegemony or Empire', *Foreign Affairs*, 82(5): 154–61.

Ferguson, N. (2004) *Colossus: The Rise and Fall of the American Empire* (London: Allen Lane).

Frank, A. G. (1966) 'The Development of Underdevelopment', *Monthly Review*, September: 17–31.

Friedberg, A. (1988) *The Weary Titan: Britain and the Experience of Relative Decline* (Princeton, NJ: Princeton University Press).

Fukuyama, F. (1992) *The End of History and the Last Man* (Harmondsworth: Penguin).

Fulton, J. (1987) 'Religion and Politics in Gramsci: An Introduction', *Sociology of Religion*, 48(3): 197–216.

Gaddis, JL. (1987) *The Long Peace: Enquiries into the History of the Cold War* (Oxford: Oxford University Press).

Gamble, A. (1996) *Hayek: The Iron Cage of Liberty* (Cambridge: Polity Press).

Gamble, A. (2009) *The Spectre at the Feast* (Basingstoke: Palgrave Macmillan).

Gamble, A. and Payne, A. (1996), *Regionalism and World Order* (Basingstoke: Palgrave Macmillan).

Gates, B. (2010) 'Foreword', in P. Petit (ed.), *Earth Capitalism: Creating a New Civilisation through a Responsible Market Economy* (New Brunswick, NJ: Transaction Publishers).

Germain, R. (2010) *Global Politics and Financial Governance* (London: Routledge).

Germain, R. and Kenny, M. (1997) 'Engaging Gramsci: International Relations Theory and the New Gramscians', *Review of International Studies*, 24(1): 3–21.

Gibbon, E. (1789) *The History of the Decline and Fall of the Roman Empire* (London: Strahan & Cadell).

Giddens, A. (1998) *The Third Way* (Cambridge: Polity Press).

Giddens, A. (2000) *The Third Way and its Critics* (Cambridge: Polity Press).

Gill, S. (1990) *American Hegemony and the Trilateral Commission* (Cambridge: Cambridge University Press).

Gill, S. (ed.) (1993) *Gramsci, Historical Materialism and International Relations* (Cambridge: Cambridge University Press).

Gill, S. (1994) 'Political Economy and Structural Change: Globalising Elites in the Emerging World Order', in Y. Sakamato (ed.), *Global Transformation: Challenges to the State System* (Tokyo: UNU).

Gill, S. (1995) 'Globalisation, Market Civilisation and Disciplinary Neoliberalism', *Millennium*, 24(3): 399–423.

Gill, S. (1998) 'European Governance and New Constitutionalism: Economic and Monetary Union and Alternatives to Disciplinary Neoliberalism in Europe', *New Political Economy*, 3(1): 5–26.

Gill, S. (2000) 'Towards a Post-Modern Prince? The Battle in Seattle as a Moment in the New Politics of Globalisation', *Millennium: Journal of International Studies*, 29(1): 131–40.

Gill, S. (2003) *Power and Resistance in the New World Order* (Basingstoke: Palgrave Macmillan).

Gill, S. (ed.) (2012) *Global Crisis and the Crisis of Global Leadership* (Cambridge: Cambridge University Press).

Gills, B. (ed.) (2000) *Globalization and the Politics of Resistance*. (Basingstoke: Palgrave Macmillan).

Gilpin, R. (1981) *War and Change in World Politics* (Cambridge: Cambridge University Press).

Gilpin, R. (1987) *The Political Economy of International Relations* (Princeton, NJ: Princeton University Press).

Gilpin, R. (2001) *Global Political Economy: Understanding the International Economic Order* (Princeton: Princeton University Press).

Goldstone, J. (2011) 'Rise of the TIMBIs', *Foreign Policy*, 90 (December).

Gough, J. (2004) 'Changing Scale as Changing Class Relations: Variety and Contradiction in the Politics of Scale', *Political Geography*, 23(2): 185–211.

Gough, J. (2014) 'The Difference Between Local and National Capitalism, and Why Local Capitalisms Differ from One Another: A Marxist Approach', *Capital & Class*, 38(1): 197–210.

Gramsci, A. (1971) *Selections from the Prison Notebooks* (London: Lawrence & Wishart).

Gramsci, A. (1985) *Selections from Cultural Writings* (London: Lawrence & Wishart).

Gramsci, A. (1992) *Antonio Gramsci – Prison Notebooks*, *Vol. 1* (New York: Columbia University Press).

Gramsci, A. (1995) *Further Selections from the Prison Notebooks* (Minneapolis, MN: Minnesota University Press).

Gramsci, A. (1996) *Antonio Gramsci – Prison Notebooks*, *Vol. 2* (New York: Columbia University Press).

Gramsci, A. (2007) *Antonio Gramsci – Prison Notebooks*, *Vol. 3* (New York: Columbia University Press).

Grandin, G. (2006) *Empire's Workshop: Latin America, The United States and The Rise of the New Imperialism* (New York: Metropolitan Books).

Grugel, J. and Riggirozzi, P. (2012) 'Post Neoliberalism in Latin America: Rebuilding and Reclaiming the State after Crisis', *Development and Change*, 43(1): 1–21.

Gruner, W. (1992) 'Was There a Reformed Balance of Power System or Cooperative Great Power Hegemony?', *American Historical Review*, 97(3): 725–32.

Haas, R. (1997) *The Reluctant Sheriff: The United States After the Cold War* (New York: Council on Foreign Relations).

Hainsworth, P. (ed.) (2000) *The Extreme Right in Western Europe* (London: Routledge).

Hall, P. and Soskice, D. (2001) *Varieties of Capitalism: The Institutional Foundations of Comparative Advantage* (Oxford: Oxford University Press).

Hall, S. (1988) *The Hard Road to Renewal* (London: Verso).

Hall, S. (1996) *Stuart Hall: Critical Dialogues in Cultural Studies* (London: Routledge).

Hall, S. (1998) 'The Great Moving Nowhere Show', *Marxism Today*, November/December: 9–14.

Hall, S. (2011) 'The Neoliberal Revolution', *Soundings*, 48: 9–28.

Hall, S. (2012) 'The Saturday Interview' (with Z. Williams), *The Guardian*, 11 February.

Halliday, F. (2009) 'International Relations in a Post-Hegemonic Age', *International Affairs*, 85(1): 37–51.

Hardt, M. and Negri, A. (2000) *Empire* (Cambridge, MA: Harvard University Press).

Hardt, M. and Negri, A. (2004) *Multitude* (Harmondsworth: Penguin).

Harman, C. (1977) *Gramsci versus Reformism*. (London: Socialist Workers Party), 5–29.

Harmes, A. (2012) 'The Rise of Neoliberal Nationalism', *Review of International Political Economy*, 19(1): 59–87.

Harvey, D. (2003) *The New Imperialism* (Oxford: Oxford University Press).

Harvey, D. (2005) *A Brief History of Neoliberalism* (Oxford: Oxford University Press).

Hayek, F. (1931) *Prices and Production* (New York: Augustus M. Kelly).

Hayek, F. ([1944]/2001) *The Road to Serfdom* (London: Routledge).

Hilley, J. (2001) *Malaysia: Mahathirism, Hegemony and the New Opposition* (London: Zed Books).

Hirschman, A. (1945) *National Power and the Structure of Foreign Trade* (Berkeley, CA: University of California Press).

Hobsbawm, E. (1962) *The Age of Revolution: Europe 1789–1848* (London: Abacus).

Hobsbawm, E. (1975) *The Age of Capital: 1848–1875* (London: Abacus).

Hobsbawm, E. (1987) *The Age of Empire: 1875–1914* (London: Abacus).

Hobsbawm, E. (1994) *The Age of Extremes: 1914–1991* (London: Abacus).

Holloway, J. (2002) *Change the World without Taking Power: The Meaning of Revolution Today* (London: Pluto Press).

Huntington, S. (1996) *The Clash of Civilisations and the Remaking of World Order* (New York: Simon & Schuster).

Hurrell, A. (2007) 'One World? Many Worlds? The Place of Regions in the Study of International Society' *International Affairs*, 83(1): 127–46.

Ignatieff, I. (2003) *Empire Lite: Nation-Building in Bosnia, Kosovo and Afghanistan* (Harmondsworth: Penguin).

Ikenberry, J. (2001) *After Victory: Institutions, Strategic Restraint and the Rebuilding of Order after Major Wars* (Princeton, NJ: Princeton University Press).

Ikenberry, J. (2004) 'Liberalism and Empire: Logics of Order in the American Unipolar Age', *Review of International Studies* 30(4): 609–30.

Ikenberry, J. (2006) *Liberal Order and Imperial Ambition: Essays on American Power and International Order* (Cambridge: Polity Press).

Ikenberry, J. (2008) 'The Rise of China and the Future of the West', *Foreign Affairs*, 28(1): 23–37.

Ikenberry, J. (2011) *Liberal Leviathan: The Origins, Crisis and Transformation of the America World Order* (Princeton, NJ: Princeton University Press).

Ikenberry, J. and Kupchan, C. (1990) 'Socialization and Hegemonic Power', *International Organization*, 44(3): 283–315.

Ikenberry, J. and Moon, C. I. (eds) (2008) *The United States and North East Asia: Debates, Issues and New Order* (Lanham, MD: Rowman & Littlefield).

IMF (International Monetary Fund) (2013) 'Africa's Rising Exposure to China: How Large Are Spillovers Through Trade?', IMF Papers, Washington, DC.

Iriye, A. and Cohen, W. (1989) *The United States and Japan in the Post-Cold War World* (Lexington, KY: University Press of Kentucky).

Ives, P. and Short, N. (2013) 'On Gramsci and the International', *Review of International Studies*, 39(3): 621–42.

Jacques, M. (2009) *When China Rules the World* (Harmondsworth: Penguin).

Jessop, B. (2011) 'Rethinking the Diversity of Capitalism: Varieties of Capitalism, Variegated Capitalism, and the World Market', in G. Wood and C. Lane (eds), *Capitalist Diversity and Diversity within Capitalism* (London: Routledge).

Jessop, B. (2012) 'The World Market, Variegated Capitalism and the Crisis of European Integration', in P. Nousios, H. Overbeek and A. Tsolakis (eds), *Globalisation and European Integration: Critical Approaches to Regional Order and International Relations* (Abingdon, UK/New York: Routledge).

Johnson, R. (1986) 'What Is Cultural Studies Anyway?', *Social Text*, 16(4): 38–80.

Johnson, R. (2007) 'Post Hegemony? I Don't Think So', *Theory, Culture and Society*, 24(3): 95–110.

Joseph, J. (2002) *Hegemony: A Realist Analysis* (London: Routledge).

Kagan, R. (2003) *Of Paradise and Power: America and Europe in the New World Order* (New York: Alfred A. Knopf).

Kagan, R. (2008) *The Return to History and the End of Dreams* (New York: Vintage).

Kagarlitsky, B. (2002) *Russia under Yeltsin and Putin* (London: Pluto)

Kagarlitsky, B. (2014) *From Empire to Imperialism: The State and the Rise of Bourgeois Civilisation* (London: Routledge).

Kaldor, M. (2003) *Global Civil Society: An Answer to War* (Cambridge: Polity Press).

Kaplan, R. (2005) 'How We Would Fight China', *The Atlantic Monthly*, June.

Kapstein, E. and Mastanduno, M. (eds) (1999) *Unipolar Politics* (New York: Columbia University Press).

Keohane, R. (1984) *After Hegemony: Cooperation and Discord in the World Political Economy* (Princeton: Princeton University Press).

Keohane, R. and Nye, J. (1977) *Power and Interdependence: World Politics in Transition* (New York: Little, Brown).

Keynes, J. M. ([1926]/2004) *The End of Laissez-Faire* (New York: Prometheus Books).

Kiely, R. (2010) *Rethinking Imperialism* (Basingstoke: Palgrave Macmillan).

Kindleberger, C. (1966) *Europe and the Dollar* (Cambridge, MA: MIT Press).

Kindleberger, C. (1973) *The World in Depression 1929–1939* (Berkeley, CA: University of California Press).

Kindleberger, C. (1981) 'Dominance and Leadership in the International Economy', *International Studies Quarterly*, 25: 242–54.

Kindleberger, C. (1983) 'On the Rise and Decline of Nations', *International Studies Quarterly*, 27: 5–10.

Klare, M. (2004) *Old and Blood: The Dangers and Consequences of America's Growing Dependency on Imported Petroleum* (New York: Metropolitan Books).

Kofman, E. and Youngs, G. (2003) *Globalisation: Theory and Practice* (London: Pinter).

Krasner, S. (1976) 'State Power and the Structure of International Trade', *World Politics*, 28 (3): 317–47.

Krasner, S. (1983) *International Regimes* (Ithaca: Cornell University Press)

Krasner, S. (1996) 'The Accomplishments of International Political Economy', in S. Smith, K. Booth and M. Zalewski (eds), *International Theory: Positivism and Beyond* (Cambridge: Cambridge University Press).

Krauthammer, C. (1990) 'The Unipolar Moment', *Foreign Affairs*, 70: 23–33.

Krauthammer, C. (2002) 'The Unipolar Moment Revisited', *National Interest*, 70: 5–17.

Krauthammer, C. (2004) *Democratic Realism: An American Foreign Policy for a Unipolar World* (Washington, DC: American Enterprise Institute for Public Policy Research).

Krugman, P. (2008) *The Return of Depression Economics* (New York: W.W. Norton).

Krugman, P. (2012) 'Nobody Understands Debt', *New York Times*, 1 January.

Kynaston, D. (2007) *Austerity Britain, 1945–1951* (London: Bloomsbury Publishing).

Laclau, E. (1977) *Politics and Ideology in Marxist Theory* (London: New Left Books).

Laclau, E. (2000) 'Identity and Hegemony: The Role of Universality in the Constitution of Political Logics', in J. Butler, E. Laclau and S. Zizek (eds), *Contingency, Hegemony, Universality: Contemporary Dialogues of the Left* (London: Verso).

Laclau, E. and Mouffe, C. (1985) *Hegemony and Socialist Strategy* (London: Verso).

Lampton, D. (2008) *The Three Faces of Chinese Power: Money, Might and Minds* (Berkeley, CA: University of California Press).

Lane, D. (1996) *The Rise and Fall of State Socialism* (Cambridge: Polity Press).

Layne, C. (2006) *The Peace of Illusions: American Grand Strategy from 1940 to the Present* (Ithaca, NY: Cornell University Press).

Layne, C. (2009) 'The Waning of US Hegemony: Myth of Reality', *International Security* 34 (1): 147–172.

Lebow, R. (2003) *The Tragic Vision of Politics: Ethics, Interests and Order* (Cambridge: Cambridge University Press).

Lebow, R, and Kelly, R. (2001) 'Thucydides and Hegemony: Athens and the United States', *Review of International Studies*, 27(4): 593–609.

Lechner, F. and Boli, J. (2012) *The Globalisation Reader* (4th edn) (Oxford: Basil Blackwell).

Lefebvre, H. (1991) *The Production of Space* (Oxford: Basil Blackwell).

Lefebvre, H. (2008) *Critique of Everyday Life* (London: Verso).

Lenin, V. I. (1939) *Collected Works* (Moscow: Progress Publishers).

Lenin, V. I. (1965) *Collected Works*, vol. 27 (London: Lawrence & Wishart).

Lenin, V. I. (1992) *State and Revolution* (Harmondsworth: Penguin).

Leviter, L. (2010) The ASEAN Charter: ASEAN Failure or Member Failure? *NYU Journal of International Law and Politics*, 43: 159–210.

Lim, K. F. (2013) 'Socialism with Chinese Characteristics', *Progress in Human Geography*. Available at http://doi10.1177/0309132513476822.

List, F. (2005a) *National System of Political Economy I: The History* (New York: Cosimo).

List, F. (2005b) *National System of Political Economy II: The Theory* (New York: Cosimo).

List, F. (2005c) *National System of Political Economy III: The System and the Politics* (New York: Cosimo).

Little, R. (1995) 'International Relations and the Triumph of Capitalism', in S. Smith and K. Booth (eds) *International Relations Theory Today* (Cambridge: Polity Press).

Louw, M. E. (2007) *Everyday Islam in Post-Soviet Central Asia* (London: Routledge).

Luxemburg, R. (1976) *The National Question* (New York: Monthly Review Press).

Luxemburg, R. ([1913]/2003) *The Accumulation of Capital* (London: Routledge).

MacDonald, P. (2009) 'Those Who Forget Historiography Are Doomed to Republish It: Empire, Imperialism and Contemporary Debates about American Power', *Review of International Studies*, 35(1): 45–67.

Macartney, H. (2010) *Variegated Neoliberalism: EU Varieties of Capitalism and International Political Economy* (London: Routledge).

Macartney, H. and Shields, S. (2011) 'Demystifying the Transnational: Finding Space in Critical IPE', *Journal of International Relations and Development* 14 (3): 375–83.

Machiavelli, N. ([1532]/1984) *The Prince* (Harmondsworth: Penguin).

Madsen, A. (1980) *Private Power: Multinational Corporations for the Survival of our Planet* (London: Abacus).

Malthus, T. (1798) *An Essay on the Principle of Population* (London: J. Johnson).

Mann, M. (2004) 'The First Failed Empire of the 21st Century', *Review of International Studies*, 30(4): 631–53.

Mason, P. (2012) *Why It's all Kicking Off Everywhere: The New Global Revolutions* (London: Verso).

Marsden, L. (2008) *For God's Sake: US Foreign Policy and the Christian Right* (London: Zed Books).

Marx, K. (1977) *Collective Works* (Oxford: Oxford University Press).

Mastanduno, M. (1997) 'Preserving the Unipolar Moment: Realist Theories and U.S. Grand Strategy After the Cold War', *International Security*, 21(4): 49–88.

Mastanduno, M. (2002) 'Incomplete Hegemony and Security Order in the Asia-Pacific', in J. Ikenberry (ed.), *America Unrivaled: The Future of the Balance of Power* (Ithaca, NY: Cornell University Press).

Mayer, N. (2007) 'Transformation in French Anti-Semitism', *International Journal of Conflict and Violence*, 1(1): 51–60.

Mazarr, M. (2003) 'George W. Bush: An Idealist?', *International Affairs*, 79(3): 503–22.

McKeown, T. (1983) 'Hegemonic Stability Theory and 19th Century Tariff Levels in Europe', *International Organisations*, 17(1): 73–91.

Mearsheimer, J. (1990) 'Back to the Future: Instability in Europe After the Cold War', *International Security*, 15(1): 5–52.

Mearsheimer, J. (2001) *The Tragedy of Great Power Politics* (New York: W.W. Norton).

Mearsheimer, J. (2004) 'The Rise of China Will Not be Peaceful at All', *The Australian*, 18 November.

Mearsheimer, J. (2009) 'Reckless States and Realism', *International Relations* 23 (2): 241–56.

Mearsheimer, J. and S. Walt (2003) 'An Unnecessary War', *Foreign Affairs*, 134(1): 50–9.

Meiggs, R. (1972) *The Athenian Empire* (London: Clarendon Press).

Miliband, R. (1969) *The State in Capitalist Society* (London: Weidenfeld & Nicolson).

Minford, P., Mahambare, V. and Nowell, E. (2005) *Should Britain Leave the EU? An Economic Analysis of a Troubled Relationship* (Cheltenham: Edward Elgar).

Mirowski, P. (2013) *Never Let a Serious Crisis go to Waste: How Neoliberalism Survived the Financial Meltdown* (London: Verso).

Mirowski, P. and D. Plehwe (eds) (2009) *The Road from Mont Pelerin: The Making of the Neoliberal Thought Collective* (Boston, MA: Harvard University Press).

Mises, L. von (1934) *The Theory of Money and Credit* (London: Jonathan Cape).

Mises, L. von (1949) *Human Action: A Treatise on Economics* (New Haven, CT: Yale University Press).

Moore, P. (2010) *The International Political Economy of Work and Employability* (Basingstoke: Palgrave Macmillan).

Monteiro, N. (2011) 'Rest Assured: Why Unipolarity is not Peaceful', *International Security*, 36 (3): 9–40.

Morton, A. (2007) 'Waiting for Gramsci: State Formation. Passive Revolution and the International', *Millennium*, 35(3): 597–621.

Morton, A. (2010) 'The Continuum of Passive Revolution', *Capital & Class*, 34(3): 315–42.

Morton, A. (2011) *State and Revolution in Modern Mexico: The Political Economy of Uneven Development* (Lanham, MD: Rowman & Littlefield).

Mouffe, C. (ed.) (1979) *Gramsci and Marxist Theory* (London: Routledge).

Mowat, R. B. (1922) *A History of European Diplomacy 1815–1914* (London: Edward Arnold).

Mowle, T. and Sacko, D. (2007) *The Unipolar World: An Unbalanced Future* (Basingstoke: Palgrave Macmillan).

Mudde, C. (2007) *Populist Radical Right Parties in Europe* (Cambridge: Cambridge University Press).

Mun, T. (2000) *England's Treasure by Foreign Trade* (London: Forgotten Books).

Murphy, C. (1994) *International Organisation and Industrial Change: Global Governance since 1850* (Cambridge: Polity Press).

Murphy, C. (2008) *Global Institutions, Marginalisation and Development* (London: Routledge).

Murray, K. (2012) 'Christian "Renewalism" and the Production of Free Market Hegemony', *International Politics*, 49(2): 260–76.

Murray, K. and Worth, O. (2013) 'Building Consent: Hegemony, "Conceptions of the World" and the Role of Evangelicals in Global Politics', *Political Studies*, 61(4): 731–47.

NASSCOM (National Association of Software and Services Companies) (2013) 'Annual Report 2012/2013'. Available at:, http://www.nasscom.in/sites/default/files/Annual_Report_2012-13.pdf.

Nattrass, N. (2011) 'The New Growth Path: Game Changing Vision or Cop Out?', *South African Journal of Science*, 107(3/4): 1–8.

Nederveen-Pieterse, J. (2000) 'Globalisation North and South: Representations of Uneven Development and the Interaction of Modernities', *Theory, Culture and Society*, 17(1): 129–37.

Neumann, I. (1996) *Russia and the Idea of Europe* (London: Routledge).

Nexon, S. and Wright, T. (2007) 'What's at Stake in the American Empire Debate', *American Political Science Review*, 101(2): 253–71.

Nye, J. (1990) 'Soft Power', *Foreign Affairs*, 80: 153–71.

Nye, J. (2004) *Soft Power: The Means to Success in World Politics* (New York: Public Affairs).

O'Brien (1999) 'Imperialism and the Rise and Decline of the British Economy, 1688–1989', *New Left Review*, 238: 48–78

O'Brien, P. and Cleese, A. (2002) *Two Hegemonies: Britain 1846–1914 and the United States 1941–2001* (Aldershot: Ashgate).

O'Neill, J. (2001) 'Building Better Global Economic BRICs', *Goldman Sachs: Global Economics Paper*, 66.

O'Neill, J., Wilson, D., Purushothaman, R. and Stupnytska, A. (2005) 'How Solid are the BRICS?', *Goldman Sachs: Global Economic Papers*, 134.

Odom, W. and Dujarric, R. (2004) *America's Inadvertent Empire* (New Haven, CT: Yale University Press).

Okumu, W. (2009) 'The African Union: Pitfalls and Prospects for Uniting Africa', *Journal of International Affairs*, 62(2): 93–111.

Overbeek, H. (2000) 'Transnational Historical Materialism: Theories Of Transnational Class Formation and World Order', in R. Palan (ed.), *Global Political Economy* (London: Routledge).

Overbeek, H. and van Apeldoorn, B. (eds) (2012) *Neoliberalism in Crisis* (Basingstoke: Palgrave Macmillan).

Overbeek, H., van Apeldoorn, B. and Nölke, A. (eds) (2007) *The Transnational Politics of Corporate Governance Regulation* (London: Routledge).

Oye, K., D. Rothschild and Lieber, R. (eds) (1979) *Eagle Entangled: US Foreign Policy in a Complex World* (New York: Longman).

Palan, R. and Abbott, J. (1996) *State Strategies in the Global Political Economy* (London: Pinter).

Panitch, L. and Gindin, S. (2003) 'Global Capitalism and American Empire', in L. Panitch and C. Leys (eds), *The New Imperial Challenge* (London: Merlin).

Panitch, L. and Leys, C. (eds) (2003) *The New Imperial Challenge* (London: Merlin).

Panizza, F. (2005) 'Unarmed Utopia Revisited: The Resurgence of Left-of-Centre Politics in Latin America', *Political Studies*, 53(4): 716–34.

Park, Y. J. and Alden, C. (2013) '"Upstairs" and "Downstairs" Dimensions of China and the Chinese in South Africa', in U. Pillay, G. Hagg and F. Nyamnjoh (eds), *State of the Nation: South Africa 2012–2013* (Cape Town: HSRC).

Paterson, B. (2009) 'Trasformismo at the World Trade Organisation', in M. McNally and J. Schwarzmantel (eds), *Gramsci and Global Political: Hegemony and Resistance* (London: Routledge).

Paul, R. (2008) *The Revolution: A Manifesto* (New York: Grand Central Publishing).

Paul, R. (2009) *End the Fed* (New York: Grand Central Publishing)

Peck, J. (2007) 'Variegated Capitalism', *Political Geography*, 31(6): 731–72.

Peck, J. (2010) *Constructions of Neoliberal Reason* (Oxford: Oxford University Press).

Peck, J. and Tickell, A. (2002) 'Neoliberalising Space', *Antipode*, 34(4): 380–404.

Petras, J. (2003) 'Whither Lula's Brazil? Neoliberalism and "Third Way" Ideology', *Journal of Peasant Studies*, 31(1): 1–44.

Perkmann, M. and Ngai-Ling, S. (eds) (2002) *Globalisation, Regionalisation and Cross-Border Regions* (Basingstoke: Palgrave Macmillan).

Phillips, N. (2005) 'The Americas', in A. Payne (ed.), *The New Regional Politics of Development*, (Basingstoke: Palgrave Macmillan).

Pijl, K. van der, (1984) *The Making of an Atlantic Ruling Class* (London: Verso).

Pijl, K. van der, (1998) *Transnational Classes and International Relations* (London: Routledge).

Plehwe, D., Walpen, B. and Neunhoffer, G. (eds.) (2006) *Neoliberal Hegemony: A Critique* (London: Routledge).

Polanyi, K. ([1944]/2001) *The Great Transformation: The Political and Economic Origins of Our Time* (Boston, MA: Beacon Press).

Polanyi, K. (1968) *Primitive, Archaic and Modern Economies* (New York: Anchor).

Porter, B. (ed.) (1972) *The Aberystwyth Papers* (Oxford: Oxford University Press).

Posen, B. R. (2003) 'Command of the Commons: The Military Foundation of US Hegemony', *International Security*, 28(1): 5–46.

Poulantzas, N. (1980) *State, Power, Socialism* (London: Verso).

Radnema, M. and Bawtree, V. (eds) (1997) *The Post-Development Reader* (London: Zed Books).

Ramo, J. (2004) *The Beijing Consensus* (London: Foreign Policy Centre).

Rashid, A. (2002) *Jihad: The Rise of Militant Islam in Central Asia* (New Haven, CT: Yale University Press).

Reifer, T. (ed.) (2004) *Globalisation, Hegemony and Power: Antisystemic Movements and the Global System* (Boulder, CO: Paradigm).

Rennstich, J. (2004) 'The Phoenix Cycle: Global Leadership Transition in a Long-Wave Perspective', in T. Reifer (ed.), *Globalisation, Hegemony and Power: Antisystemic Movements and the Global System* (Boulder, CO: Paradigm).

Roberts, K. (2007) 'Repoliticising Latin America: The Revival of Populist and Leftist Alternatives', *Woodrow Wilson Center Update on the Americas*, November.

Robinson, N. (2012) 'The Edges of Europe, the "Eastern Marches" and the Problematic Nature of a "Wider Europe"', in G. Strange and O. Worth (eds), *European Regionalism and the Left* (Manchester: Manchester University Press).

Robinson, W. I. (2005) 'Gramsci and Globalisation: From Nation-State to Transnational Hegemony', *Critical Review of International Social and Political Philosophy*, 8(4): 1–16.

Rosamond, B. (2000) *Theories of European Integration* (Basingstoke: Palgrave Macmillan).

Rosamond, B. (2012) 'The Discursive Construction of Neoliberalism: The EU and the Contested Substance of European Economic Space', in G. Strange and O. Worth (eds), *European Regionalism and the Left* (Manchester: Manchester University Press).

Rosecrance, R. (1976) *America as an Ordinary Country* (Ithaca, NY: Cornell University Press).

Rosenberg, J. (1994) *Empire of Civil Society* (London: Verso).

Rostow, W. (1960) *The Stages of Economic Growth* (Cambridge: Cambridge University Press).

Rothermund, D. (2009) *India: The Rise of an Asian Giant* (New Haven, CT: Yale University Press).

Rothbard, M. (1994) *The Case Against the Fed* (Auburn, AL: Ludwig von Mises Institute).

Rothkopf, D. (1997) 'In Praise of Cultural Imperialism', *Foreign Policy*, 107: 38–53.

Ruggie, J. (1993) 'Territoriality and Beyond: Problematizing Modernity in International Relations', *International Organizations*, 47 (1): 139–74.

Ruggie, J. (1995) 'The False Premise of Realism', *International Security*, 20(1): 62–70.

Rupert, M. (1995) *Producing Hegemony: The Politics of Mass Production and American Global Power* (Cambridge: Cambridge University Press).

Rupert, M. (2000) *Ideologies of Globalization* (London: Routledge).

Russett, B. (1985) 'The Mysterious Case of Vanishing Hegemony; or, is Mark Twain Really Dead?', *International Organizations*, 39(2): 207–31.

Said, A. and Simmons, L. (1975) *The New Sovereigns: Multinational Corporations as World Powers* (London: Prentice-Hall).

Said, E. (1978) *Orientalism* (Harmondsworth: Penguin).

Said, E. (1993) *Culture and Imperialism* (London: Vintage Books).

Said, E. (2003) *Culture and Imperialism* (London: Chatto & Windus).

Salamini, L. (1981) *The Sociology of Political Praxis: An Introduction to Gramsci's Thought* (London: Routledge).

Sassoon, A. S. (1982) *Approaches to Gramsci* (London: Writers & Readers).

Saull, R. (2012) 'Rethinking Hegemony: Uneven Development, Historical Blocs and the World Economic Crisis', *International Studies Quarterly*, 56(2): 323–38.

Scerri, M. (2013) 'South Africa', in M. Scerri and H. Lastres (eds), *BRICS: The Role of the State* (London: Routledge).

Schroeder, M. (1992) 'Did the Vienna Settlement Rest on a Balance of Power?', *American Historical Review*, 97(3): 683–706.

Schweller, R. and Pu, X. (2011) 'After Unipolarity: China's Vision of International Order in an Era of US Decline', *International Security*, 35(1): 41–72.

Scott, J. (1990) *Domination and the Art of Resistance* (New Haven, CT: Yale University Press).

Seligson, M. (2006) 'The Rise of Populism and the Left in Latin America', *Journal of Democracy*, 18(3): 81–95.

Shields, S. (2012) *The International Political Economy of Transition: Transnational Social Forces and Eastern Central Europe's Transformation* (London: Routledge).

Shields, S. and Macartney, H. (2009) 'Finding Space in Critical IPE: A Scalar-relational Approach', *Journal of International Relations and Development*, 14(4): 375–83.

Shirk, S. (2004) *How China Opened Its Door* (Washington, DC: The Brookings Institution).

Silver, B. (2014) 'Reshuffling of the World Proletariat', Paper presented to the XVIII ISA World Congress of Sociology, Yokohama, Japan, 13–19 July.

Sklair, L. (1990) *Sociology of the Global System* (London: Pearson).

Sklair, L. (2000) *The Transnational Capitalist Class* (Oxford: Basil Blackwell).

Slaughter, A. M. (2008) 'Wilsonianism in the Twenty-First Century', in J. Ikenberry, T. Knock, A.-M. Slaughter and T. Smith (eds), *The Crisis of American Foreign Policy: Wilsonianism in the Twenty-first Century* (Princeton, NJ: Princeton University Press).

Smith, A. ([1776]/1993) *Wealth of Nations: A Selected Edition* (Oxford: Oxford University Press).

Steger, M. (2005) *Globalism: Market Ideology Meets Terrorism* (Lanham, MD: Rowman & Littlefield).

Stelzer, I. (2004) 'Introduction', in I. Stelzer (ed.), *The Neo-Con Reader* (New York: Grove Press).

Stephens, M. (2014) 'Rising Powers, Global Governance and Liberal Global Governance: A Historical Materialist Account of the BRICS challenge, *European Journal of International Relations*. Available at: http://dx.doi.org/10.1177/1354066114523655.

Stiglitz, J. (2002) *Globalisation and Its Discontent* (New York: W.W. Norton).

Strange, G. (2006) 'The Left Against Europe: A Critical Engagement with New Constitutionalism and Structural Dependency Theory', *Government and Opposition*, 41 (2): 197–229.

Strange, G. (2011) 'China's Post-Listian Rise: Beyond Radical Globalisation Theory and the Political Economy of Neoliberalism', *New Political Economy*, 16(5): 539–59.

Strange, S. (1987) 'The Persistent Myth of Lost Hegemony' *International Organizations*, 41 (4): 551–74.

Strange, S. (1988) *States and Markets* (London: Pinter)

Syme, R. (1939) *The Roman Revolution* (Oxford: Oxford University Press).

Taggart, P. and A. Szczerbiak (eds) (2008) *Opposing Europe? The Comparative Party Politics of Euroscepticism* (Oxford: Oxford University Press).

Telo, M. (2007) *European Union and New Regionalism* (Aldershot: Ashgate).

Thucydides (1972) *History of the Peloponnesian War* (Harmondsworth: Penguin).

Tomlinson, J. (1991) *Cultural Imperialism* (London: Continuum).

Trotsky, L. (1977) *The History of the Russian Revolution* (London: Pluto).

Valdes, J. (1995) *Pinochet's Economists* (Cambridge: Cambridge University Press).

Vezirgiannidou, S. E. (2013) *The United States and Rising Powers in a Post-Hegemonic Global Order*, 89(3): 635–51.

Walker, R. (1994) 'Social Movements/World Politics', *Millennium*, 23(3): 669–700.

Wallerstein, I. (1979) *The Capitalist World Economy* (Cambridge: Cambridge University Press).

Wallerstein, I. (1985) 'The Relevance of the Concept of the Semi-Periphery to Southern Europe', in G. Arrighi (ed.), *Semiperipheral Development* (Beverly Hills, CA: Sage).

Wallerstein, I. (ed.) (2004) *The Modern World-System in the Longue Durée* (Boulder, CO: Paradigm).

Waltz, K. (1979) *Theory of International Politics* (Reading, MA: Addison-Wesley).

Waltz, K. (1993) 'The New World Order', *Millennium*, 22(2): 187–95.

Waltz, K. (2000) 'Structural Realism after the Cold War', *International Security*, 25(1): 5–41.

Watson, A. (1992) *The Evolution of International Society* (London: Routledge).

Watson, A. (2007) *Hegemony and History* (London: Routledge).

Warren, B. (1980) *Imperialism: Pioneer of Capitalism* (London: Verso).

Weyland, K. (2004) 'Assessing Latin American Neoliberalism', *Latin American Research Review*, 39(3): 143–9.

Williamson, J. (2012) 'Is the "Beijing Consensus" Now Dominant?', *Asia Policy*, 13: 1–16.

Williams, R. (1977) *Marxism and Literature* (Oxford: Oxford University Press).

Williams, R. (1980) *Culture and Materialism* (London: Verso).

Williams, R. (2003) *Who Speaks for Wales: Nature, Culture, Identity* (ed. D. Williams) (Cardiff: University of Wales Press).

Wohlforth, W. (1999) 'The Stability of a Unipolar World', *International Security*, 24(1): 5–41.

Woollard, K. (1985) 'Language Variation and Cultural Hegemony: Towards an Integration of Sociolinguistic and Social Theory', *American Ethnologist*, 12 (4): 738–48.

World Bank (2010) *Development and Climate Change* (Washington, DC: World Bank).

World Bank (2012) *World Development Indicators 2012* (Washington, DC: World Bank).

World Bank (2013) *World Development Indicators 2013* (Washington, DC: World Bank).

Worth, O. (2002) 'The Janus-like Character of Counter-hegemony: Progressive and Nationalist Responses to Neoliberalism', *Global Society*, 16(3): 297–315.

Worth, O. (2005) *Hegemony, International Political Economy and Post-Communist Russia* (Aldershot: Ashgate).

Worth, O. (2007) 'Reengaging the Third Way: Regionalism, the European Left and "Marxism without Guarantees"', *Capital & Class*, 93: 93–109

Worth, O. (2008) 'The Poverty and Potential of Gramscian Thought in International Relations', *International Politics*, 45(6): 633–49.

Worth, O. (2009) 'Unravelling the Putin Myth: Strong or Weak Caesar?', *Politics*, 29(1): 53–61.

Worth, O. (2011) 'Recasting Gramsci in International Politics', *Review of International Studies*, 37(1): 373–93.

Worth, O. (2012) 'Accumulating the Critical Spirit: Rosa Luxemburg and Critical IPE', *International Politics*, 49 (2): 136–54.

Worth, O. (2013) *Resistance in the Era of Austerity: Nationalism, the Failure of the Left and the Return of God* (London: Zed Books).

Worth, O. (2014) 'The Far Right and Neoliberalism: Willing Partner or Hegemonic Opponent?', in R. Saull, A. Anievas, N. Davidson and A. Fabry (eds), *The Longue Durée of the Far-Right: An International Historical Sociology* (London: Routledge).

Worth, O. and Moore, P. (ed.) (2009) *Globalization and the 'new' Semi-Peripheries*. (Basingstoke: Palgrave Macmillan).

Wu, F. (2010) 'How Neoliberal Is China's Reform? The Origins of Change during Transition', *Eurasian Geography and Economics*, 51(5): 619–31.

Xiaochuan, Z. (2009) 'Reform the International Monetary System', *BIS Review* (Basel: Bank for International Settlements).

Yates, J. and Bakker, K. (2013) 'Debating the "Post-neoliberal Turn" in Latin America', *Progress in Human Geography*. Available at: http://doi: 10.1177/0309132513500372.

Young, H. (2012) 'European Union Coordination at the United Nations', PhD thesis, University of Limerick.

Young, R. (1995) *Colonial Desire: Hybridity in Theory, Culture and Race* (London: Routledge).

Yahuda, M. (2006) *The Post-Cold War in Asia and the Challenges to ASEAN*. (Singapore: Institute of South East Asian Studies)

Yúdice, G. (1995) 'Civil Society, Consumption, and Governmentality in an Age of Global Restructuring: An Introduction', *Social Text*, (45): 1–25.

Zapatistas, The (1998) *Zapatista Encuentro: Documents from the First Intercontinental Encounter for Humanity and Against Neoliberalism* (New York: Seven Stories Press).

Index

208   *Index*

3International Relations (IR) *cont.*
  realism   8–9, 16, 20, 52, 60
  unipolarity   xix, 9–10, 42, 52–5,
    60, 101, 112, 136, 172
Iraq War   54, 112
Ireland   35, 103, 109, 125
Islam   24, 130, 136, 142, 158–60,
  163
Italy   23, 25, 36, 43–4, 68, 74–5,
  103–4, 151, 162

Jefferson, T.   55
Jintao, D.   114
Johnson, R.   78
Joseph, J.   65

Kashmir   142
Kautsky, K.   4, 64–5
Kenny, M.   69, 72, 84
Keohane, R.   22, 48, 70, 171, 180
Keynes, J. M.   38, 91, 153, 155
  Keynesian economics   79,
    88–91, 99, 102–3, 107, 135,
    148, 152–3
Kindleberger, C.   46–7, 52, 70
Kohl, H.   93, 106
Krauthammer, C.   60

Lebow, N.   xi, 3, 21
Lefebvre, H.   77–9, 85
Lehman Brothers   101
Lenin, V.I.   xix, 46, 124, 160
  hegemony   4, 15, 147, 64–5
  State and Revolution   64–5
Liberia   55
Linguistics   15
List, F.   26, 36
Lloyd George, D.   35
Lord Liverpool (Robert Jenkinson)
  32
Louis XVI   26
Lugo, F.   141
Lula, L. I. da S.   118–19, 140, 146

Luxemburg, R.   57–8, 64, 156,
  160

Machiavelli, N.   26, 39, 66–7,
  101, 147, 172
Malaysia   163
Malthus, T.   35
Marshall Plan   43–4
Marx, K.   64, 66, 83, 180
  hegemony   63–6
  Marxism   xviii, xix, 3–6, 12–13,
    16, 58, 59, 69, 80, 171
  Marxist-Leninism   46
  post-Marxism   15–17, 82–3
  Marxism Today   79
Mastanduno, M.   9
Mearsheimer, J.   112
Meiggs, R.   3
Mercantilism   25–30, 37, 110,
  117, 123, 137
Mercosur   131–2, 140
Mexico   45, 99, 123, 139, 154
Mill, J. S.   35
Millennium   13, 69
Mises, L. von   88–9, 105, 161,
  161
Modernization theory   9, 97
Monnet, J.   44
Mont Pelerin Society   88–92, 105
Morales, E.   139–40
Morton, A.   74–5
Mouffe, C.   xvii, 15–16, 64, 82–4,
  166
Mowle, T.   53
Mun, T.   26
Murphy, C.   71

Napoleonic Wars   30–2, 56
National Interest   9, 52
Nationalism   36, 71, 81, 85, 100,
  106, 149, 161, 174
  far-right groups   156–8
Negri, A.   57, 61